THE GREENSBORO READER

The University of
North Carolina Press
Chapel Hill

The Greensboro Reader

Edited by
Robert Watson
and
Gibbons Ruark

In memory of

RANDALL JARRELL
DIANE OLIVER
LETTIE ROGERS

CONTENTS

FICTION

ACKNOWLEDGMENTS

The editors are grateful to the following authors and publishers for permission to reprint the works listed below:

JAMES APPLEWHITE, "Tree in the Rain." Reprinted from *The Young American Poets*, edited by Paul Carrol (Big Table Books: Follett Publishing Company), 1968.

FRED CHAPPELL, "A Property of Hope." First published in *The Saturday Evening Post*, May 9, 1964. Coypwright © 1964 by Fred Chappell. Reprinted by permission of McIntosh, McKee & Dodds.

KELLY CHERRY, "The Getaway" and "For Alice, Whom He Marries One Year Later: The Proposal." *The Greensboro Review*, December, 1966.

JEAN FARLEY, "Bed Rider" and "She Sees Pallbearers Coming on Snow." *The Sewanee Review*, Summer, 1967. "Night Horse," *Southern Review*, Spring, 1968.

CAROLINE GORDON, "The Captive." Reprinted with the permission of Charles Scribner's Sons from *The Forest of the South* by Caroline Gordon. Copyright 1945 by Caroline Gordon.

HIRAM HAYDN, "Virgil's Manuscript." From *Report from the Red Windmill*. Copyright © 1967 by Hiram Haydn. Reprinted by permission of Harcourt, Brace & World, Inc.

BERTHA HARRIS, "Catching Saradove." *The Greensboro Review*, December, 1966.

RANDALL JARRELL, "Art Night." Reprinted with the permission of Alfred A. Knopf, Inc. from *Pictures from an Institution* by Randall Jarrell. Copyright © 1954 by Randall Jarrell. "A Girl in a Library," Copyright © 1952 by Randall Jarrell.

X. J. KENNEDY, "Little Elegy," Copyright © 1967 by X. J. Kennedy. "Cross Ties" and "Loose Woman" by permission of X. J. Kennedy.

ROBIE MACAULEY, "Legend of the Two Swimmers." From *The End of Pity* by Robie Macauley. First Printed in *The Kenyon Review*. Copyright © 1957 by Robie Macauley.

HEATHER ROSS MILLER, "Gilead." From *The Wind Southerly*. Copyright © 1967 by Heather Ross Miller. Reprinted by permission of Harcourt, Brace & World, Inc.

THOMAS W. MOLYNEUX, "Before, Once." *The Sewanee Review*, Summer, 1967. Copyright 1967 by Thomas W. Molyneux.

DIANE OLIVER, "Key to the City." Reprinted from *Coraddi*, Winter, 1964.

PATRICIA PETERS, "Sidewalk Bone," "Tin Can," and "Easter." *The Greensboro Review*, December, 1967.

LAWRENCE JUDSON REYNOLDS, "That Grand Canyon." Reprinted from *Intro I*, Bantam Books, 1968.

WM. PITT ROOT, "Passing a Sawmill at Night," *The Catalyst* and *Academy of American Poets Anthology of College and University Poetry, 1960-66*. "The Firstborn," *The Virginia Quarterly Review*, Fall, 1967. "The Grandfather," *The Greensboro Review*, December, 1966.

JESSIE ROSENBERG, "A Garden Down the Street." By permission of the author. All rights reserved by Jessie Rosenberg.

GIBBONS RUARK, "A Blind Wish for Randall Jarrell." First appeared in the September, 1967, issue of *Poetry*. Copyright 1967 by The Modern Poetry Association. Reprinted by permission of the Editor of *Poetry*.

ALLEN TATE, "The Immortal Woman." First appeared in *The Hound and Horn* in 1932. Copyright © 1968 by Allen Tate.

ELEANOR ROSS TAYLOR, "After Twenty Years," "Bulletin," and

"Pause, in Flight." First appeared in the January, 1966, issue of *Poetry*. Copyright 1966 by The Modern Poetry Association. Reprinted by permission of the Editor of *Poetry*.

PETER TAYLOR, "A Cheerful Disposition." *The Sewanee Review*, Spring, 1967. Copyright 1967 by Peter Taylor.

ROBERT WATSON, "An Elderly Ghost Has His Say." Reprinted from *A Paper Horse*, Atheneum, 1962. Copyright © 1962 by Robert Watson.

Royalties from *The Greensboro Reader* will go to the support of *The Greensboro Review*.

EDITORS' NOTE

Every contributor to the reader has either received a degree from the University of North Carolina at Greensboro or has been a full-time teacher in the English Department. Each has published or has ready for publication at least one book of poetry or fiction. In one sense the reader is not representative of Greensboro writing because space limitations forced us to slight novelists, which means that Jackson Burgess, Lettie Rogers, Jan Coxe Speas, Sylvia Wilkinson, and others could not be properly represented. Both Doris Betts and Frances Gray Patton, we regret to report, have been stolen from us by the late Jessie Rehder in her *Chapel Hill Carousel.* And for obvious reasons of space we have been unable to include many excellent story writers and poets. Both Arturo Vivante and Thomas Kirby-Smith joined our staff after we had completed this volume. If we had been able to include a section of essays, Noel Perrin, one of a handful of genuinely witty essayists in America today, would have been represented. We are hoarding these and other writers for *Greensboro Reader Number 2.*

ROBERT WATSON
GIBBONS RUARK

FOREWORD

When I arrived in North Carolina fifteen years ago to teach at what was then called the Woman's College of the University of North Carolina, a mythology had already grown up about the writers on the campus. One of the very first stories I heard was that in the late thirties Robert Lowell lived in a tent on the front lawn of the Allen Tate house because Ford Madox Ford was occupying the only guest room. A few years later, I learned from Peter Taylor that my version was not completely accurate: Ford Madox Ford had told the Tates that he didn't want Robert Lowell in the house for fear Lowell would write a poem about him. And Robert Lowell did: "Ford Madox Ford," which he included in his volume *Life Studies*. Then some spoil sport said, "Why that didn't happen in Greensboro; it happened in Tennessee." Anyway, by the time I arrived, a mythology had already grown up about writers in Greensboro, a city where very fittingly the largest hotel is named "The O' Henry."

Michel Oresset, in an article called "La Litterature Américaine en 1964" that appeared in *Les Nouvelles Littéraire*, said, "Greensboro parait être un véritable centre d' activité Littéraire dans le Sud actuellement." Yet the news from Paris had not reached Robert

Lowell in New York who, two years later in an essay on Randall Jarrell, refers to us as a "little-known Southern college for girls in Greensboro, North Carolina." When I arrived, Lettie Rogers, the novelist, said to me, "Throw a stone in North Carolina and you will hit a writer." If you don't like writers, you might kill two with one stone on this campus. Until I looked at the faculty listing for the English Department before I was hired, I too thought that I might be coming to teach at a "little-known Southern college," but after I read the names of Randall Jarrell, Robie Macauley, Lettie Rogers, and Peter Taylor, I couldn't name an English department in the nation that to me seemed more distinguished.

I once asked Randall Jarrell why he thought writers found Greensboro congenial. He gestured toward the campus and said, "See, it's Sleeping Beauty." Many writers and artists visiting here from New York City are appalled at the thought of anyone's living in Greensboro: dull, middle-class, suburban Greensboro, a "city of parking lots," as Lewis Mumford once called it; far from a metropolis, far from the sublime beauties of mountains and sea, a campus with none of the historic greatness of a Harvard or a Yale. Yet a great poet could live on a mountain and only come down twice in his life, and a great fiction writer could complete most of his work in jail—as many have. What New York (or Paris, or London) can give a writer is a reputation. And it seems to me that writers who are fearful of leaving New York and who are condescending about the provinces are really fearful of losing their reputations. Reputation, of course, is only fashion, a product of the market place. In New York reputations can be manufactured just like garments in the garment industry and are apt to be no more enduring. I say this as someone who grew up in the metropolitan area, occasionally has lived in New York, and enjoys it.

If someone asked me what Greensboro offered a writer, I would answer, "Boredom." What I mean is this: Greensboro puts the writer to his own resources, and he can compose without becoming entangled in the fads of the market place. Greensboro can give him a clarity of vision so that he understands his competitors are not the writers whose pictures appear on the covers of *Time* or *Newsweek* or who are approved by *The New York Review of*

Books or win Pulitzer Prizes or National Book Awards. His competitors are the great writers of the past—and future. In fact he realizes that he has no competitors; this knowledge can keep him from becoming a provincial writer.

Greensboro is a congenial city. Its people are hospitable to writers; its newspapers write friendly editorials about them. And the administration of the University has been kind to writers. At my undergraduate college, writing courses were offered to students to prove to them that they couldn't be writers. In Greensboro every year the writing teachers half expect the next Keats or the next Jane Austen to be enrolled in the sophomore writing class.

Twenty-five years ago Marc Friedlaender, then Professor of English, and Winfield H. Rogers, Head of the Department, in collaboration with other departments, founded the Arts Forum. Distinguished writers were invited each spring to read from their works, to lecture, and, most important, to discuss student writing from this and other campuses in the nation. In 1946 the Arts Forum issue of *Coraddi*, our undergraduate literary magazine, printed stories by Flannery O'Connor and Mac Hyman; poems by both Anthony and Roger Hecht, Donald Justice, and Edgar Bowers. In later Arts Forum issues of *Coraddi*, undergraduate poems appear by James Dickey, Donald Hall, Joel Oppenheimer, James Wright, William Goodreau, and Robert Mezey, all at that time unknown. Student writers came to attend the sessions from all the nearby campuses; others traveled from such distant places as Kenyon, Dallas, Harvard, and Vassar. Over the years student work was criticized by Lionel Trilling, Robert Penn Warren, Elizabeth Bowen, Frances Gray Patton, Karl Shapiro, Saul Bellow, William Blackburn, John Crowe Ransom, Robert Lowell, Flannery O'Connor, Andrew Lytle, Henry Rago, Guy Owen, Stanley Kunitz, Adrienne Rich, and many others. Within the last decade writing forums imitating our pattern have flowered. *Coraddi* magazine continues to flourish: last year in a national competition it was ranked third in the country, after San Francisco State and Yale.

Two years ago when we began to accept candidates for the Master of Fine Arts degree in significant numbers, we founded *The Greensboro Review* specifically for our graduate students in writing. Three of the five stories published in the second issue—stories by David Ackley, Bowman Beaufort, and Lawrence Judson Reynolds—were listed as "Distinctive Short Stories of 1966" in *The Best American Short Stories* edited by Martha Foley and David Burnett.

Many people, especially Europeans, poke fun at writing courses. They have a point. No teacher, no class assignments can make anyone a poet or fiction writer. In England, at least in the past, a young writer could always run down to London with his manuscript, obtain introductions to literary circles, and have his work read and criticized by established writers. America is too large for such cozy traditions; it doesn't have a single literary center comparable to a London and Paris of the past. Writing courses, visiting writers, Arts Forums are the modern American substitutes for the older continental traditions. What the young writer wants most of all is sympathetic readers who will treat his work with seriousness and care. He seeks writers, rather than critics or scholars, because only the writer knows the craft. Never again in his life will he probably hear so much—good and bad—about his writing. And what about the danger of imitation? Aren't the students apt to turn out carbon copies of their teacher's work? The stories and poems in this book, with their great variety of subject matter and style, answer this question.

Introductions to books of this kind tend to be self-congratulatory, the author a name dropper; mine is no exception. The spirit of literature is restless and fickle. It may inhabit a place or an institution for a period of time, then pack its bag never to return. Luck has been on our side. For three decades Greensboro has been a friend of the spirit.

ROBERT WATSON

AN INTRODUCTION

Randall Jarrell

ART NIGHT

My wife and I were Gertrude's only old acquaintances at Benton; sometimes we were sorry that this was so. She called one morning to ask whether we could come by for her that night—it was Art Night; "Sidney's in New York," she said, "and I feel that As A Novelist I ought to go." I replied senselessly: "That's odd—my wife's in New York too, with the car. Do you suppose she and Sidney have run off with the car?" Gertrude was silent for a moment; she didn't like jokes about Sidney. Then she said, "That's silly." I tried to think of something to say that would make up for what I had said: that my wife certainly wouldn't have run away with *Sidney,* that *Sidney* certainly wouldn't run away with anybody, that—I said, "Yes, that was silly," and told Gertrude that I could come for her anyway, that someone was taking me.

It was Dr. Rosenbaum. When we got to Gertrude's I jumped out of his car and then paused, transfixed. Gertrude's apartment was on the second floor; it had a little balcony; Gertrude was sitting on the balcony holding in her hand an enormous Mexican glass; inside her apartment a phonograph was playing, louder than I had heard a phonograph play before. Gertrude held up her glass, waved it—quite a good deal spilled —and called out to me, "Look, Jack Daniel's! Mama sent it to me for my birthday."

I said, wonderingly: "Your mother! For your birthday! I didn't even know you had one."

"Didju think they found me under a cabbage-leaf?" Gertrude asked, laughing girlishly. Something about her laugh attracted her; she repeated it. She was all dressed up: her voice, her flushed smile, everything about her gave an impression of reckless but secure gaiety. "Come on up and have a drink," she said.

"You come on down; we don't want to miss any of *Art Night*."

"O.K.," said Gertrude; "be right down. Just let me finish this drink." She finished it in three swallows, without visible effect; I watched without belief; but when she repeated, "Be right down," she had become for the moment a contralto.

As she walked to the car the music came to a climax: the orchestra itself seemed to have turned into a drum. I said to Gertrude, raising my voice: "I believe you've left the phonograph on."

She answered, "It'll turn itself off; it's automatic." Then she said—but she didn't make it the first time, stopped, and repeated carefully, in a voice of real elevation: "And what if it does not?"

The time had come. I said, "Gertrude, say hello to Dr. Rosenbaum; he's going to drive us over to school."

Gertrude stopped. She stopped as a tribe of Indians, walking in single file through the forest, stops when its chieftain sees a snake. She stared into the Simca.

Dr. Rosenbaum said in a terribly deep voice, "*Guten abend, gnädige Frau!*" Gertrude said nothing. I opened the door of the car; after a moment I said, "I'll—let me sit in the middle."

Gertrude said, "Pray do."

Dr. Rosenbaum said, "There is no middle." This was so; between the two bucket seats there was only the gear shift. I could have asked Gertrude to sit in my lap, and yet. . . . I got myself into the space behind the seats; there was room for everything but my head. Gertrude sat down and folded her hands in her lap; I reached over her shoulder and shut the door.

We started away; for a while the strains of the music followed us. I said, "What is that, Gertrude? It's very impressive."

She answered, "It's—" then she paused, and said surprisedly: "I can't remember."

"It's *Ce qu'on entend sur la montagne*," said Dr. Rosenbaum; "what we call the *Bergsymphonie*."

"That's right," said Gertrude. Then she said, "That's *right*." She was silent for a moment, collecting herself. Then she began to talk. At first it was hard for her to pronounce some of the words, but from the first what she had to say was witty and coherent—by the time we got to Benton her mother might as well have sent her sachet. No liquor could influence Gertrude like an audience.

WHEN WE got inside the gallery, the first thing we saw was Sona Rasmussen. Miss Rasmussen was half Japanese, half Norwegian; she came from Honolulu. She was a fat, tiny, shiny woman: with a different paint job, and feelers, she would have looked exactly like a potato-bug—I used to think of her as part of a children's story in which there were Reginald Chipmunk, and Dorothy Thrush, and Sona Potato-Bug, and many other innocent, foolish, and agreeable creatures.

Miss Rasmussen made welded sculpture. Her statues were

—as she would say, smiling—untouched by human hands; and they looked it. You could tell one from another, if you wanted to, but it was hard to want to. You felt, yawning: It's ugly, but is it Art?

Miss Rasmussen also designed furniture; but people persisted in sitting down in her sculpture, and in asking "What is that named?" of her chairs. This showed how advanced her work was, and pleased her; yet when she laughed to show her pleasure, her laugh sounded thin and strained. Gertrude said about her work, "She was a shipyard welder during the war, and the sculpture just naturally followed." When this was repeated to Miss Rasmussen she said hotly, "Oh, *that* again! It was an aircraft factory—and besides, I'd thought of it *long ago*."

She liked Benton, and Benton liked her; but she had had difficulties during her first term. President Robbins said to her, after two of her freshmen had burned themselves severely: "A welder's torch is *not* a thing with which just any freshman can be entrusted, Miss Rasmussen." Miss Rasmussen said that you couldn't shelter students forever, but after that she had her freshmen stick to wood, mobiles, and Cold Iron. Her advanced students were a different affair: she and they, in their goggles and masks, looked wonderful, like racetrack-drivers about to give a Nō play.

Gottfried and Gertrude and I arrived, first, at the wooden half of the sculpture. All the statues, to show that they were statues, were mounted on little black pedestals. Off to the side there was one statueless pedestal; Gertrude looked at it a long time, in silent admiration; I had to persuade her to leave it.

Some of the statues looked like improbably polished *objets trouvés*, others looked as if the class had divided a piece of furniture among themselves, lovingly finished the fragments, and mounted the result as a term's work. The passing sculptors —and Miss Rasmussen, who did not pass, but stood there like a sentry—found Gertrude's voluble admiration for their works offensive; she exclaimed about the one she liked best, "Why, you can *see* yourself in it! What I wouldn't give for that in bird's-eye maple!" She went on to say to Miss Rasmussen: "How *do* you and your pupils get this *wonderful* finish?" Miss Rasmussen did not reply: she looked as if she were half Japanese and half Ethiopian. Gertrude continued artlessly, "I always use linseed oil and rottenstone, myself; but to tell the truth, Miss Rasmussen, a little old-fashioned elbow grease is what it really takes." She said this with a cheery laugh; she was enjoying herself, and if people didn't know enough to get out of the way, they would have to suffer for their ignorance.

After looking at ten or twenty of these statues you muttered to yourself, "I wish wood didn't *have* any grain"; a few more and you were sorry that there is such a thing as wood— were sorry, that is, until you came to the Ores and Metals section of the sculpture. First came the mobiles—and they were mobile: if you breathed hard that part of the gallery looked like dawn in a cuckoo-clock factory. Then came the welded statues: they were made, apparently, of iron twine, with queer undigested knots or lumps or nodules every few inches, so that they all looked like representations of part of the root-system of an alfalfa plant, or that of almost any legume. Sometimes a statue had four legs and was an animal; sometimes it had two legs and two arms, and was a man. But sometimes it had neither arms nor legs, and was an abstraction.

Gertrude said softly, though not so softly as I could have wished: "Why don't riveters do sculpture, too?" But when she applied the word *fragile* to a statue with less than its share of lumps, Miss Rasmussen broke in stormily: "*Fragile!* You couldn't break that with a hammer! Let me tell you, every joint in that is *welded.*"

Gertrude gave her a surgeon's smile; you expected Gertrude to say, "More ether, nurse. This woman is conscious." Then she remarked in a speculative voice, "Have you ever stopped to

consider, Miss Rasmussen, just *why* your statues are so thin?"
By now the patient, poor fat thing, was beginning to be sorry
that she had come to; I said before Gertrude could go on: "I
love your statues, Miss Rasmussen," not even crossing my
fingers as I said it; and Gottfried said that *dey madt him feel
goodt ven he lookedt at dem.* Gertrude looked at me for a
moment; then she looked at Gottfried for a moment; then she
laughed. It was a placing laugh. When the ripples of this
laugh had died, she quoted clearly: "Kind hearts are more than
coronets, And simple faith than Norman blood."

Miss Rasmussen began to tell Gottfried and me about her
statues. Some of what she said was technical, and you would
have had to be a welder to appreciate it; the rest was aesthetic
or generally philosophic, and to appreciate it you would have
had to be an imbecile.

WE CAME to the paintings next. There had been quite a
good painter at Benton the year before, a mild, absent, indifferent man, with hair like a string bag; when he resigned he
said genially, "You don't need *me*." He had been replaced by
a painter who painted animals in marshes—or jungles: all
glowed. This man stood looking out over his herds, the ring-
straked, speckled, and spotted; he wore a turtleneck sweater
and a black beard, and smiled a complacent smile, as if he had
just said to you in an English novel, "I thought you'd ask that."

The paintings varied, though not much. The students loved
their teacher, it was plain: there were a great many beasts of
prey, in forests and marshes, all looking like feral Florence
Nightingales. I said to Gertrude, finally: "Gertrude, for God's
sake stop saying *Tiger, Tiger, burning bright!*" Then I said
to Gottfried, "Say something!" He said, "What can I say?"

The animals were recognizably animals, and that was about
all you could say for them—but it was something you could
not have said for any of the other paintings there. The stu-

dents had learned all the new ways to paint something (an old way, to them, was a way not to paint something) but they had not had anything to paint. The paintings were paintings of nothing at all. It did not seem possible to you that so many things could have happened to a piece of canvas in vain. You looked at a painting and thought, "It's an imitation Arshile Gorky; it's casein and aluminum paint on canvasboard, has been scratched all over with a razor blade, and then was glazed —or scumbled, perhaps—with several transparent oil washes." And when you had said this there was no more for you to say. If you had given a Benton student a pencil and a piece of paper, and asked her to draw something, she would have looked at you in helpless astonishment: it would have been plain to her that you knew nothing about art. By the time a Benton artist got through exploiting the possibilities of her medium, it was too dark to do anything else that day; and most of the students never learned that there was anything else to do.

Gertrude had begun an animated conversation with the painter; her first sentence was, "Tell me, have you ever thought of doing illustrations for *The Jungle Book?*" I thought it unfair of her to talk so much of the suppressed aggressions that manifested themselves in his work, since it was plain from his part of the conversation that he was not a man who suppressed aggressions. Against many conversationalists he would have had quite a good chance: he spoke not as the scribes but with authority, and was untroubled by any of the doubts that intelligence brings in its train. He looked truculent to begin with; within five sentences he was looking baffled and truculent. To Gertrude's extended, unfavorable, but really quite brilliant comparison of his jungles with those of Max Ernst and the Douanier Rousseau, he retorted: "I'm not interested in other painters' paintings."

Gertrude looked at him with delight, and said: "You're from the West Coast, aren't you?"

"What do you mean?"

"Well, aren't you?"

"How did you know?"

Gertrude said modestly, "Oh, I just knew." Then she said, "I'll bet I can tell you who your favorite writer is, too."

"Who?"

"Henry Miller."

The painter laughed triumphantly, and exclaimed: "Wrong! D. H. Lawrence."

Gertrude smiled and said to him, "You're older than I thought"; and to me, "Well, it's a moral victory, anyway."

I said, "Gertrude, don't you think we ought to be finding some seats for the performance?"

She answered, "Christ, you're a—a sobersided man. We can always sit in Dr. Rosenbaum's lap." Then she said to the painter, winningly: "You come too." He said, "Well, I—" But Gertrude, staring at him thoughtfully, murmured: "D. H. Lawrence!" Then she said to me, aside: "Still, I suppose he's doing well to *have* a favorite writer. I think Cézanne was right about painters, don't you?—*le peintre est en general bête.*"

Gertrude's French was so bad that anyone could understand every word of it. But there was no light, either of comprehension or of increased anger, in the painter's glittering eyes; they went on looking intense. Gertrude said again: "D. H. Lawrence! . . . But don't you *really* think Giono beats him at his own game?"

I said, "Gertrude, the seats, the seats!"

Gertrude was opening her mouth; before *D. H. Lawrence!* could come out I pulled her away. She went reluctantly, calling back to the painter a feeling goodbye.

We found two seats, though with difficulty; Gertrude and Gottfried sat down, and I lowered myself to the floor beside them. I noticed that as Gottfried sat down in his seat, and as I sat down in the aisle, we gave a soft strange sigh. Had we too once, long ago, made jokes, said unkind things, been hushed by our worried responsible fellows? We sat there like unleavened Sunday School superintendents, and Gertrude sparkled to the rows around; unsuspecting children would come up to talk and we would tense ourselves, making ready to push them away before Gertrude could go off in their hands.

THE LITTLE auditorium was already full, but a third of Benton remained to be seated. Girls sat in girls' laps; girls sat on the floor, as if at a party; standing girls lined all the walls; athletic girls sat on the hall's Tudor rafters, swinging their shorted legs. (There was disagreement on how to dress for Art Night. Half the girls dressed as if for a date, and were unrecognizable to their teachers, who had never seen them except with their shirt-tails out, in shorts or blue jeans; the rest came with their shirt-tails out, in shorts or blue jeans.) The audience discussed what they had seen and what they were going to see; they pointed, called greetings, rustled like leaves; but, mostly, they giggled. Great visible waves of giggles would sweep across the hall; the girls looked like the choir and furniture of Heaven, but they sounded like bats.

The President sat in the front row, his leg over the arm of his seat, his good profile turned toward his audience; from time to time his laugh would soar up under the giggles of the girls—an unaffected laugh, full of spontaneity and enthusiasm and boyish artless life. He was going to get his thirty-seventh merit badge tonight, Gertrude told her row; some were silent, some gave a shocked and wicked laugh.

The program was already twenty minutes late, but behind the curtain you could hear things being dropped, things being dragged across the stage. But finally a messenger came to the President; he rose; he—

Just at that moment Mrs. Robbins came in. She appeared at the back of the auditorium; she was dressed in—well, she always seemed to be dressed in what she called *a tea gown,* but this was a tea gown with a fringe and sequins. There was a long delay while she made her way to the seat beside the President. I mean this literally: there was no way there, she *made* it. You felt that she had signed a compact with the devil to stumble over or to step upon, to say *Sorry!* to, every person sitting in the center aisle. Mrs. Robbins was always one to apologize, necessarily or unnecessarily, and you could see how she felt: it was a pity to leave unused for even an hour a *Sorry!* so superior as hers.

The President was greeted with loving silence. He said that we had already seen what Benton could do in painting and in sculpture, and now we would see what Benton could do in drama and in the dance. The Department of Drama was going to perform a new adaptation, made especially for us by Mrs. Caraccioli, of Strindberg's *The Spook Sonata;* and the Department of Dance and the Department of Music would give a dance-drama called *The Life of Nature,* with a score especially composed for it by Benton's Composer in Residence, Gottfried Rosenbaum. (Gottfried smiled guiltily.) Last, to sum up the significance of all that we had seen that night, we would have the privilege of hearing a distinguished visitor, Charles Francis Daudier, speak on Art and the Democratic Way of Life.

Mrs. Caraccioli had adapted *The Spook Sonata* according to her lights, the lights of Benton: it was a nightmare still, but a nightmare with social significance. And yet, where *we* were, it was pure delight. As an actor said to me afterwards, "There was one part of that audience that, I don't care what we said, they laughed." Gertrude's improvised variations on Strindberg, sketched out in a rapid whisper, had the seats around her helpless with laughter; as they had giggled once, so, now, they laughed. Gottfried muttered to me—and his voice was almost loving—"Oh, but she is good! I have underjudged her. She is a *truly* witty woman."

When the play was done, Gertrude looked around at her audience in wordless triumph; during the intermission she received congratulations smilingly. It was during this intermission that the President spoke with so much emotion, to the Head of the Department of Literature, of Camille Batterson. He even went on to say: "And this fall we were, perhaps, too hasty."

"Too hasty?"

"In giving up Mr. Gumbiner so soon, I mean." But then he said—and he smiled like the newly created angels, who cannot yet believe their bliss—"Only twenty-three more days!"

But Gertrude was tired, now; after a few minutes of *The Life of Nature* she said surprisedly, "Why, it's a child's point of view ballet"—this was so—and a few minutes later she said that the prima ballerina had "a bottom of good sense"—whether this was so I don't know, but she did stay on all fours most of the time, like the animals—and that was all Gertrude said; we sat and dully watched the dancers. We missed *The Spook Sonata*.

The girl who was a girl—all the rest of the girls were creatures of the forest—had been hurt by life, and the plants and animals helped her to understand. You saw everything through her Awakening eyes. I tried to, to name the birds without a gun, and to be all right because it was almost over—I told myself this over and over—but mostly I tried to find something to *do:* I would have played Ghosts, I would have played Lotto, I would have played Animal Grab. It seemed to me that generations of me would be born, and live their lives out, and die gladly, and still not have got through *The Life of Nature*.

After a while *The Life of Nature* ended: the girl, awake now, was borne off on the shoulders of the forest, and the President introduced Charles Francis Daudier.

Mr. Daudier spoke to us for—for some years, we felt. It was the speech a vain average would make to an audience of means.

Gertrude had heard him give the speech before; so had I; Gottfried never had; yet Gottfried knew it better than we did, because Gottfried was older than we were, and had heard that speech more times than we had.

After a while I could no longer hear what Mr. Daudier was saying, and I just looked at him. There were waves like heat waves in the air of the auditorium, so that his face would get big and indistinct, and then small and indistinct; sometimes I would realize that it had disappeared altogether, that I hadn't seen it for minutes, and I would grope my way back to seeing it.

It was a wonderful face. Mr. Daudier—the name is pronounced *Dod*yer—came from a Huguenot family that had settled in Massachusetts very early, and become a sort of example to the Puritans. Gertrude used to call him Old Rocky Face. The name suited him: compared to *him*, Dante looked like Little Black Sambo's mother, Black Mumbo.

Mr. Daudier had been pushed up and down New England several times, head-first, by a glacier; this face was what was left. (Or, from another point of view, New England was what was left.) And yet he kept talking about Love; it was always *Love*, never *love*, and when he said *Love* a strange light would come over his face, and make you want to hate your neighbor. He looked *much* more like a stone than stones do: he not only knew that he was right, he knew that he was good—and he recognized the fact that other people weren't; his face had a look of such grave, muted, self-righteous complacency that it seemed a seventeenth century engraving designed to illustrate Socrates' *Nothing can hurt the good man.*

I kept looking into this face while it weighed itself; then a hand wrapped it in some paper, paper that looked like grey moss, so that I said to my wife, who had come back from New York with Sidney: "He's got a haircut." My wife and Sidney and the face began to applaud; the girl in the aisle beside me gently shook my head—it was in her lap—and said, "You've been asleep." They turned on the lights in the auditorium. I was confused, and as I sat up said foolishly: "Thank you for taking care of me." The girl answered: "I've been asleep."

The audience got up slowly, and walked away uncertainly —the girls to their dormitories, the teachers and their wives and husbands to the President's, to meet Mr. Daudier. "Come on," said Gertrude; her face was that of the characters in the *Lays of Ancient Rome* when they swear something upon the ashes of their fathers.

THE FURNITURE of the President's house had been picked by Mrs. Robbins and an interior decorator, and looked as if it had been picked by two interior decorators. Except for photographs and a teddy bear of Derek's, the house was institutional. Mr. Daudier stood in front of the fireplace waving off compliments on his speech, and trying to repress a smile of justified complacency. The President stood by him, alertly beaming. He and Mr. Daudier got along well: they had everything but their views in common.

When the President started to introduce Gertrude to Mr. Daudier, Mr. Daudier halted him, and exclaimed affably, "Why, Gertrude and I are old friends—we've met half a dozen times."

Gertrude replied in a bleak voice, "I'm sure we must have; I just don't remember."

Mr. Daudier was taken aback. He began to remind Gertrude of occasions; Gertrude visibly did not listen, and after a moment broke in, "You remind me of *some*one, though. Haven't you a brother?"

"I? A brother?"

"I could have sworn you had a brother. You mean every time I see the name Daudier it's you?"

Mr. Daudier said that of course Daudier was an old name, a fairly well-known name in New England, but that—

"You're the poet?"

Mr. Daudier said, in the deprecating tone in which Americans refer to poetry, that he *had* published several volumes of verse. Gertrude murmured softly, "*Several!*" and went on to ask him about some anthologies. They were his. Some people are great strawberry-fanciers, or soccer-fans, or stamp-collectors. Mr. Daudier was a great anthologist: he made anthologies all the time. Once a man wrote that we see many men with a passion for gambling, but none with a passion for running gambling-houses; I think that Mr. Daudier, by his anthologies, disproved this remark. And he was a prominent literary critic: he had a column of criticism, every week except the last two weeks in August, in the best-known literary weekly; he was a director of a club that picked books for readers who didn't know what to read; there are radio-programs which have several critics blame, and several critics and the author praise, some recent book, and Mr. Daudier was generally on one side or the other; during the school year he would lecture to colleges, and when the school year was over he would make commencement addresses to them or get honorary degrees from them; he was the chief reader of a publishing-house, he was one of the vice-presidents of the American branch of the Académie Francaise; you saw one-act plays by him, if you fell among anthologies of one-act plays; he even wrote informal essays. ("*Now* I know who it is I've been confusing you with," cried Gertrude; "Christopher Morley!" "*Who?*" "Christopher Morley. Oh, I know you haven't any beard; I was just confused. It was those informal essays.") But mostly he talked about great books—about a hundred of them; I don't know why he stopped at a hundred, but he did, and let the rest go; he must have made up his mind that it was no use trying to get people to read more than a hundred. There were two things he was crazy about, the thirteenth

century and Greek: if the thirteenth century had spoken Greek
I believe it would have killed him not to have been alive in it.
He didn't know anything about, or care anything for, science,
unless it was several hundred years old—or several thousand,
for choice; he loved it then. He would say, "What do *we* know
that Aristotle didn't know?" But he wouldn't let you tell him;
it was a rhetorical question. He had diabetes and used to get
an injection of insulin every day, but I don't believe he ever
got one without wishing it were Galen giving it to him.

He wasn't a Catholic, just a fellow traveller, but he did the
Church more good than half a dozen ordinary *monsignori*.
He couldn't talk for five minutes without mentioning Aquinas
—Aquinas, or Thomas Jefferson. He would say it was sad how
rusty your Greek got when you'd been out of college as long
as he had; but if he read it a tenth as much as he talked about
it, I don't see how his Greek could have got rusty. (I think it
must have got worn away with use, the way a beaver's teeth
do.) And he loved to read the *Divine Comedy* aloud to you,
especially if you didn't know Italian; he would translate it to
you as he went along. And he could tell you what Aristotle
thought about *anything*. He was a liberal education in himself
—a conservative one, I mean.

But it was his novels that seemed to interest Gertrude most.
She said in a queer tone, the tone a mother uses when she
doesn't want to wake her baby: "I was very interested in what
you said about the failure of the modern novel, and about the
modern novelist's needing to go back to Fielding."

"You were?"

"Oh yes," replied Gertrude. "I've read one of your novels;
that was why I was interested. It was a novel named—named—"

"*The Firmament of Time?*"

"No."

"*The Greatest of These?*"

"No, not that."

"*A Cock for Aesculapius?*"

"No, some other."

"I haven't written any other."

"It must have been one of them, then. It was a novel about —about—well, it's been some time since I've read it, but I remember thinking that the critics had been *most unfair* to it." Mr. Daudier had a queer look on his face, as if he were a box of mixed nuts, but mostly peanuts; but you could see that he agreed with *this* remark down to the last cell of his toenail.

"Now, *I'm* a novelist, and naturally I'm prejudiced: I want a novel to be *by* a novelist—you know, a real professional job; but I don't think a *critic* ought to be like that, do you? It's his duty to make allowances. *He* ought not to judge a—an unpretentious novel by a beginner as if it were *War and Peace*. I think he ought to judge it by the *spirit*, not just by the letter, and forgive it all those little technical errors an amateur just naturally makes."

I had read that if you let a seed grow for a while it can crack a boulder; and I could see, now, that this was so. We all looked at Mr. Daudier and thought: "He's not half so insensitive as he seems."

Gertrude paused, to give him a chance to say something; but as he did not say anything, she went on: "The moment I started your book I remember feeling—it was such a refreshingly *different* feeling: why, this is the sort of book I used to read when I was a girl, a real *old-fashioned* novel. I felt as if I were just about to curl up in a window-seat with *Little Women*. And that's the sort of thing you can't fake—I'll bet *you've* often curled up in a window-seat with *Little Women*."

The President, looking as if he were worrying about Mr. Daudier, tried to take him off to the others, but Gertrude seized Mr. Daudier by the arm and said firmly: "I know everybody wants him, but I want him first. There're simply *thousands* of things Mr. Daudier and I have to say to each other.

You know, little trade-secrets. For instance, what you said about the ideal education being manual labor and Greek. Now, I was interested in that. I'll bet all of us were interested in *that*. I've seen it somewhere else, though. Who said that first?"

Mr. Daudier said that he thought he'd said it first, though he might have read it somewhere else and forgotten; my heart was hardened, and I said: "I think it's Auden." Mr. Daudier looked at me like Pyrrho the Sceptic. Gertrude said, "Yes, that must be right," and gestured towards me, saying: "*He* knows Auden by heart, practically." Then she got back to business: "What you said about manual labor and Greek, that they're the ideal education, that made me think of Cassandra. I mean, when the Greeks captured her and made a slave out of her, she could have cheered herself up by thinking that at least she was going to get an ideal education. And that was so about *any* Greek slave—any slave that was a foreigner to begin with, and didn't know Greek. But there's one thing that bothered me: how could any *Greek* get an ideal education? *They* already knew Greek."

Gottfried said, helpfully, that *dey didtn't needt an ideal edtucation*: *DEY vere Greeks.*

Gertrude said, "Now take St. Thomas. Did St. Thomas know Greek?"

The President's eyes lit up. He said quickly, "I've read something interesting about St. Thomas—oh, I just happened to come across it in some history or other I was reading—that, that interested me very much because it's so different from people's ordinary idea of him. Did you know that St. Thomas Aquinas was so fat that they had to cut out a hole for him to sit in, at the dinner-table?"

"Of course," said Gertrude. She continued, fixing Mr. Daudier with her absorbed stare: "Now take you. Do you think readers like *you* so much because you know Greek?"

Mr. Daudier said, "Well—"

Gertrude waited for a moment, to let him go on; when he didn't she went on herself: "No, sir! [Here she gave a strange little smile. I think that she was amused at herself for having said *No, sir*: it was overdoing it, but who would see or care? She had the contempt for her audience that the real virtuoso so often has.] The common man likes you," exclaimed Gertrude, "because he feels that you're speaking directly *to* him."

Mr. Daudier looked rather pleased, but surprised, too.

"And why shouldn't he?" cried Gertrude. "*You've* never lost the common touch—I think you *are* a common man."

The look on Mr. Daudier's face was so complicated that I was sorry I had ever thought him simple. But also—but also, for a moment, he looked like a poor stupid old man; I thought, "He hasn't a chance."

"Yes, that's the way it is," Gertrude exclaimed. "You know, Swift once wrote to Pope—or Pope once wrote to Swift, *I* don't care—that there's one sure sign of a true wit: all the dunces are leagued against him. You take a writer like you, and nobody's leagued against him: they're *for you*. And the reason for *that* is, you never say one single word that they couldn't—that every one of them wouldn't say himself. Oh, I know a lot of people think you're a reactionary, but they don't hold it against you. They know that at heart you're exactly the same as they are. It was a good idea to get you to talk on art and democracy—anyway, on democracy: I think you're a really democratic writer. . . . Now take what you said about all modern novels being bad."

Mr. Daudier said that he hadn't called, and didn't think, *all* modern novels bad.

"Oh no," replied Gertrude, "just all except yours."

But a wail from the staircase interrupted Gertrude. It was Derek. He stood there in his pajamas, staring out at us unseeingly; his neck and shoulders were hunched like an animal's. "Poor dear, has he had his nightmare!" cried Mrs. Robbins;

she went to him and, with surprising awkwardness, tried to console him. He seemed unable to see or hear her, but her touch comforted him; after a little he stopped trembling and allowed himself to be led back upstairs to bed. I felt so sorry for them both, at that instant, that I cursed myself for noticing that she called him *Pammy's little boy.* During the whole time he never said a word.

Mrs. Robbins didn't come back for some time; when she returned Gottfried and I said goodbye to her, explaining that we wanted to get back to Irene, who hadn't felt too well that evening. Mrs. Robbins was uneasily gracious to us. Gertrude was staying; as we walked to the door she came up to me and, drawing me aside, said happily: "I've always meant to have a little heart-to-heart talk with that guy."

I said something, I don't know what, but my voice was so halfhearted that Gertrude's face fell. I thought, "No, it isn't fair; she doesn't know any better." I felt as you do when your cat brings you a bluejay it has caught; the cat knows no better and the bluejay deserves no better, but just the same. . . . I thought, *Poor Gertrude*; I realized that, in a funny way, I was fond of Gertrude. I said. "You were really good tonight, Gertrude. Did you hear what Gottfried said about you?"

"No, what?"

"He said that you are—" and I imitated his voice—"a *truly vitty voman.*"

She tried not to show it, but she was pleased; she said goodbye, and as she went off to find new audiences, new victims, I said after her: "Goodbye, Gertrude. I'll see you soon."

I had been living in another world—a dream world, as they say—for a couple of hours, and had awakened from it. I went out dejectedly. Gottfried seemed depressed, too. I suppose that at that moment, for us, Miss Rasmussen and the painter and Charles Francis Daudier and Gertrude were only Dereks. The world had reminded us that, underneath anything any of us could say about, it existed.

The Rosenbaums had in their living room one of the longest sofas I have ever seen; when we got there Constance was asleep at one end of it and the cat at the other; Irene was reading. She said, "How was it?" I said, "Awful, awful."

"What was Daudier like?"

"He's a—he's a poor stupid old man," I answered.

We sat down, got ourselves something to drink, talked a while; it was quiet outside, quiet inside; the light fell on the Persian's rumpled fur, on Constance's sleeping head, and it was more peaceful than, for a while, I could believe. Irene kept on reading.

The cat was thirsty or else just dreaming: she lapped for a moment and then stopped lapping. But she had stopped with her tongue out of her mouth, and it made her snore; finally she woke, jumped up, shook herself, and walked out of the room.

Gottfried said to Irene—he spoke, absentmindedly, in German—"What readest thou?"

"A poet—an English one. I've come to a part about a singer."

"A singer of opera?" I asked, smiling at her.

"I think of *lieder*. I will read it to you.

> *I have oft heard*
> *My mother Circe with the Sirens three*
> *Amidst the flowery-kirtl'd* Naiades
> *Culling their Potent hearbs, and balefull drugs,*
> *Who as they sung, would take the prison'd soul*
> *And lap it in* Elysium, Scylla *wept*
> *And chid her barking waves into attention,*
> *And fell* Charybdis *murmur'd soft applause:*
> *Yet they in pleasing slumber lull'd the sense,*
> *And in sweet madness rob'd it of it self,*

But such a sacred, and home-felt delight,
Such sober certainty of waking bliss
I never heard till now."

Gottfried said, in amazement, "Why, it is better than
Hölderlin, almost"; I repeated silently, *And O poor hapless*
Nightingale thought I,/How sweet thou sing'st, how near the
deadly snare. "Let me see it, Irene," I said. "There's something further on that I've often thought is—that I want to read
to you." I found what I wanted and read it aloud:

The leaf was darkish, and had prickles on it,
But in another country, as he said,
Bore a bright golden flower, but not in this soyl:
Unknown, and like esteemed, and the dull swayn
Treads on it daily with his clouted shoon,
And yet more med'cinal is it than that Moly
That Hermes *once to wise* Ulysses *gave.*

All of us had, I think, the same rueful smile; Gottfried repeated, "And yet more med'cinal is it than that *Moly*/That
Hermes once to wise *Ulysses* gave"; and Irene said soberly,
with the little mock-pedantic intonation she had gained from
her life among the Germanic peoples: "Yes, this is so."

I yawned—it seemed to me that Gertrude, and Mr. Daudier,
and Miss Rasmussen, and *The Life of Nature* were thousands
of years away—and said contentedly to Gottfried: "Take me
home. And I guess we'd better wake up Constance and get
her home—she'll be having to go to work in the morning."

"There is no need," said Irene. "I do not want her waked.
I will cover her with a blanket and set the alarm-clock, and in
the morning I will make breakfast for her and take her to the
school."

I said goodbye to Irene, and as Gottfried and I left she
went upstairs to get the blanket.

POETRY

Eleanor Ross Taylor

AFTER TWENTY YEARS

After twenty years in France
Do you dream in French, my son? . . .
Home . . . ca existe encore.
Still, still exists Flagg Bros. store,
With new glass front, but behind
The dilapidated sheds
And packed road lined with maypops
Where you talked to the white horse.

Gloved, hatted, I kneel here
Where you by the sky-blue windows
Sang Onward Christian Soldiers.
For I have needed pardon
Since the morning we found Dad
In the garage (It is hard
To be a father without
A son). I screamed, and without
A son to be a widow.
Shall I pray your pardon too?
Prince of Peace, absolve all warriors,
My warrior of the bow and arrow.
Your old girl married money.
She's grown stout. (*He* has ulcers.)

Last year they were in Nice
Not Normandy. . . .
My glove's rouge, with lipstick
Or with teeth. . . . Curse *men*, curse *free*—
God vault your freedom!
Oh the acres of undistinguished

Crosses make me sick.
Mother could mark Papa's grave
In the churchyard a mile from home,
By its firs and shaft. . . .
Your nothing grave. . . .
                    Shame!
God I am of little understanding. . . .
But with God all things are possible. . . .
Give my son another life—
A Norwood ugliness, a bourgeois rot,
Dust and concrete, Falcons and Mustangs, not. . . .

BULLETIN

It's Dr. James gone wild
Who used to save life
Smite him
Transfusing the enemy
Maul him
Bandaging the firing squad
Wrest off his gun
And if his arm come with it
And his head
The wet roots clinging thereunto,
The warm roast carved:
Wash the liver
Wash the lights
Breathe life into the lungs
The valves, the wheelchair;
Cherish this white-suited
Uncouth, incurable angel
Unfold his newspaper
Unfold his hand
Run his finger under the commercials
You grow better
You will not die
It says here
You will not die
You grow better
O surgical hands
Hero of the corps
St. Devil

PAUSE, IN FLIGHT

Late August. The wind stays awake all night
Thinking of autumn. The crickets wonder
Out loud about the future. . . . Damn the past.
Damn the past. . . . Fall is yonder,
The constellation we are travelling to.
No, we are where it is travelling to
From a distance, a time, long overdue,
Extinguished before the hunter put
The gun over his shoulder. Will these trees
Be the last to receive
This light? The crickets, apprehensive,
Give ear. This light, this autumn, this hunter—
Comes already dead. Who
Flutters featherless into the leaves?

Wm. Pitt Root

PASSING A SAWMILL AT NIGHT

The road was straight. A gully braced by stumps
plunged from the edge. Beyond it, a fall field
widened through the darkness toward a clump
of trees etched in fire against the sawmill wall.
Slowing down, I watched the bright smoke
scatter ashes dying into stars.

Years before, without a word spoken,
my father stopped the jeep as we hunted his farm.
Our years together ending, the stubble behind us bright
with frost, we watched a distant mill's dark walls
pulse with swollen squares of fire. "At night,"
he told me (he still moves through the smells
of oil and gunpowder, night itself,
reaching to release the brake), "a man knows
more than can be learned of death, or life."

I stopped the car slowly. My wife leaned
against my arm, asleep. Across the road,
through the living trees, the taken burned.

THE FIRSTBORN

Our first child
    was early, "easy"
they told her, and telling me
    she smiled,
pretended to smile. The pillow case
was white, the sheet-stains hidden, her face
familiar, strange.
    And full of guilt
beyond delivery, I felt
    as strange
as Adam joining Eve, feigning pride
while I brought her a rose bright as blood.

THE GRANDFATHER
At a Family Picnic

From wave to wave a flat rock skips,
skids. An edge catches. It flips and sinks.
Each time he throws, the watch in his pocket clinks

on the coins and collected pebbles. How many trips
he's made back here, to pry stones from their chinks.
  From wave to wave each flat rock skips,
  skids till it catches its edge, flips, and sinks.

His wife complains, insists that his pocket rips
from carrying "sharp, dirty stones." She thinks
aloud, "he's my oldest child." Their grandson blinks.
  From wave to wave the flat rock skips,
  skids. When it catches an edge, flips and sinks,
  the water twinkles. He flinches. The watch in his pocket
    clinks.

Jean Farley

THE NIGHT HORSE

I awake an hour before dawn
And still she grazes there,
Slipped somewhere out of the field of sight
But ripping and chewing spring grass
Which grows longer now, gaining momentum:
After the first low hesitant start
It pours forth from the ground
Almost as fast as rain went in.
The horse grazes on the edge of attention;
Half between sleep and feigning sleep,
I dare not look too close or she will go.
Now that there are leaves the wind blows
Like a bear turning over from sleep—
Stirs and rustles and goes.
Silence then, the horse I cannot see
Grazing in the dark at the edge of the woods.
If I could go to her as simply
As the single night song of a bird
Reaches out of the woods—
Reach for her mane and be on her back—
The wind turns over, dawn begins
And the babble of many small birds.

BED RIDER

Strength was once my stand
I think and having thought,
Draw my lids against the leaning of a wall.
I see myself implant a foot
On the hatchmarks of a broad brown floor—
Which slips aside as though to dance
One matronly measure on the side of a wave
Before blundering into the trough.

I settle sideways
Into a sea of darkness
Which must diminish me like sleep
To powers I never lost—
For when someone opens at daylight
A door in my head
The room and I flap hugely once
Like a drowning moth.

All day my legs lie sunken in cloth.
My forearms crossed upon my chest
Are helves the women put aside
While with their fingers and their biddy eyes
They tend my body like a garden.
Its crops are more dreadful than dust—
And there at night reopen the craterous sores
Which they discuss.

Scritch-scratch, scritch-scratch they go,
And in each abrasion they savor
The barren outermost lands
I long ago lost—
Old cabbage head tossed in a sea
Of senseless, solitary fault,
I feel the water lapping, loosening
The innermost leaves of my thought.

SHE SEES PALLBEARERS COMING ON SNOW

If, instead of taking away,
They lifted your long white body dead
And bent it with the strain
Of stringing an unstrung bow,
Bent it until inward cold sinews gave
And it broke at the sockets of your legs—

You would sit then and I
Would sit behind and to one side,
Avoid the field of your eyes
And, thinking us alive,
Would watch your cheek where the beardness shows.
For once you go white into frozen ground
This patch of stubble will grow
Upward, upward, to melt your fine-grained snow.

X. J. Kennedy

LITTLE ELEGY
For a Child Who Skipped Rope

Here lies resting, out of breath,
Out of turns, Elizabeth
Whose quicksilver toes not quite
Cleared the whirring edge of night.

Earth whose circles round us skim
Till they catch the lightest limb,
Shelter now Elizabeth
And for her sake trip up Death.

CROSS TIES

Out walking ties left over from a track
Where nothing travels now but rust and grass,
I could take stock in something that would pass
Bearing down hell-bent from behind my back,
A thing to sidestep or go down before,
Far-off, indifferent as that curfew's wail
The evening wind flings like a sack of mail
Or closeup as the moon whose headbeam stirs
A flock of cloud to make tracks. Down to strafe
Bristles of grass a hawk falls—there's a screech
Like steel wrenched taut till severed. Out of reach
Or else beneath desiring, I go safe,
Walk on, tensed for a leap, unreconciled
To a dark void all kindness.
                     When I spill
The salt I throw the Devil some and, still,
I let them sprinkle water on my child.

LOOSE WOMAN

Someone who well knew how she'd toss her chin
    Passing the firehouse oglers, at their taunt,
    Let it be flung up higher than she'd want,
Just held fast by a little hinge of skin.
Two boys come from the river kicked a thatch
    Of underbrush and stopped. One wrecked a pair
    Of sneakers blundering into her hair
And that day made a different sort of catch.

Her next-best talent—setting tongues to buzz—
    Lasts longer than her best: it still occurs
    To wonder if she'd been our fault or hers
And had she loved him. Who the bastard was,
Though long they asked and notebooked round about
    And turned up not a few who would have known
    That white inch where her neck met shoulderbone,
Was one thing more we never did find out.

Heather Ross Miller

GILEAD

You come from a long house,
A long stone house of prayers.
River Sundays and muddy barefoot praise
Damned up the days of your summer riot.

I don't know that house.
My house was a windmill,
Moss-stacked and tall,
A dim green glimmer in the heat.

We look in the book of your house:
The men and their women peel brownly,
And their legends stiffly crack.
You say:
> "Grandpa went round on Sunday morning
> To every house;
> Knocked on its door with his big blue knife,
> And collected his nigger rent."

Your Grandpa wore several white beards,
Not one, but several,
Rippling across his old face like frosty vines.
And your Grandma held a German silver purse,
A grey crushed mesh of vanity.
The cradle, church, and churn had left famine,
Flood, no fire.
She was more buttonhook than woman.

Grandma and Grandpa rose to their river church on
    their river Sunday
In the green rush of a river-strangled May.
There the hollow wives sat beside their strange mates,
And the twining ivy starved with God.

When they returned,
Stiff and hot in the new spring balm of Gilead,
He was calm.
He picked up the poker
And struck her, the wife of his bosom.
Severely, methodically, without passion,
The black soot streaked her pale old-fashion skin.
She put up her hands,
Like poor old ivory fans
Left over from a masquerade.

Then he left her by the best hearth,
Swept bare of fire,
In the stiff front room where a tall mantel clock
Ticked stupidly;
And the frozen stares of her children
Stared frozenly out their heavy oak frames.
He went to his barn,
To his rope that he had thrown up over the loft beams
In the cool, fluttering, early morning.
"There is a tree in Gilead
That shall heal the sin-sick soul."
The field lark sang.
The horses frisked;
Their big veins twitched with the blood-push.
He stood,
Still calm.
Oh, balm of Gilead,
Sweet mint of my father,
Caress me.
You have said these gifts are mine:
The big blue knife, the stiff buttonhook,

Grey German silver, sweet balm of Gilead.
But I say I don't know that house.
In the still early morning,
Let us flee.
Let us take the balm and steep it into sweet tea.
The book of my house is full of blank pages.
No green river riot rages
In the cool clover-white of my house.

When their Sunday is over,
And the muddy feet have stamped out the mounds of
    their praise,
We can walk on to higher grounds in warmer days,
Through the rank wild green,
Easy, quiet, faintly incarnadine.

Patricia Peters

SIDEWALK BONE

Something majestically clumsy was slaughtered,
Devoured and then its thigh bone carelessly
Tossed on the sidewalk or rather by night
Trash cans are raided and expressed.

In daylight that bone is shoddy and degrading
Like a specimen from a shallow Indian grave
Sprinkled with sapless leaves like scales or ashes.
But at night it is brighter

Than ivory and glowers
Beside those cans as if it might
Batter them into urns or kettledrums.
Also it flies through gaping eyes to detonate the back of my
    skull

Where darkness invades like molten lava
Until I am entranced like a bucket rusting
On a pump primed so that that filthy bone
Siphons my strength

Like a leech or a skin
Filling with wine or a grape
Bending its vine toward the ground or a seed
Erupting into a jungle where twining branches seal the air
    like cattle into pens.

EASTER

Spring limber dances twirls and lifts up hands.
So Grandfather on a juvenescent day
Came striding from the grave as
Naked as a ghost ill-fitted
In a flat fedora,
Divested of decay
Came marching through the door.
Himself beyond a doubt
Since he was mantled
In retired years,
An air of being kite-like to our floor.
Of course our shock
Was strong but greater still
His charge of not recalling
Where he was
Or why
Why memory
Should reappear in life-
Begotten shells to shoot without the
Walls of our dried love
To crash like hyacinths past stationed
Bulbs past coffin shroud
And raise a fragrance quite beyond themselves.
Small wonder that he sighed and
Faded out again
Or we were whipped like tinder through the wailing room.

TIN CAN

Somebody kicked a tin can in the night
And I was in a speedboat at the Falls;
The trees were filed away in paper sheets
And from the eaves the bats swung out like bells.

My mind was ringing with the swipe of time.
The stars were rattling in a comet's wake;
The air exhaled like sand inside a wave;
A heartbeat was a parachute downwind.

I waltzed, a speck of dust, through specious skies
And heard clear rust impinge on tripping veins;
Somebody kicked a tin can out of sight
And open windows battered down the night.

James Applewhite

TREE IN THE RAIN

I came out into the wet night
Wondering if windows of my car were down.
Keen drops needled into the slick grass.
The town was deep in a rustle of rain
Fresh-smelling as flapping wash.
I settled into a chair, willing to wait,
Thought of the earthworms stirring—

Still, in spite of my drowse
The young tree shaped like a cloud
Across the street seemed poised, aware.
I sensed the inside of it rain-rubbery,
Clammy like a wet raincoat,
With scratching branches and with leaf-edges
That would tickle like bugs;
And yet it dreamed itself
Listening like the ears of earthworms
Under their lids of mud.
A sensation trickled into me of it
Risen like an earth-pulse into the showering
Sky, like a single cupped palm
Catching drink, or cupped, hearing.

I felt the cold sound naked on my skin.

A WOMAN FIFTY

Her husband at work, she'd take a pill. Four
O'clock. Then alone in the house, even her pets
Laid still by the sun, she'd muse behind draperies,
While heat took the town, upon people:
                             Charlotte so thin
And fragile, whose helpless long nails fluttered
Before housework like a caught bird's feathers;
Who heard of her death in the mourning dove's cry,
Who drove white and sickly to the doctor's (she said):
Meeting her lover.
                    Mrs. Whittaker on the edge of town,
The bank president's widow. How could one live so?
What was a witch? Trees gathered over the house
As she thought. Dark leaves as surely live things dead
As bats' skin clung to its roof, that peaked
And rose in accumulated shade, as light leaked
From fields beside through bright grass back to the sky.

"Yellow shade of the bathroom is tissue of skin.
Marble-hard putty around window panes seems
The substance of nails: old, brittle, chalky,
As if beyond those fingers wrinkled to the tips.
And the louver under her roof is open,
Wood slats broken as the paint is parched
On that rusty, rough-straked front,
And in and out under the starry night
Spin bats with beautiful bones under skin
Of their wings, that are repulsive and naked come day
But now seem skeltons keen as the starlight.
And the arc-winged birds at dusk, pale sky
In the hollows of their brains, or why should they
Come so, at evening? And she is lonely,

With old newspapers stacked, cut flowers withering
In dust, red petals gone rust and brittle.
Old high shoes she has, and the bushes in front
Straying and starved as a cry in the fields at night.
Leaves scatter on splintery twigs that pierce the space,
Behind them mosquitoes weave over dry leaves
In the sill's corner by a wicker chair, then through
The rust-weak front door screen I think
Into the hall, where a velvet hanging
Makes light too dim to see through, but as if
The sight of your eyes would touch it
And feel the rustle. She will be out of sight,
Her bird's head upswept hair and tip-toe
Walk kept still behind a door, shadowed in a closet.
But she will have in her skull the evening
Light like sickle-winged swallows, her hands
As starlight-shaped as the bats'. She will
Be waiting at evening, tense and unseen,
Too timid to visit, her laughter covered,
In an undisclosed pressure of herself
Like a child's held breath, a light clamped tight
In her skull behind closed lips, clenched eyes.

I pray she feels the flow in and out of swallows,
Bats with bones in their wings beautiful as hands."

Kelly Cherry

THE GETAWAY

East of the sun,
West of the moon,
South from Tennessee,
                    Benjamin John
Lies loafing; but the wide brass bed
Like a plumped-up anecdote
Seems to say,
"You are a dream-ridden fool
Who is no exception nor any rule."
                    Benjamin John,
Riding the fevers of 3 A.M.,
Yanks the top sheet over.
To this lackluster, easy, leggy girl
Stretched out in shadow,
He would say,
"Wash the anchovies,/While I pour the wine"
In the words of a crazy Greek,
Cynical, lyrical.
She sleeps in her grand and blockish bed,
                    Benjamin John.
O this dull indolence. . .
O this lack of clarity; *fuzzy* pretense. . .
Lack of rhythm, drama, sense. . .
He will pack his toothbrush;
Solo, straddle and spur a llama to Chile or Peru. . .
                    Mad as a hatter, like a child
He buries his face in her tangled hair
And wishes this small, wild prayer:
I'm hiding, I'm hiding, and no one knows where.

FOR ALICE, WHOM HE MARRIES
ONE YEAR LATER: THE PROPOSAL

Long distance.
"How are you?" "Fine.
How are you?" "Fine."
Restlessly, restlessly,
Pines scrape the sky.

Silence. Then together.
"Sorry, you go on." "No,
You go on." "Sorry."
Looking off, he gathers
Night in his eyes.

In the dark room
He moves alone
Restlessly, restlessly.
Asleep he becomes
A drowned bird washed
Ashore, bill, plume
Pared to the bone,
A skeleton.

ELEGY FOR A DYED REDHEAD

Sitting, she
toys with this thing.
How her hair flickers and burns! . . . matches
the blush her cheek commands.

She is Chicago raging. She blows
hot, blows
cold. In the middle of the night,
we both are burning bright.

In the middle of the night I dreamed
she crumbled, ashes
raining on my head
like a storm of dust or curses.
I laid her down among the dead.

Gibbons Ruark

THE RIDE

The dark car idles at my doorway.
The driver's seat is empty. No matter.
I have known for a long time what to do.
Turn off the radio. Turn off the light.
Lock the house behind you. I lock the door,
Cross the walk, climb into the humming car.
Somewhere in the dark a catch releases
And the car slides forward like a subway.
Settle back. Sink in the deep seat. I do.
When I press the button by the silver
Ash tray, a window rises on a greased
Track and seals me up in the plush back seat.
It isn't long before my breathing clouds
The glass. I reach for the ash tray but I
Can't reach it. Now my feet won't touch, won't touch
The floor. Driver, driver, where are we going?
A voice with the sound of a radio
Says "Downtown. Downtown to see the F.B.I."
It's *not* my breath. It's smoke from Daddy's cigar.
I sit beside him in the long black car.
As we glide down Pennsylvania Avenue
The driver winks at me in the mirror
And I whistle back through Daddy's microphone.
Let's go to the zoo tomorrow, can we?
If I press the button by the ash tray
I can roll the window in between us
Up and down. I roll it down, I roll it up,
It sticks. Driver, where are we going?
Driver, driver . . . The driver's seat is empty.
Hello. Click. Hello. Click. Can you hear me?
When I drop the mike and reach out to tap
The window, my hand turns into a sponge.

A BLIND WISH
FOR RANDALL JARRELL

Sometimes all the roads seem dark.

But in that darkness trees and animals
Take slow shape under an enormous will.

The field between the lost world and the world
You gently foundered in is woods again,

The bearded man and boy in tennis shoes
Now grow together in a single tree,

Or run with the blood of a single fox,
Leaping and falling in the deepening forest.

POLIO

The snore of mid-summer flies at the screen,
Afternoon's tepid fog crawling my sleep.
In my unrelenting dream the fire truck
Peals round the corner, and when I wake
The sirens still confound me. From the wobbly
Room I stumble to my mother's door,
A shifting blur in the wall before me.
Her limbs are weak and rumpled on the sheet.
The empty braces glint. Their brightness hurts.
Pale pillow, damp hair, my father's shadow
Straining over her, sweat at his armpits,
Straightening, bending, straightening her leg.
Like knives her shrill cries peel the heavy air,
But he keeps at it, forcing tears back till
His eyes ache. The veins map out his anguish.
His false teeth tighten on that work of love.

Robert Watson

AN ELDERLY GHOST HAS HIS SAY

This Halloween I'll just stay put at home.
An old ghost, my grave grows on me: warm shrubs,
An oak, asters, my flesh their sap, their leaves,
And their dead leaves my food; my voice the owl,
Wind or what I choose. I am content,
Content as I was never home in life,
My restlessness, mind scattered, gone to seed.

It took some getting used to I'll tell you.
At first my wet best suit began to shrink
And I swelled up like biscuit dough until—
The bone, wood box split. And I was born again:
A child playing in dirt, his parents gone.
Worst was that stone men stuck on top of me—
To keep me in, remind me of my name—
Heavy as my memory of childhood,
Weighed down with that trash they teach in school,
But the oak kicked down, weeds ate up the stone.
Here it's mindlessness that counts. A fleshpot
I was and am. You should have seen me glow
In youth, this youth with neighbors' bones
Dancing, mingling in dark. But that's behind,
Behind me in my wild phosphorescence.
A ripe corpse now of two hundred halloweens,
I find this grave is good enough for me.

Gossip has it my wife has turned black cat.
Agnes was always bad luck, bad luck for me,
Licked clean in her black Sunday dress she wore

To church to purr, claws closed in her black muff.
She thought she'd be a spirit when she'd die.
A spirit? When I'm solid as a mudpie.
To be dead you can't be squeamish, must be
A part of what Agnes could never bear.

Some lovers hide near graves as I once did,
Impatient, wanting my hard earned change,
Straining an hour in my lap; find, weep
That all this buckling on another fails.
Here it is our nature, law: I am my neighbor.
I am worn thin with what men above call sin.
Even in my dust age lust blows me on
To lace with other flesh, birds, beasts,
Grass and men. In spring a child once came here
And ate a wild strawberry at my foot.
And ate a little part of his great, great
Grandfather's left big toe. Do you smell smoke?

In fall when boys play with matches in the leaves,
Piled as comforters for my snug winter's nap,
I turn nervous, fear fire spreading out of hand
In which I die again, not to be buried
In cool, moist ground, sweet darkness of earth's flesh,
In which I mix, change each day, spread my arms
Out to the living world which lives in me:
My nightmare is fire that burns me to the clinker
Men call soul, and I am tossed to heaven,
Hell—who cares?—some other birth far away
From ashes of my accustomed lover earth;
To sit with that creature who was my wife;
To burn forever in fire of her yellow eyes,
Raked by metal claws: a mouse that black Agnes
In her superiority would have had me be.

Randall Jarrell

A GIRL IN A LIBRARY

An object among dreams, you sit here with your shoes off
And curl your legs up under you; your eyes
Close for a moment, your face moves toward sleep . . .
You are very human.
                              But my mind, gone out in tenderness,
Shrinks from its object with a thoughtful sigh.
This is a waist the spirit breaks its arm on.
The gods themselves, against you, struggle in vain.
This broad low strong-boned brow; these heavy eyes;
These calves, grown muscular with certainties;
This nose, three medium-sized pink strawberries
—But I exaggerate. In a little you will leave:
I'll hear, half squeal, half shriek, your laugh of greeting—
Then, *decrescendo*, bars of that strange speech
In which each sound sets out to seek each other,
Murders its own father, marries its own mother,
And ends as one grand transcendental vowel.
(Yet for all I know, the Egyptian Helen spoke so.)
As I look, the world contracts around you:
I see Brünnhilde had brown braids and glasses
She used for studying; Salome straight brown bangs,
A calf's brown eyes, and sturdy light-brown limbs
Dusted with cinnamon, an apple-dumpling's . . .
Many a beast has gnawn a leg off and got free,
Many a dolphin curved up from Necessity—
The trap has closed about you, and you sleep.
If someone questioned you, *What doest thou hear?*
You'd knit your brows like an orangoutang
(But not so sadly; not so thoughtfully)
And answer with a pure heart, guilelessly:

I'm studying. . . .
                        If only you were not!
Assignments,
            recipes,
                    the *Official Rulebook*
Of Basketball—ah, let them go; you needn't mind.
The soul has no assignments, neither cooks
Nor referees: it wastes its time.
                            It wastes its time.
Here in this enclave there are centuries
For you to waste: the short and narrow stream
Of Life meanders into a thousand valleys
Of all that was, or might have been, or is to be.
The books, just leafed through, whisper endlessly . . .
Yet it is hard. One sees in your blurred eyes
The "uneasy half-soul" Kipling saw in dogs'.
One sees it, in the glass, in one's own eyes.
In rooms alone, in galleries, in libraries,
In tears, in searchings of the heart, in staggering joys
We memorize once more our old creation,
Humanity: with what yawns the unwilling
Flesh puts on its spirit, O my sister!

So many dreams! And not one troubles
Your sleep of life? no self stares shadowily
From these worn hexahedrons, beckoning
With false smiles, tears? . . .
                        Meanwhile Tatyana
Larina (gray eyes nickel with the moonlight
That falls through the willows onto Lensky's tomb;
Now young and shy, now old and cold and sure)
Asks, smiling: "But what is she dreaming of, fat thing?"

I answer: She's not fat. She isn't dreaming.
She purrs or laps or runs, all in her sleep;
Believes, awake, that she is beautiful;
She never dreams.
                    Those sunrise-colored clouds
Around man's head—that inconceivable enchantment
From which, at sunset, we come back to life
To find our graves dug, families dead, selves dying:
Of all this, Tanya, she is innocent.
For nineteen years she's faced reality:
They look alike already.
                    They say, man wouldn't be
The best thing in this world—and isn't he?—
If he were not too good for it. But she
—She's good enough for it.
                    And yet sometimes
Her sturdy form, in its pink strapless formal,
Is as if bathed in moonlight—modulated
Into a form of joy, a Lydian mode;
This Wooden Mean's a kind, furred animal
That speaks, in the Wild of things, delighting riddles
To the soul that listens, trusting . . .
                    Poor senseless Life:
When, in the last light sleep of dawn, the messenger
Comes with his message, you will not awake.
He'll give his feathery whistle, shake you hard,
You'll look with wide eyes at the dewy yard
And dream, with calm slow factuality:
"Today's Commencement. My bachelor's degree
In Home Ec., my doctorate of philosophy

In Phys. Ed.
          [Tanya, they won't even *scan*]
Are waiting for me. . . ."
                              Oh, Tatyana,
The Angel comes: better to squawk like a chicken
Than to say with truth, "But I'm a *good* girl,"
And Meet his Challenge with a last firm strange
Uncomprehending smile; and—then, then!—see
The blind date that has stood you up: your life.
(For all this, if it isn't, perhaps, life,
Has yet, at least, a language of its own
Different from the books'; worse than the books'.)
And yet, the ways we miss our lives are life.
Yet . . . yet . . .
                    to have one's life add up to *yet!*

You sigh a shuddering sigh. Tatyana murmurs,
"Don't cry, little peasant"; leaves us with a swift
"Good-bye, good-bye . . . Ah, don't think ill of me . . ."
Your eyes open: you sit here thoughtlessly.

I love you—and yet—and yet—I love you.

Don't cry, little peasant. Sit and dream.
One comes, a finger's width beneath your skin,
To the braided maidens singing as they spin;
There sound the shepherd's pipe, the watchman's rattle
Across the short dark distance of the years.
I am a thought of yours: and yet, you do not think . . .
The firelight of a long, blind, dreaming story
Lingers upon your lips; and I have seen
Firm, fixed forever in your closing eyes,
The Corn King beckoning to his Spring Queen.

FICTION

Peter Taylor

A CHEERFUL DISPOSITION

I. At The Airport

The Episcopal service he had of course known would be unabridged and unaltered. But the attendant rituals— the gathering at the house the night before, the repeated trips to the mortuary, the closeted audiences with the bereft one (the dead brother's widow)—all of those old practices, it seemed to Frank Lacy, might easily have been abandoned or changed beyond recognition. After all, people didn't *live* quite the way they had twenty-five years before! . . . When he had first decided that he and Janet should go out to attend his brother's funeral, it hadn't really been clear to him why or how he came to the decision; for, the truth was, he had not often gone to visit the brother when the brother was alive. The deceased brother was known to have grown quite rich in recent years, but, then, Frank himself had more than sufficient means. And so it wasn't that. Although he prided himself on being a person of cheerful disposition, it may actually have been an interest in the funeral proceedings themselves that had made him decide to go. Because as soon as he had arrived on the funeral scene, as soon as he was face to face with the very sad circumstances that had brought him home, he found that he could think of almost nothing but how like the funerals of his long-ago childhood this one was. Everything about it was the same. And somehow he had expected it all to be quite different.

Aboard the Whisperjet, on the way out from New York, he had kept trying to imagine just what his own role, the role of a brother, would be. Would he and his surviving brother, Alfred, and perhaps his brother-in-law, his sister Norma's husband, be expected to wear black bands on their arms? Or was it only the Catholics who did that, nowadays? He couldn't decide whether he and Janet ought to go first to the funeral home or to the widow's house or to the motel where they were going to stay. (They had declined to stay with any of the relatives.) . . . Yet as soon as he had set foot on his native soil, at the airport, everything had become remarkably easy. His dead brother's chauffeur had turned up to meet them and had taken them directly to the mid-town motel. From that point on, the course seemed perfectly inevitable. He and Janet went first to the widow's house, and after a brief audience with that poor, distraught woman, they moved on to the funeral home where the deceased brother's remains were resting temporarily. It all seemed very natural, very familiar, very much like the old days when hardly six months could pass without the family's having to give an honorable burial to some old timer amongst them. At any rate, it had positively done Frank Lacy's heart good to see how little funerals had changed.

It seemed that from the moment he stepped off the plane from New York everything had gone so very—well, so felicitously. There was no other word for it. He had received his first impression when he peered out through the tiny window, just after the plane landed, and saw the uniformed chauffeur waiting for them there at gate number seventeen. He had never seen the ruddy-faced fellow in the dark uniform before. He had not known who, if anyone at all, would be there to meet him and his wife. Yet hadn't he somehow known at once who the fellow was? As soon as he saw him standing behind the little chain at gate seventeen, he *knew*. And the presence of the chauffeur struck him at once as representing—well, a happy decision, a quite delightful decision, on somebody's part. There was no other phrase for it. Surely if a member of the family had come instead of the chauffeur, the first gloomy exchanges might have been awkward in that public place. He was very glad indeed to see the chauffeur, and when a few minutes later the big, well-scrubbed hand reached out to take his small carry-on bag, Frank could barely resist clasping the hand and giving it a cordial pumping.

Then, at the front entrance to the airport, Frank was to experience another pleasant surprise. After obtaining the baggage checks from Janet (it was always Janet who looked after the tickets and baggage checks when they travelled) the chauffeur had gone on ahead of them to fetch their two pieces of plaid luggage that would presently arrive on the conveyor belt. Frank and Janet moved along the wide concourse to the terminal building at a leisurely pace and then rode the escalator down to a lower level. Upon finally reaching the front entrance they pased on outside, the automatic doors opening gracefully, effortlessly before them and then closing gracefully, effortlessly behind them. It was an early morning flight they had come in on—what a beautiful October morning it was, too!—and except for the taxis, there were but two cars parked by the curb at the main entrance. The first was a low, long, black sedan. Assuming this to be the kind of car his brother would have owned, Frank seized the handle to the rear door and tried to open it. He did so rather absent-mindedly, not really looking at the car itself but over its glossy black top toward the expanse of cloudless blue sky to the west. When the handle didn't yield and he realized that the door was firmly locked, he peered down inside the car and saw that someone else's matched luggage—some travelling-man's sample cases, actually—all of a very dark leather and with many straps and buckles, was laid out in a depressingly neat row along the back seat. Frank quickly released the handle, and turning to Janet he said jubilantly: "This is not our car! We've come to the wrong car!"

Janet, who still had not seen the sample cases inside and who of course trusted more in her own efficiency than in her husband's, took a step forward to try her hand at the door. But Frank stopped her. At that moment he had spied his dead brother Ralph's chauffeur coming toward them. The fellow was bouncing along, carrying all of their rather gay, holiday-looking luggage as though it weighed nothing. The green-and-red-plaid suitcases swung from his mighty hands; the little calf-skin carry-on was tucked under his capable, long right arm. He was a stout, healthy-looking fellow, probably in early middle-age, and with large ears and heavy jowls which made one trust him immediately. As he approached them now, in his natty, well-fitted uniform, he wore a broad grin on his face and was shaking his head from side to side. At the same time, he repeatedly tilted his head away from the long, low, black car and toward the vehicle just behind it. Frank returned the man's cheerful grin and gave an understanding nod. With a tug at Janet's sleeve he led her to the second car.

And, oh, what a tremendous reprieve the second car seemed. It was a lovely, sea-green convertible with gleaming chrome hubcaps! This reprieve was greater even than that of having the chauffeur turn up instead of some of the family. Frank at once guessed the circumstances, and the chauffeur obligingly confirmed his guess: All other family cars being in use, they had sent for him and Janet in a car belonging to one of his late brother Ralph's college-age sons. Well, *that* was certainly a happy turn of fate! And while the driver was loading the luggage into the trunk of the convertible, Frank found himself wondering if he mightn't ask to be allowed to take the wheel. It even occurred to him that they might put back the plastic top and ride in the open—so fine a day it was, with the autumn air somehow suggesting spring rather than winter. But after a quick glance at the composed and self-possessed chauffeur, who was just then closing the lid of the car's trunk, Frank did manage to restrain himself.

Nevertheless, it was in that spirit that they made their drive into town. Frank kept pointing out familiar sights to Janet, she not being native to this part of the world, and noted for her the changes that had taken place on the otherwise familiar scene. He missed certain old monuments to his youth. But, still, he confessed he found the approach to the city much improved. It soon came out that he and the chauffeur were exact contemporaries. Before long, neither of them could mention any vanished landmark without the other's remembering it and recalling still another. The atmosphere in the car could not have been more congenial. To Frank Lacy it seemed surprising that this agreeable fellow, the chauffeur, had not gone farther in life. Yet on the other hand he envied his still living here at home, driving about town all day with no responsibilities, not worrying about how his career was progressing or what complications the next rung up the ladder might bring or whether the next rung might be down the ladder. Here was at least one man in his early forties who was not still questioning whether he had followed the right career, whether he mightn't still be happier in "the academic life" or perhaps in "the book-publishing field."

After they had got nearly into town, Frank asked the chauffeur about certain night-spots that used to lie along the route. The chauffeur burst into laughter. The very mention of the places delighted him. His laughter was so infectious that even Janet's voice could be heard in a quiet tittering. Those places, said the chauffeur, had all moved out to the north and east sides of town, and they were operating on a much larger scale. The pity was, added this very humane chauffeur, that such teen-agers as he and Frank had been, when they knew those places, could no longer afford to patronize them. But Frank felt little sympathy for the current teen-agers. He was only glad to hear that the dear old toughs and dear old floozies who ran the joints had prospered and were moving up in the world. It seemed a splendid town to be coming home to, regardless of the mournful circumstances. Every street they turned into looked as though it had been newly paved. There was not a lawn that had not been seeded with winter grass, and when, here and there, an urn or a windowbox appeared it was invariably freshly planted with luxuriant greenery. As they drew closer into the city and into the older neighborhoods, it was evident that most of the houses had been very recently refurbished. There was no dinginess anywhere. Under the bright sky, everything seemed to have fairy-tale perfection about it. It was the way he had, as a child, sometimes imagined the old neighborhoods must have looked when they were new, before he was born, even.

II. At The Funeral Parlor

About the funeral arrangements themselves there was nothing that did not seem entirely appropriate and well-conceived to Frank. In the first place, everything seemed so private, so personal. Even the mortuary itself had once upon a time been somebody's private residence. Frank could almost, though not quite, recall the name of the family that had once upon a time lived there. In fact, he could very definitely remember a little thirteen- or fourteen-year-old girl who gave a supper party there on one occasion and a dance on another. They had danced in the wide front hall until after eleven o'clock! But since that little girl was not a girl who matured into an even passably attractive young woman, he was sure that he had never been in the house at any later time. But still the funeral home was just *such* a house as the houses he had frequented during his last, best years at home. If only that little girl had developed along more attractive lines, then the house might well have been amongst the very ones. This thought was somehow consoling. And during the two days between his arrival on the Whisperjet and the actual funeral service at the church, Frank tended to cherish the "watches" or "shifts" he took at the familiar-seeming mortuary. So long as he was posted there, shaking hands and chatting with the dead brother's host of in-laws and with his own long-unthought-of-relatives—so long as he was there he enjoyed a sense of his own undiminished vitality, and a childlike illusion of *relating* to all about him. He discovered that he even took some pride in the provincial stylishness of the people who came to sign the mortuary register. It was an experience unlike any he had known in many years and was not one he could possibly have imagined himself finding satisfaction in again.

Afterward, Frank felt that in all the funeral proceedings there had been for him only one difficult moment. No, there had been two; the second that came to mind was simply the more happily forgotten of the two. At any rate, upon arriving at the church for the funeral service he had made a fairly silly mistake. Stepping out of the undertaker's grey-upholstered Cadillac, to which he and Janet had been assigned, he immediately crossed the pavement to the church steps and seized the hand of one sweetly smiling funeral director. Momentarily he had mistaken the man for one of his bereaved sister-in-law's relations. He was not sure which one of them it was but he imagined he saw a family resemblance! And during that moment how he had welcomed the sweetness and warmth of that undertaker's smile! It was a pretty awful gaffe on his part, and only the sympathetic blush on Janet's cheek, when she came up beside him, told him for certain what he had done.

The other difficult moment had come the previous afternoon. It was quite the reverse in its character and was considerably more painful to recall. In the parlor at the mortuary he had touched the elbow of a slight, stooped, dark-suited man who stood gazing out through the plate-glass front window of the old mansion. Supposing the man to be one of the "staff," Frank had intended asking him where he might find a rest room. But the solemn face that presently showed itself to Frank, revolving slowly on the slender neck and without the body's giving any sign of movement, was none other than his brother Alfred; Frank's first and only thought was that the question which he had been prepared to ask would be long remembered in the family if it got asked. It would be thought so *like* him to have to go to the *bath* room at such a time and in such a place. It would bring back to them so *many* memories of what he had been like as a little boy. But since he could not immediately invent another question to substitute, he offered his brother in its stead only a big, silent, sickly smile. He anticipated the response would be a deep scowl. But he was mistaken. Alfred's solemn expression was replaced by a smile so mournful and yet so detached that Frank felt the sickliness and the cheapness of his own smile. And then Alfred had turned away to the window again without a word's having passed between the two brothers.

The small shock from not recognizing Alfred's back did not have its effect upon Frank until the back was turned to him again. The effect was Frank's refusal almost to believe his own eyes—to believe that the funereal little figure at the window, with the baldspot on the grey head, could really be his brother. Thinking, afterward, of the unlikely face that had been shown him, he felt that it was more like the face of a man of seventy than of one barely fifty. And for a moment he had the strange conviction that it was not their older brother Ralph who was dead at all, but this middle brother Alfred. . . . Presently, though, Frank got hold of himself. After all, he had had an urgent physical need to consider at the moment; he was in search of a rest room. There would surely be one somewhere on the first floor of an old mansion like this one. As he drew away from Alfred his wife threw him a questioning glance from beside the high oak mantelpiece where she had been standing with his sister Norma. Her glance gave him strength. He decided that he should and could endure his discomfort until they made another trip back to their motel.

III. At The Motel

At the funeral home, and at the widow's residence too, everything moved slowly—almost as in a slow-motion movie. And of course it seemed quite right that it should. But at the motel where Frank and Janet were put up, it was a different matter. At the motel, all of their activities—all of their comings and goings, that is—went on at the senselessly accelerated rate at which life normally moves nowadays. Even when they felt they could allow themselves twenty minutes or half an hour for a nap, they threw themselves down on the twin beds hurriedly and without even turning back the buff-colored bedspreads. And usually they did not actually succeed in dropping off to sleep—not even Frank, who had a marked talent for catching a quick nap. At best, Frank merely lay there with his eyes closed and managed to make his mind a blank. At second best, he gazed up at the stuccoed ceiling and reflected upon how much less grim and depressing the proceedings were than he had anticipated they would be. "I don't really know why I came," he would say to himself at these moments, "but I am glad I did. It really satisfies something in one—satisfies one's sense of ritual."

Or sometimes when Janet discovered that he was awake,

when they both were supposed to be napping, she drew him into conversation. And it was during those intervals when they were alone in their motel room that Frank would explain to Janet the identity of the various family friends and the myriad relatives whom she had met since they arrived. Janet was not Frank's first wife, nor even his second—if that matters. (What *does* it matter, Janet and Frank not being people who live out there in one of those places where things are more difficult?) She had not known Frank's parents when they were alive and she had met his sister and his brothers only briefly when they had made flying trips up East. The other relatives she could not differentiate amongst at all. But when Frank explained to her who the relatives were, she lay on her bed in the motel, listening carefully, her mind clicking away, storing up all the information.

Frank Lacy knew that this was the nearest his wife could ever come to making *her* mind a blank. He knew that her brain was always pecking away, clicking away at something or other, whether she were in the magazine office where she worked or in the big co-operative apartment which they owned in Manhattan. He was not like that, himself. Under ordinary circumstances he could drop off in a nap almost anywhere and at almost any time, and usually woke feeling greatly refreshed. At night he sometimes seemed to go to sleep the moment his head touched the pillow, though he not infrequently woke a few minutes later, from a seemingly endless dream, to find Janet still going over events of the day or planning events of the morrow. Moreover, he liked this trait of his wife's (so unlike the dominant traits of his first and second wives, with their sloppy, unhappy, neurotic tendencies, their empty intellectualism). He was a man who prided himself on his own happy, healthy disposition, and he found it reassuring to know that his wife was always involved in some practical problem for which there *was* some solution. It seemed wonderfully characteristic of her that as soon as she arrived on the scene of the funeral she took on duties and responsibilities, began listing the names of the callers at the funeral home and later on, at the residence, began making lists of those who sent telegrams, those who sent flowers, those who sent in food for the family's meals.

His wife was, in other words, business-like about the funeral and in some degree gave order to a scene where there had previously been almost none. But once, when they were lying on their beds in the motel, Frank had wished to congratulate Janet on this achievement, and she had then sat up very straight on her bed to say, "Oh I am able to be practical about all this because I am not emotionally involved. You must remember that I never really knew the poor man. Your brother's death is not at all something real to me." Usually, during these brief intervals at the motel, however, the two of them would lie on their twin beds, with their eyes mindlessly scrutinizing the stuccoed ceiling, and would make only random and very objective remarks on the mournful proceedings at the funeral home and at their poor sister-in-law's house, as though it were all something taking place hundreds of miles away.

IV. THE VISITORS

That was how it was at the motel—as if they were far, far removed from the funeral scene. And that was no doubt why, on the night after the actual funeral service, it came as such a shock when Frank's sister Norma and her husband George, still dressed in their dark funeral garments, burst in upon them there. Somehow his sister's presence was not like that of another person but like the presence of a strange, new spirit that had come into their midst. Suddenly, without knowing that he was listening to the words she spoke, Frank sensed that Norma had come at that near midnight hour for the sole purpose of contradicting all his own impressions of the past two days. Norma's view, which she expressed in whispered words that filled the motel room, was that it had been the most "dismally depressing" funeral she had ever witnessed! The attendant events had been "miserably grotesque"! All in all, it was the most mismanaged funeral there had ever been in the family. Finally seating herself on the stool at the dressing table, she focussed her attention directly on Frank and said, "But it didn't have to be so, Frank. It was all brother Alfred's doing. It was Alfred's doing. You know it was, Frank."

For some time, Frank could not make out why it was that their brother Alfred was to be blamed. He couldn't make out how Norma considered the funeral had failed or what exactly it was that was supposed to have been brother Alfred's "doing." All that he could be certain of was that his impressions of the past forty-eight hours were not the same as Norma's and that her view of how things had gone was somehow a threat to his peace. He took up the nightcap, which Janet had made him just before his sister and her husband arrived, and sipped at it. "The truth of the matter is," he heard Norma saying now, "yes, the truth is that our dear, sweet Alfred is just a damned awful liar."

At the sound of those words Frank heard Janet rattle two glasses together in the bathroom, where she had gone to make drinks for Norma and George. He sprang to his feet and stuck his head through the bathroom doorway to ask if she had broken a glass. She hadn't, of course, and with an impatient shake of her head she sent him back to their guests in the bedroom. It was, of course, characteristic of Janet to find a way of busying herself in times of tension. There was nothing for him to do but to return to Norma and George. "A damned awful liar," Norma repeated as soon as he showed his face again. Frank thought it was clearly an absurd charge to hurl at poor, mild-mannered, withered-up Alfred. But, anyway, Frank was not interested in Alfred's alleged lies—not yet. And when Norma began on the failings of their dead brother's widow, he wasn't interested in that either. It was still the discrepancy between his own and his sister's view of the funeral proceedings that interested him and disturbed him and kept him from giving her his full attention.

The substance of Norma's charges was that Alfred was, himself, a sick man, a dying man—"He keeps it a deep secret what his trouble is, but it is *serious*, Frank"—and that Jennifer, the widow, had made her husband's life such a misery that the poor man had *wanted* to die. "She was jealous of him to the very end and resented his taking his final leave of her." It was because the surviving brother was "in a decline," of course, that he found the elder brother's death so disturbing. He had been a dreadful nuisance during the last months of the illness. He had accused the doctors of "doing Ralph in" and accused the hospital staff of all manner of neglect. That, principally, was how and wherein he was a liar. And the fact that Norma's husband was on the hospital board made matters no easier and no less embarrassing for anybody!

"I couldn't help noticing how different Alfred was from you at the funeral," Norma told Frank. "His morbidity communicated itself to everyone. But you have always been different from Alfred, Frank. You are so blithe, so gay, so free. I have watched you all through the past two days. You have such serenity, or sublimity."

As for the widowed Jennifer, Norma had never seen a widow behave so badly. She had done nothing about the funeral arrangements. She had "secreted" herself in her upstairs sittingroom and permitted people to come there to commiserate with her, to come and "view" her, so to speak, instead of letting them view poor Ralph. Even at his own funeral she was in competition with him! Her orders were that no one was to view him in his casket. And no one, not even his own sister, had been allowed to do so.

While Norma was delivering herself on the subject of her

widowed sister-in-law, Frank had kept his eyes on Janet. She was seated again on her bed, having served the drinks, and with her left hand she was smoothing the furrows and wrinkles in the bedspread. Then, after a moment, he saw her turn to straighten the small travelling-clock and the glass ashtray on the bedside table, and then straighten the shade on the lamp there. He supposed it was part of her being a "professional woman" that she should be embarrassed and made uneasy by the behavior of purely domestic females like Norma. She found it particularly painful, he knew, to hear one woman gossip about or berate another woman in the presence of men. That she should identify herself with such a creature as Norma, or even Jennifer, seemed almost incredible to him because he considered that she, Janet, steered the wonderful middle course between that of the entirely domestic female animal and that of the neurotic female intellectual. Perhaps she kept her admirable balance merely by keeping busy, by involving herself always only in what was real. She had got up now from her place on the bed, and she had got up to *do* something. It would be something useful, he had no doubt. And how different her bearing was from Norma's as she went across the room. Perhaps it was altogther because she had her mind on her own business, even if it were business she invented as a diversion. Anyway, she walked directly to her suitcase, found a box of Kleenex, and in the absence of napkins to wrap about the cold glasses she was soon offering the squares of tissue to all present.

Accepting a sheet of Kleenex, Norma addressed herself to Janet: "I am saying these things to Frank because Frank sees things with his own truth-seeing eyes. He always has. He already knows what I am telling him. Our brother Ralph *wanted* to die! He wanted to die because for nearly thirty years his life had been nothing but a torture living under the roof with Jennifer. He waited till all their children were married and gone, and then he just went to bed and died. Our brother

Ralph was a gentleman, Janet. And to him that seemed the only way out. Jennifer knows that's why he died, and now she's ashamed to show her face." Rising from the bed where she had been sitting during this last denunciation, Norma set her empty glass on the bedside table and again came and stood directly before Frank. "What he did is hard for us to understand, isn't it, Frank? We can't understand how someone could *want* to die. For me the hardest part is to understand how a woman could bring herself to be so cruel, so demanding of a man as to make him want to leave her even if the only way to do it was by dying. Oh, poor, poor, dear Ralph!" All at once, turning away from Frank and toward George, Norma gave way first to sobbing and then to full-fledged weeping. George came rushing to her and took her in his arms.

"Poor baby," said George, stroking her hair and pressing her head to his shoulder. "It's been a trying time for her." Frank and Janet came immediately to their feet, of course, but they stood speechless, trying to show sympathy in their facial expressions. "We only meant to drop in and say goodbye," explained George to his hosts. And then, addressing Norma: "But we're tired, aren't we? And we shouldn't have let ourselves get so worked up." In no time, it seemed, he and Norma were gone. Their departure was so hasty, in fact, that it had somewhat the same shocking effect upon Frank and Janet as their arrival had.

V. Beyond The Rest Room

When they were alone in the motel again, Frank and Janet looked at each other with open-mouthed expressions, each seeming to ask if those people had really been there or if he or she had only imagined it. Glancing at the clock on the bedside table and seeing how far past midnight it now was, Frank suddenly sat down on the bed and began removing his shoes. "Our plane leaves at a quarter past seven," he said. "We'll never make it if we don't get some sleep.

Janet was still standing by the door, her head cocked to one side, plainly going over in her retentive mind all that Norma had said. "Oh, we'll make the plane, never fear," she said with a vague smile. "That's one I most certainly won't let us miss."

In the middle of untying his second shoe, Frank paused with his fingers on the strings. "Her tears were real, you know," he said.

"Yes, she's scared stiff," Janet replied at once. "I don't know whether she's more scared she'll die or scared George will want to die—and manage to." Frank watched her as she came over and picked up the two empty glasses on the bedside table near him. "They're *all* of them scared nearly out of their wits," she said gravely. "Were they this way, Frank, when your parents died?"

"No, not at all." He removed his second shoe and began pulling at his tie. "But Ralph is the first of our generation to go. That's what's put the fear of God in everybody." Janet continued to move about the room, picking up glasses and pieces of Kleenex. From the bed Frank said, "Alfred probably wasn't right about the doctors and the hospital. I suspect Norma's analysis of him is correct to a point. But she's no less a liar than he. That business about Jennifer was mostly rot, and so was that about Ralph's wanting to die. Norma and Jennifer were never friends. Jennifer came in and stole her handsome big brother when she was just twelve, and Norma has never forgiven her. Moreover, anyone can see how Norma treats George. It's a case of judging others by yourself."

Janet stood with the four tumblers on a tray which she had taken from the dresser. "What are you going to do with those?" Frank asked.

"I'm going to rinse them in the lavatory, so the room won't smell so alcoholic when we struggle out of bed at six a.m."

"Very good," he said with an approving smile.

But she remained standing there with the aluminum tray and the glasses. "They are all so frightened for themselves," she said, "that they haven't had a real thought of Ralph. What was he like?"

"He was a very usual sort of man, if there is such a thing. He was ten years older than I, and so we weren't together much when we were growing up. It's hard to say much about him. He was a little bit hen-pecked, I suppose. Suddenly I feel that I didn't really know him well enough to come to his funeral."

"Oh, I'm glad you came," Janet said. "You've been very good. They needed someone with your cheerful disposition. I know it has been difficult for you, and you've done wonderfully. Somehow, I've suspected the worst moment for you must have been when you stepped off the plane and didn't really know what was ahead of you."

"I thought it would be so, myself," he said. "But it wasn't bad, and after that, everything came so easily that I haven't really minded. It is you who have been wonderful. You've done so much. They couldn't have run the funeral without you."

"It hasn't been hard for me, Frank," she said, "because I didn't know the man who died. That makes an enormous difference. I would have felt I was intruding if I hadn't kept busy." Then, as she turned away toward the bathroom, she said with a broad smile, "Maybe I've found my real vocation. I think I might become a fine funeral director."

It was not thirty seconds later that Frank heard the crash in the bathroom. The sound was unmistakable. Janet had spilled the glasses off the tray. He leaped off the bed and ran in his sock feet to the bathroom door, arriving just in time to see Janet drop the tray itself on the tile floor, and plunge her hands into the lavatory where the glasses had fallen. And simultaneously he heard her somewhat muffled cry of pain.

"What is it, my dear!" he exclaimed in a whisper.

Janet straightened herself and turned around at once. In the lavatory he had a glimpse of the broken glasses. "I stumbled," Janet explained, smiling faintly and looking rather pale, Frank observed. "I stumbled over that rug." Frank looked down and saw that there was a small, white mat on the floor, but he had not seen her stumble on it. When he looked up again, he saw the red lines beginning to show on her wrists and on her left thumb, where the broken glass had cut her. Suddenly the blood from her wrists began to flow rather profusely, as he had often seen it do from the nick of a razor on his cheek or neck. He noticed that Janet was observing it with intense interest. She looked pale, and her eyes seemed to have darkened.

"I am *so sorry*," he said, reaching for a towel. As he wiped away the first flow of blood, he noticed how her hands were trembling.

Her voice was as calm as usual, though. "There is some alcohol and a box of Band-Aids in my suitcase," she said. "They're in my little kit, on the left side." Before going to fetch the kit, he smiled at her and winked, because her efficiency was often the subject of joking between them. She not only returned his smile; she threw back her head and laughed aloud.

"You're all right?" he said, before going to her suitcase. She stopped laughing, but a big grin remained on her face. . . . When he was applying the alcohol he saw that the trembling had increased and he noted to himself that there was no response to the application of the alcohol, no evidence of its stinging. When he had applied the last Band-Aid, around her thumb, he looked up into her face and saw that her lips were drawn tight and that there were tears in her eyes. Then, throwing back her head again, she began laughing and crying simultaneously. He took her by the shoulders firmly, repeating her name over and over again. But this had no effect upon her.

He put his arm about her and pulled her into the bedroom. "You've been under more of a strain than you know," he said. "You're tired and it's so late." It was so unlike her to become hysterical that he felt at a loss to know what to do for her. "We must get hold of a doctor," he said. But Janet shook her head. Several minutes passed, during which he first walked about the room with her, then tried to get her to lie down. Again and again he suggested that they should summon a doctor, but each time she shook her head and tried to indicate that she would be all right presently. There were continued repetitions of this exchange between them, yet for more than ten minutes Janet remained in a state of hysteria, mostly crying but with occasional bursts of laughter. Somehow Frank managed at last to get her out of her clothes and into her nightgown, and managed also to get himself undressed and into his pyjamas. And when he lay down he took her into his bed with him and held her in his arms. At last he heard and felt her sobbing quite simply and normally, like a tired child, on his shoulder, and he knew that she would sleep soon.

He lay awake in the dark long after he heard her breathing evenly in her sleep. He would not let his mind dwell upon the subject of what her hysteria had meant, except to reproach himself for having said that Norma was no less a liar than Alfred—for having put it in those terms. Finally, while he still held her in his arms, the words came silently to his lips, "She is no less afraid than the others." Although he held the wife whom he loved very close beside him, he felt utterly alone. But why is it not so for me, too? he asked himself. Why was he not hysterical, too? he wondered. Was his cheerful disposition really only shallowness? Would Janet come to feel, as those neurotic women before her had, that he was without depths of feeling? But something in his nature would not let him pursue such a subject, not lying there in the dark and after such a day as this one had been. He set himself to thinking, instead, of the ride from the church to the cemetery that afternoon, when he had actually experienced a kind of joy and transport that had been the crowning satisfaction to his pilgrimage home. Since the church had been a downtown church and the cemetery was in the eastern-most suburbs, it had been a long ride through the town he knew best in the world and through the section of that town that he knew better even than the section near the airport. And when the procession came to within a mile of the cemetery Frank recognized that instead of the woods and the truck farms which used to line the road, there was now, first of all, "Maggie's Place"—which name he saw spelled out in large cut-out letters along the peak of a steeply gabled roof. Next was a low, rambling brick building situated in an acre of asphalt and with electric letters over the entrance spelling "The Palms." And soon after that was a modern glass-and-brick structure with an awning-covered walk stretching out to the curb, and on the awning printed in bold, red letters: "The Embers, formerly Popeye's."

He had barely been able to suppress a smile, or even perhaps a loud guffaw. For those establishments were obviously the elaborated juke joints, the very ones, which he had frequented on the south end of town twenty-five years before. He felt an impulse, almost irresistible—though not quite, not quite —to spring out of the grey-upholstered Cadillac, with its jump-seats and its foot-rests and its old-fashioned handstraps at the sides, to spring out and run into one of those night-spots for at least one quick afternoon-drink. He had only sat blinking his eyes, of course, as the Cadillac continued to creep slowly along in the procession. For one moment, in the rear-view mirror, his eyes met the eyes of the oily-haired young driver of the car, so impersonal, so indifferent, so unlike the eyes of brother Ralph's middle-aged chauffeur! The young driver seemed so perfectly trained, so utterly, so perversely resigned to driving the car at this mercilessly slow speed past "Maggie's

Place," past "The Palms," past "The Embers, formerly Popeye's." As though there were no difference between these
places and the high-rise apartments, the office buildings, or all
the ranch houses and split-levels they had passed earlier! Frank
looked down at his hands and quietly crossed his ankles on the
grey carpeted floorboard. But he was not deceived. He was not
deceived, he told himself. Out there was life! And none of
the others in the car with him—neither his widowed sister-in-
law's sister, or said sister-in-law's sister's husband riding in the
front seat with the driver, or that couple's two boys perched
on the jump-seats, or even Janet—none of the others with him
in the car knew where life was. And being a man of cheerful
disposition he smiled inwardly at himself. But while one part
of him smiled inwardly with cool irony, at the same time he
felt a great surge of joy welling up inside him. The proprietors,
the employees, the habitués of those establishments were free
as none of those in the car with him were; those denizens of
the night world in his hometown were the first really free people he had ever known, were the first evidence he had en-
countered, at seventeen, that there was such freedom from the
confines the other members of his family knew. In his own
way he had followed their example. As Norma had said of
him tonight, he was so blithe, so free! And that was why he. . . .
He went off to sleep quite suddenly, in the middle of his un-
finished and perhaps unfinishable sentence. His line of thought
did not continue in any half-waking dream, as it sometimes will
do. He fell into a deep sleep at once and into a deep dream
that seemed to derive in no way from his thoughts about the
funeral procession that afternoon. He was in the mortuary
again. He had just received Alfred's smile and exchanged
glances with Janet and Norma, standing over by the high oak
mantelpiece. But instead of taking strength from Janet's glance
and deciding that he should and could wait, he lowered his
eyes and made his way past the two women, across the new-

looking carpet, and toward the wide front hallway. It was dangerous to poke about too much in one of these places, he thought. One never knew what one might come on. But suddenly, while hesitating in the doorway, he remembered that he had been in this very house before—long, long ago—and had danced in this hallway till eleven o'clock! Could he possibly remember?—Yes! Or maybe it was only his knowledge of *such* houses as this one. Of course, it would be under the stairway, toward the end of the hall. Presently he had opened the panelled door, and there it was. And it was just as he remembered it or knew it had to be—the tiled floor, the large oval lavatory with the handsome mirror set in the wall above, and of course the capacious toilet bowl and tank. It was all just as he would have expected, except that the porcelain was whiter and was antiseptic-looking in a way that it couldn't have been in somebody's house, and the fixtures on the lavatory were polished like steam-fittings on a battleship. He found that he could pass on around and beyond the lavatory and the toilet, and because of that somehow he did not need to use the toilet. Now he was in another, larger part of the room where the floor and walls were tiled and where there was, on the ceiling and along one wall, a maze of highly polished chromium pipes. Presently he realized that he was actually in a long, tiled corridor, and he saw approaching him from the far end two men wearing rubber gloves and white smocks. They drew nearer and passed him without speaking, but he recognized one of them as brother Ralph's chauffeur and the other as the man he had shaken hands with on the church steps. "I suspected you were deceiving me all along and were doing double duty," he said, though not loud enough for them to hear.

At the end of the corridor he passed into an extremely large room in which the floors, the walls, and even the ceiling were tiled in white and in which were great coils of polished pipes, also some large vats, and one huge bottle in which was a full-

grown foetus. Turning away, so as not to have to look at the
giant foetus, he saw on the other side of the room, toward which
all of the pipes finally led, a grey coffin with its lid open. He
recognized it at once as Ralph's coffin, the very coffin he had
seen in the back parlor earlier and which the widow had or-
dered should not be opened. "Well," he said to himself, "there's
skullduggery here." As he spoke, he heard a door open behind
him. He whirled about and saw that through the door, beyond
which he could see daylight, two aproned delivery-men were
bringing in groceries. They bore a strong likeness to the chauffeur and the funeral director he had seen a few moments before. They went across the room and passed through a door
that opened on a descending stairway. He heard them descend
the wooden stairs and then come up again immediately. When
they reappeared, they were carrying bushel-baskets of garbage.
He followed them to the outside door and saw them dump the
garbage, baskets and all, into an old-fashioned garbage wagon
to which a mule was hitched. He recognized the area outside
as one of the narrow, rat-infested alleys of the town, alleys
which had always repelled and frightened him as a small child
but which a few years later became a delight to him. As he
stepped back inside, he sensed that he was being followed by
the two men in aprons. Presently he saw that, unmindful of
him, they were heading for the coffin. "That's my brother," he
asserted, and began walking faster, trying to reach the coffin
before they did. "That's my brother in the coffin," he said
with still more force. And one of the men said to the other,
"Who does he think he's fooling?" . . . He now rushed to the
coffin and looked inside. The man he saw laid out on the
tufted silk looked years younger than Ralph, though everybody
had said, hadn't they, that Ralph had aged so? He realized that
there was an inscription on the side of the coffin and got down
on his knees to read it. It read: "Here lies our brother, Frank
Lacy."

He tried to cry out to the two men, "Oh, no, it's a mistake!" But he woke instead, sitting up on the side of the bed, making ugly, guttural noises in his throat.

"What is the matter, Frank?" he heard Janet say—from far away, it seemed. She had moved to her own bed while he slept.

Frank, who was still only half awake, pretended he was coughing. "I guess I've got to quit smoking," he said.

"Yes, they're like nails in your coffin," said Janet, who seemed less than half awake. Then she laughed and said, "But you quit smoking more than a year ago."

Frank gave a little half-grunt, half-laugh and fell back on his bed. "We'd both better try to sleep," he said, feeling ashamed of his foolish effort to deceive Janet about his nightmare, "or we'll never get up in the morning." Yet, against his better judgment, he lay there in the dark with his eyes wide open. In the past a visit home had meant a glimpse of childhood and youth to him. But it wouldn't mean that again. Ralph had been the first of them to go. Alfred wouldn't be with them long. In time, Norma would die—and George and Jennifer. But he was not coming back to their funerals. Home was not a glimpse of childhood any longer. And home was no place for him—not at his age. Tomorrow he would rise early and take the plane back to New York. For, yes, home was something he could put behind him. If only, he thought, still lying with his eyes open in the dark, if only the dream born of being home was something he could put behind him, also.

Jessie Rosenberg

THERE'S A GARDEN
DOWN THE STREET

She saw three of her mother in the lighted glass panels painting a thin blue color on her eyelids. Then her father came into the bedroom with his shirt and tie on and no pants. He was holding one shoe out in front of him like a dead fish.

"Where's the goddam shoelace?" he said, shaking the shoe.

Dina giggled from the bed and her mother's elbow slipped on the dressing table. The blue color jerked up to one eyebrow. She glared at Dina through the mirror.

"Why are you in here? Why aren't you watching Kenny?" Her voice sounded like thin wire, and her hands were busy, rubbing at the blue smear. Her mother hardly talked at all, except in that tight voice or in front of company, when she sounded like somebody Dina didn't know.

"Cause he's in the bathroom is why."

"The shoelace?" her father said again, ignoring Dina.

"Daddy looks silly," Dina said, pointing to his white legs.

He looked at her then with no expression on his face, only raising the shoe in the air a little higher so that she said quickly, "Kenny was eating it a minute ago. He chews on everything."

"Why." It wasn't a question. Sometimes her father just said "why" and then wouldn't move for a few minutes. Now he stood in the middle of the bedroom looking silly.

"In the second drawer," her mother said, making funny shapes with her mouth in the mirror.

"Is stupid Mrs. Lockard coming tonight?" Dina asked, propping her chin on her elbows.

Her mother stopped scrootching up her lips and looked at her through the glass, her blue eyelids narrowing. "Yes, dear pet—good old stupid Mrs. Lockard." Her voice was like sugar and it meant she was getting mad.

Dina heard the bureau drawer slam and then her father was sticking his white legs into his trousers. When she stopped watching him, she heard her mother's dress going zzzip like a match striking in the closet and then Kenny came to the door. He stood there blinking for a moment behind his rimless glasses, looking like a little white rabbit, and then he found Dina.

"Open up, open up," he said then, bouncing from one bare foot to another. "She's here. She's here. Open the door, open up."

"For chrissake, somebody let the old bat in." Her father was lacing his shoe.

Dina's mother waved toward her with a cigarette in her hand and Dina slid off the bed, following Kenny down the narrow hall.

Mrs. Lockard entered as usual, wrapped like a bear in her grey, wet-smelling coat, carrying a knitted bag with sequins on it and the evening paper. She nodded at Dina and Kenny and, without speaking, walked into the kitchen. They stood in the living room and heard her putting the kettle on.

"She hates us," Kenny said from the doorway, biting his

thumbnail. He looked up at Dina. "What're we going to do tonight?"

"Shhh!"

"What for?" he said louder.

Down the hall their parents' voices mixed together like a small whining noise and then her father shouted toward them, "Close the door, damn it."

Dina took the door away from Kenny's hand and slammed it hard. Then she motioned him to the couch and they flopped down into one corner.

"Stop chewing your finger, stupid, and listen: they aren't as dumb as you think. Only sometimes. They'll catch us if we aren't careful."

"They don't know nothing," Kenny whispered loudly.

"Anything."

"Just because you're older than me doesn't make you Jesus."

"And just cause Daddy says that doesn't mean you can. You don't even know about Jesus."

"I know as much as you—two years isn't so much, smarty."

Dina pulled his thumb from his mouth.

"I know something you don't know about—we can go tonight when the T.V. gets her." He put his finger back inside his cheek.

"Where? What kind of place?"

Kenny shrugged deeper into the couch and looked up at Dina through his oval glasses. "It's a statue," he said, mouthing the words around his finger. "It's in this big garden in Hillary Circle. A great big statue of this woman." He looked at her for a moment blinking fast, then he took his thumb out of his mouth and looked at it. "She doesn't have any clothes on."

"How big?"

"Big as Mother. Bigger. I come up to her knees."

"You sure?"

"Yeah, we found it today when we were playing tag—you

go through these trees in this big yard and there she is, just standing there. With no clothes on."

"I'd rather go catch goldfish in Mrs. Kelly's fountain."

"Wait'll you see this, Dina—just wait—those goldfish aren't nothing compared to this."

"Anything."

He glared at her a minute and then he shut his eyes and started chewing on his shirt collar. She watched him sulking and then whispered "okay" just as Mrs. Lockard marched through the swinging kitchen door and her parents came down the hall, their heels clicking on the hard wood. Mrs. Lockard stood in front of Dina and Kenny with her hands folded around her middle and her parents stood behind the couch. Mrs. Lockard nodded and then Dina felt her mother's cool fingers patting her hair absently.

"You'll see they're in bed by ten," she said in her company voice.

Dina stretched her head back and looked up between her mother's hands. Upside down her mother looked like a painted statue, all white skin showing down the length of her neck and arms, the black dress carved around her breasts. Her face was set in a cold half-smile and her thin nose looked chiseled above her pale lips.

"We'll be back late, Lockard—use the guest room when you get sleepy," her father said. He was pulling at his cuff links as if they were pinching him.

Mrs. Lockard didn't even nod. She just clasped her hands tighter around her middle and rocked back on her heels.

"Give me a kiss, babies," her mother said, leaning over the couch. She smelled like a garden.

Dina held her face back again, lifting her cheek, and closed her eyes, waiting for the smell of her mother's lipstick, and then when the cold mouth brushed her face she opened one eye. Kenny didn't turn around, he was just sitting with his eyes blinking behind his glasses. She saw her mother's smile freeze and then the long fingers reached out and flicked Kenney's hair. He wrinkled up his nose and said "bye."

"Let's go," her father said, drumming on the couch with his fingers, and then Dina saw Mrs. Lockard nodding toward the door, heard the swish of silk when the door opened, and they were gone.

Mrs. Lockard stared at the door for a moment and then she yawned. "Upstairs and undressed," she said, her mouth still gaping.

"It's only eight o'clock," Dina said.

"I want to hear the bath water running in exactly three minutes and then I expect you to be in your pajamas when I come up. Now."

She looked like a lady soldier, Dina thought—all big, muscle and fat mixed together in a lump. And her hair looked like something had been scratching around in it. Mrs. Lockard only patted it a lot.

"Okay," Dina said, trying to sound disappointed. "Who goes first," she asked Kenny, "me or you?"

Kenny had his shirt collar tucked into his mouth again, so he pointed.

"Well, you come and pick up your room while I get clean then."

Kenny tried not to smile, biting down harder on his shirt collar. He nodded, and then he followed Dina upstairs, holding onto her skirt with both hands. "Gettyup," he said, flapping the skirt, and Dina walked up the stairs bent over on all fours, trying to make snorting noises. At the top of the stairs they waited, and then they heard the sound of applause and a band making old-fashioned music.

Dina leaned over the bannister. "Burp—it's Lawrence Welk time!"

"Hurry up—let's go stomp around in the tub and she'll be asleep soon. I can't wait."

They ran water in the tub and stood in it up over their ankles, splashing each other's legs.

"Don't get my dress wet, stupid," Dina said. "That's enough —get the towels."

They dipped the towels into the water and threw them on the floor. Then they tiptoed into their bedrooms and when they met on the stairs again, they were in their pajamas.

"Look sad, now," Dina whispered, and she started down the stairs, flopping her slippers hard on each step. Mrs. Lockard jerked in her chair and looked around at them.

"I want something to eat," Kenny said. "A bologna sandwich."

"You'll have bad dreams. Go on to bed now—it's almost nine."

"Can't we watch Lawrence Welk first?" Dina asked. "He's one of my favorite shows."

"You never listen when I let you watch. You always talk and ask questions. I can't even hear the music—no, go on to bed. Turn on your radio to make you sleepy."

Dina nudged Kenny in the back and they whined together, "Please?"

Mrs. Lockard stood up then and pointed behind them to the stairs. "Goodnight."

"Yeah," Kenny said and rubbed his eyes behind his glasses. "Same *to* you."

Upstairs again, they lay on Dina's bed and whispered in the dark.

"I'll give her ten," Kenny said.

"Shhh."

Downstairs the music bubbled up and after a few songs there was a slow snorting sound that rose in rhythm above the clarinets.

"There she blows," Dina whispered. "Okay—be quiet—meet you here in three minutes."

They waited for a commercial about cars to start and then they eased down the stairs and out the door while Mrs. Lockard's snores growled around the sound of engines racing.

Outside it was suddenly quiet. When the door shut on the television, the night closed around them like a net.

"Which do you like best? July or now?" Dina asked, looking down the empty street.

"Now," Kenny answered. "August is best. Feel the sidewalk? Still warm."

They rubbed their bare toes along the pavement and Dina nodded.

"Come on—you won't believe it. It's weird."

"Sure you don't want to catch a goldfish first? Remember last week when Mr. Koonce found that one we left in his mailbox?" Dina covered her mouth, trying not to laugh loud, but Kenny was already looking down toward Hillary Circle.

"We can do that later—please, Dina."

"Okay. Big deal."

"She doesn't have any clothes on," Kenny said.

"Oh, boy—is that what it is? You already told me three times. Haven't you ever even seen somebody naked before?"

Kenny blinked up at her, his little face indignant. "See Mother all the time with no clothes on and you know it, smarty. She never wears clothes—even when she does wear clothes she hardly does." His face changed then and, behind his glasses, his eyes got round. "This is different. You'll see."

They walked through the lawns of the houses, watching their footprints sink into the wet grass. Dina was chasing a firefly across the Parkinson's yard and then Kenny hissed over to her, "Through here—come on—this way," and when Dina looked again, the firefly was above the roof of the Parkinson's house, blinking like a yellow drop. She padded toward Kenny, who stood parting the bushes behind the Parkinson's garage, and then he held out his hand and she let him pull her through the shrubs. They wound their way through the overgrown dividing line between the two properties, until they were standing in deep, soft grass, like a springy carpet, and the trees stretched over them so tight that only once in a while a star glittered through the sheaf of leaves, as if it were pinned to a branch like a rhinestone.

"Okay—close your eyes now until I say," Kenny whispered.

"Why for heaven's sake? It's dark anyway."

"Just do—please."

"Okay—but if you're playing a trick on me, Kenny, I'll—"

"No." His voice was so serious, and he took her hand gently, his fingers laced between her own.

Dina shut her eyes then and squeezed his hand and then she felt him pulling her slowly forward. Her feet stumbled along behind him, testing the ground cautiously and then he stopped so abruptly in front of her that she almost fell over him.

"Now," he whispered and let her hand go.

They were standing in a clearing, a semi-circle of grass framed by trees that cut them off from the rest of the lawn, and above them the moon hung like a fat lantern, spilling light into the shadows. In the middle of the clearing, framed against the circling trees, the woman stood looking down at them. Dina felt the air suck out of her lungs, heard her breathing catch in the silence. She was a tall, full woman—standing slightly forward on one foot as if she had begun to take a step, her left leg poised carefully behind her. One arm hung simply by her hips, palm loose against her full thigh, the other raised gently to her waist, and she was almost smiling. She looked as if someone had called her and she had just begun to answer, quietly, when something had turned her into stone. But even the stone seemed human, warm—it was grey where the shadows curved around her thighs and breasts, and her feet were a pale green, as if part of the grass were seeping into her body. Under the moon's thick light, she seemed so capable of breath that Dina expected the step to be taken, waited for the upraised hand to gesture, calling them forward.

"Who is she?" Kenny whispered. "Do you know who she is, Dina?"

Dina shook her head, staring at the shadows webbed around the woman's arms. "No—but she's the only one. I know that."

They were quiet for a moment then, looking up at the smooth face, the almost smile.

"Isn't this better than Kelly's goldfish?"

Dina nodded her head slowly, unable to turn her head away from the statue, and then behind the trees circling the woman, music suddenly poured toward them, and people's voices mixed together high, laughing. The sounds drifted over the trees like voices in a dream, persistent, half-real, until as abruptly as it had begun, the music stopped, the sounds clicked like a radio turned off and only two voices were left, hollowed against the outside silence.

"Hold my drink—I want to take off my shoes." It was a woman and she laughed, and then a man was saying "Hold on—there—that's better." They were quiet for a minute and then the woman laughed again, her voice ringing brittle over the rustle of wind against trees.

"Here," she called, giggling now, "come sit with me here—I know a place," and then there was only the sound of bushes rubbing together.

Dina grabbed Kenny's hand and put her other hand over his mouth. She held him for a moment tight that way and then she let him go, only still holding his hand hard.

"Don't say a word. Where can we go—we have to go."

Kenny looked frightened. "You're hurting me," he whispered, looking down at his hand. "What's the matter, Dina—you're hurting me."

"Let's go—come on."

"Wait—it's just some people from the Adams'. Let's hide." He was excited now and he jumped up and down shaking Dina's hand like a limp rope. "Oh, boy—I told you this was better than those stupid fish. Let's hide over here—come on, hurry."

"No," Dina's face was pale as the statue's. "We have to get out of here. Please, Kenny, let's go. Now." Kenny stood still and looked at her then. She was breathing fast and her eyes were round and dark in her white face. Behind them the woman's laughter seemed to catch in the bushes; it spiraled toward them like music from a carnival—high, drunken, somehow out of tune as if it were running too fast.

"Please," Dina hissed, tugging Kenny's hand, and then they pushed through the bushes, scrambling now on their knees, back into the Parkinson's yard. They padded behind the garage, beyond the sound of the laughter now, and Kenny pulled on Dina's hand. She was still running.

"Wait, wait." He was breathing fast now. "Why-couldn't-we-stay? What's the matter?"

Dina shook her head fast, holding her stomach as if it were cramped. "I just don't feel good. I want to go home. Please, Kenny? I just got this stomach ache."

"Oh," he reached toward her, holding her arm. "I'm sorry, Dina. I didn't know you felt bad—come on. We can go slow now—don't run. It's okay if you get sick outside, nobody'll see."

Dina nodded, patting his hand on her arm. "I want to go home," she whispered, and they walked back through the wet lawns.

Inside, Mrs. Lockard stared open-eyed at the ceiling while before her on the screen Cary Grant and Myrna Loy were yelling at each other over the noise of an open convertible.

Kenny followed Dina into her room. "I'll stay with you case you need me."

"No—thanks, Ken. I just want to go to sleep."

"Sure? Want some Pepto-Bismol? Want some milk?"

"Really," Dina shook her head. "You go to bed. I'm sorry I made us come home early—next time we'll stay. Okay?"

"Sure." He watched her climb into bed.

"Aren't you going to put your pajamas on?" he asked. His eyes were blinking again and he looked like a bewildered little old man.

"Oh," Dina looked down underneath the covers. "I felt so bad I just forgot," she said, feeling her face burn in the dark room. "Yeah," and she got out of bed and stood looking down at him.

"You *sure* you're all right? I can call Dr. Maynard." He was looking at her strangely.

"You sound worse than Daddy—worry-wart. I'm fine. You go to bed—I'll put my pajamas on and tomorrow let's go back and visit the statue." She tried to sound excited, like it would be an expedition. Kenny loved expeditions.

"Okay." He walked to the door and then he just stood there. "Night."

Dina looked at him blinking at her from the door and she caught the tears in her throat. Then she ran to the door and hugged him hard.

"You're my most favorite people," she said, holding him close. She felt him stiffen with surprise. "Don't forget that." Then she spanked him on his bottom and pushed him across the hall toward his room.

"Night," she whispered before the door closed on his soft smile.

She lay on top of the rumpled covers in her room, listening to the noise of Kenny's bureau drawers slamming, then hearing the soft descent of sound as he moved around the room, turning off lights, rustling the bed covers, then quiet until she almost felt she heard his breathing slow into the purring rhythm of sleep. Inside her head, beyond the silence of her room, beyond her listening, the brittle laughter echoed, hanging like broken mirror glass behind her eyes.

Allen Tate

THE IMMORTAL WOMAN

W e never knew why she came but it was always in
October when the warm days were few, and the fallen leaves
under the thick shade stuck to the dampness on the walk that
the sun could not dry. It was usually the last of October. We
wondered how long she had been here, a round little old lady
in black holding her head up on the left side and leaning on
a heavy black cane. When I saw her I thought: she has already
passed several times. Then I remembered that was last year or
two years ago. It got so that when I saw her for the first time
in the fall, I said: it is another year. My aunt says she came
every fall for fifteen years but I know it was only in the last
four or five that she took to walking with a cane. Stringy, dead-
looking grey hair fringed the edge of the small black hat that
she wore close to her temples, and her thick glasses gave her
eyes a fixed stare. She walked steadily to the corner by the
grey brick house, crossed the street to the green bench by the
College gate, and sat down facing the house. Her clothes were
always the same and it is hard to remember what she wore.
She seemed to sink into the faded anonymity of the old street.

Only the leaves have renewed themselves here since I was a boy. On our side there are tall trees, sugar maples and sycamores, from the far corner, which is out of sight, down to the old square house where stands, heaving up the bricks in the walk, a giant oak; across the street runs the high wall of the old College. The same damp trickle has held to the wall the same patch of grey moss as long as I can remember. Early in the morning, and more distinctly in the fall, you can hear if you listen closely the clatter of the main street down by the Potomac, a low hum of noise that seems to bring with it the smell of the fishmarket. At noon there is a moment, filled always with surprise, when the sunlight falls quietly through the trees.

We see few people. Nothing happens. We never visit and no one comes to our house. I think that none of our neighbors ought to be living here. I suppose the trees know what was here, and what it was, but no one knows who planted the trees. They know something that we never hear and they contain years that we cannot see. On the third of every month Mr. Higgins comes to collect the rent. 'It's a fact now. Mark my word. It won't be five years till there's niggers in all these houses.'

There is the old brick house on the corner across from the College gate. I see first the wall running out of the side of the house down the side street. It encloses the garden, and midway along it opens, or opened once, an iron gate now a rusty green. I have never seen inside. The dull slate roof, cracked everywhere and littered over with twigs and leaves, slopes front and back; at each end, wide apart and perilously tall, two slender chimneys rise. Six windows stretch across the front of each of the three storeys. In the exact center of the house stands the door; it opens into the second floor at the end of two curved flights of stone steps, one on each side. It is a double door, two plain panels with small tarnished brass knobs set in a carved but very simply carved frame that is arched over by a fan-light of many small panes. Some of the panes are broken and the paint is peeling off the door. The house must have been built before this country was a nation, when there was no city east of the creek and Georgetown was a town in the Proprietary Colony of Maryland.

From my window I could just see the old lady where she sat on the green bench, day after day, and towards noon I got so that I began to look for the large white-haired man in blue serge, who came to take her away. A black derby high on his head gave him a little more than his real height, and although he must have been past seventy he was heavy and of powerful frame—the sort of man you would like to see on a big bay horse, cantering down a quiet street and, without changing pace or his own expression, gravely lifting his hat to the ladies as he passed. He never spoke to the old lady but with great simplicity removed his hat, holding it across his chest while she rose; then they started off, the old lady keeping an even distance in the rear. I am sure that in all these years he never uttered a word, but the old lady talked constantly, not to her husband but as if his presence made it easier for her to talk to herself. The large man—I am certain of this too—never onced looked at the old house.

And not more than twice did he fail to come for her. The first time must have been five or six years ago, when a tall very old man, who looked tall at any rate because his knees were so long, drove up in a muddy Victoria. A doctor, I am certain; his white hair flowed over his shrunken shoulders; he wore a wrinkled Prince Albert and a shining stove-pipe hat, and he held a gold-headed cane. As the carriage slowed down he moved as though he were about to get out; but he thought better of it and the old lady, old but many years younger than he, climbed slowly in. The negro boy driver turned—I remember he had on a greasy linen duster and a colorless felt hat decorated with a rooster's tail—and, with a solemn face, distinctly said: 'Good mornin', Miss Jane.' She nodded. The old doctor leaned forward and kissed her and they began talking; I could hear nothing they said. Without raising his voice the old gentleman talked more and more vehemently, pointing towards the upper windows of the house, alternately pointing and rubbing the side of his long white nose with the knob of his cane. At last she nodded, as if she had at last got a difficulty out of her mind—as if to say: Yes, that's it, I remember now. The old doctor spoke to the boy, who pulled up the reins and drove briskly down the street.

The old house has not been occupied for years. Aunt Charlotte says that people lived in it when we first came here. There were no children and I never looked much at the place. It is too elegant for poor people, and too large; too shabby, in too shabby a neighborhood, for the rich. Aunt Charlotte cannot distinctly remember the last tenants; they lived there less than a year. But the house looked shut up even then, and quite untouched, as if it were going its own way. Every year it seems to settle a little more into the ground. The windows look dimmer, defying the light to disturb the perfect shadows within.

Further than 'Miss Jane' we never knew the names of any of the people who came back to look at the house, though I must have seen the old lady and her husband, the vigorous western man, thirty or forty times a year for ten years—the time I've been an invalid—and my aunt, sewing at her machine every morning in the other front room across the hall, watched them come and go a good five years longer. You have understood that Aunt Charlotte is a seamstress. She had been a clerk in the Patent Office—snapped rubber bands around papers and envelopes, whose purpose and destiny she did not know, from nine to five—until I came back from over-seas, paralyzed. We are Pennsylvania people from a small town, Greencastle, who came here, my father and mother and Aunt Charlotte, her sister, to go into the Government service, when I was a child; my parents are dead. I went from the high-school to the war but when I was eleven or twelve I spent many afternoons at the Smithsonian and wandered over to the Fisheries and the Army Medical Museum where they keep South American mummies and wax representations of diseases, and monsters in jars. We are the only members of our family left in Georgetown. We never hear from our relatives and we are poor.

I will never forget how the old lady nodded to the doctor, as if but for a slight piece of information she knew all that the house contained; and how he nodded in return, affectionately but a little absently, not thinking very much about the house. He must have known all the people there long ago, but he had not lived there. It was that, I think, more than the old lady's coming and going that started me to thinking about her. I began to wonder where she lived, and where I myself should live since this town is not my home; and then too I ask Aunt Charlotte where the people are who ought to be living in the square house. I don't think she quite knows what I mean. She says the neighbors all came after they left, and they either forgot or never knew the name. My aunt is very busy and lately she has got so much fashionable patronage that she seems a little giddy, as giddy as an anxious old maid could ever be.

But she does good work and somehow the ladies who go to F Street have decided that a shabby street in Georgetown is the place to go. There is Mrs. Ritter, she comes in a Cadillac, I don't know where she is from; she talks about her parties, sometimes as if she and Aunt Charlotte were really together and the parties weren't hers; but one day she said, 'I just hate poor people.' But Aunt Charlotte is so innocent. The senator's daughters are pretty and they don't know what they want and they are afraid to let a sewing-woman tell them. I fall into these currents of life around me and I like to think how far away they run. When a car drives up or the knocker sounds

I roll my chair to the window and look out. I roll over to the door, open it, get behind it and wait for the lady to begin talking.

There is old Mrs. Dulany and, come to thing of it, it must have been old Mrs. Dulany who lives down near the Tenally-town Road who got all these people coming to our house.

'No, don't thank me. My dear, I don't know any of them. I just told Mrs. Roberts you did splendid plain sewing and I reckon she told some one else who told all the others.'

Every spring, every fall, Mrs. Dulany comes three or four times to have some old silk dresses made over or a new black voile. She says:

'My dear, I don't know them at all.'

Her right eye suddenly squints, and that side of her face twitches spasmodically until she holds it a moment with her hand. Then she talks on. Sometimes I go into the sewing-room when she is there. 'Mr. Hermann, you are looking better this spring.' Or 'this fall'—as it happens. She always says that, and you feel a great kindness. She gives Aunt Charlotte minute directions about a skirt. 'It don't make much difference how I look, I'm gettin' so old.'

When I wish to compose myself I close my eyes, and I can hear Mrs. Dulany's voice. It is a little cracked for she must be nearly eighty but the tone is at once sharp and fluent, and what she says is neither memorable nor foolish. She must have come in one day while I was dozing. I felt that she was there though she had not spoken, and I was startled at thinking that I knew what she was going to say.

'Well, Miss Charlotte, maybe you think this street has always been just like it is.'

As I looked across the hall Mrs. Dulany was bending a little forward, whether to see what Aunt Charlotte was doing or in some inner excitement I could not tell. The mid-morning light fell on the heap of scraps, the odds and ends of muslin and silk, velvet and bits of thread, that covered the big table where Aunt Charlotte with her aimless patience was picking about here and there. Mrs. Dulany had spoken; my aunt looked up, her eyes blank, like a surprised beetle.

'Yes'm, only I tell John it ain't as bad as it might be if my work took me out.'

Thinking the talk would go on that way I wheeled my chair back to the window—and yet I felt illuminated and pleased. The sun was just over the College wall. It struck me full in the face. It was time to put up the window and let the warm air come in. This is my greatest pleasure. The light shakes the big sycamore leaves, and the sycamore balls in the sudden heat burst, and fall softly to the ground. It is wonderful to watch the rays of sun lift the branch by my window at least a foot higher than it seems to be in the evening shade. There is a faint crackle in the air as the night mist from the river steams up out of the leaves. I knew that when I leaned over the sill I should see the old lady.

She was coming slowly up the street, head and shoulders hidden by a tree, and it struck me for the first time how she walked—as if she were being propelled from the outside, by a force that she neither knew nor could control—like the dressmaker's form in the sewing-room, moving with an even glide— a slightly stooped form for old ladies' fittings. And with a start I thought how curious it was that she needed a cane. She put little weight upon it and at regular short intervals jabbed the rubber ferule noiselessly against the bricks as if indeed that were her way of testing her distance from the ground.

There are some things we know so little about; yet I suppose I looked at the old lady with new eyes because a tone or a phrase in what Mrs. Dulany had said put something into my mind . . . I reckon you think this street has always been just like it is . . . I cannot remember what I thought she really meant, or whether I thought about it at that moment. There are times when my sight grows dim and my head whirls; I grip the wheels of my chair, move a few feet very rapidly; objects begin to reappear. I think I know things only in action; there are the surprising and intolerable crises that a trivial act of will dissipates as breath a soapbubble—those harassing swivets of the mind. I tell Aunt Charlotte that if one must be an invalid one must have a wheeled chair, not to go anywhere in but to give one something to do. I can only say that going over to the window and seeing the old lady float by was my way of understanding what Mrs. Dulany had said.

To understand even a little of what one sees one must at every moment understand more than there is to be understood, or looked at another way, a great deal less. I see, of course, very little. When I remember that the old lady stopped coming by at last, in a way that told me she would not come again, I thought how foolish it was to say that she had always looked this way or had done this or carried that. It takes years to understand the easy things: I recall the exhilaration I felt swarming over my face and eyes when I suddenly and definitely knew that no two days are alike, no person the same two days running. There was the beach down on the bay that I had been to as a child, where the shallow utmost reach of the surf deposited at each thrust a thin filament of sand, but never at the same place twice over.

I do know, of course, that the old lady held her head up a little to the left, as if she were about to sniff, that she wore black worsted mittens, and carried a black reticule that sagged under the weight of shapeless objects: the crazy stare through the thick rimless glasses and the apparently useless cane completed the miscellany of her appearance, one's sense of animated odds and ends. I thought she might fall apart, or go up in a wisp of smoke. She had merely been put together by all past generations, and she saw no need of doing anything about it; I mean that she could not have known that she had a self. The gliding ease of her step, the unshakable regularity of her habits, had all the perfection of an untested desire. I felt, as she passed that last time, though I did not know then it was the last, that she was as perfect as a cyclone, as terrible, with the same suffocating vortex inside.

I am trying, I suppose, to see what she really looked like. I cannot imagine a picture of her. Could she have sat every day for a photograph, for a whole year, always on the same plate, one image upon another, there would have appeared an outline indistinct as a distant shadow, or perhaps one should say that her picture would have been like a whisper in an empty room. Just nothing, in the sense that impalpable fear is nothing: precisely nothing at all. And then I suddenly knew that I had been hearing the voice all this time, the words from the sewing-room forming a single moment with the image in the street.

'. . . I knew them all of course, I knew them because old Cousin John Gibson, that was the father of the girls, and my own father were second cousins. And I knew Cousin Georgiana too, his wife. We used to go up there when I was a little girl and I knew them that way, but all the girls were young ladies, too old for me to be intimate with and too young to be married and have children my age. My mother said Cousin Georgiana paid a heavy price for not having any boys. That was why the family broke up. Of the four girls, only one, Mary Anne, made a good match, a Federal naval officer. Old Cousin John, their father, said a Yankee and a rebel looked about the same to him. I reckon he was right about it, for that Yankee, such a handsome young gentleman, was the only good husband any of them got.'

'Yes'm, that's what papa said, the rebel soldiers that come to Greencastle was mighty well-behaved, didn't steal a thing.

I'll just baste this hem so you won't have to try on the skirt again.'

'Yes, I don't like to stand on my feet . . . That Yankee officer brought out the shares of the other sisters—that was after the war and their father was dead—in the land down in St. Mary's. It was the worst thing they could have done. There was Anna; she never married, I reckon I ought to go to see her, she's ninety at least, lived on charity for forty years in the Home for Incurables ever since her mother died. Susan married my cousin on my mother's side, Captain Charles Sterrett. He warn't much force. Aunt Martha, the old negro woman who nursed the girls, helped them, but Cousin Charlie always said: Hadn't the white folks supported her before the war? Just like *he'd* done it. Cousin Lottie I knew best; she married a clerk at Beckitt and Wylie's, a nice deserving young man, only we never knew where he came from—old Major Beckitt said it was all nonsense, folks had to live, and the boy was well-mannered and industrious. But that boy took to drinking and Cousin Lottie supported her family with her needle. Mama said it wasn't right for old Cousin John to leave the land to the girls after they'd been raised in town. Once I heard Mama talking to somebody, that Cousin John had an awful temper, and hit Cousin Georgiana on the head with a tin cup. After that she was never the same. One time she got the old gentleman when he was very intoxicated, sewed him up in two stout linen sheets and horsewhipped him till he was sober. She was never the same after that and he wasn't either. He never touched another drop. They never said much about that tin cup, but after he was dead and buried, and Cousin Georgiana and Anna were living alone in the old house towards the end of the war, Mama showed me the place where she'd whipped him at the top of the stairs. She had one sheet already spread out; he was so unsteady she tripped him with a poker. When he fell he went right to sleep, then the old lady started sewing the other sheet over him. Mama would whisper just as we came to the old lady's door, "Who would think she could have done it?" And Cousin John left the house to his sister, when he should have left it to the girls—his sister Anne, the one that married old Mr. Posey . . .'

When she had got to the corner she stood for an instant on the kerb; and looking at her, listening to the voice from the depths of the old house, I could see her incline her head from one side to the other and gaze, rather slyly, up and down the street. I saw her peering cautiously out of a door into a dark hall. With sudden speed she sailed across the street. I suppose she really looked like that at that moment. I see her in four or five distinct scenes, imperishable glimpses, but I know that each of these scenes is composed of many particles of memory, all of them striving day and night to come together and to take form. Before she had quite sat down on the bench she began to take odd pieces of string out of the reticule, laying them across her knees—she was too round to have a lap—and after a brief pause began tying the ends together and winding it into a ball. She rolled steadily and expertly, her hands on her knees; she raised the ball to the level of her eyes, winding all the time, back and forth from her eyes to her knees. In a little while she rested. She looked around with jerks of her head but the head had a different focus from the eyes. Like a chicken pausing alertly between scratches. I suppose she was watching the house.

The sun always fell on her back, throwing the side of her face into a luminous shadow in the middle of which, from the temple to the chin, ran an almost straight line. It made her features thinner and younger. I had to look away. There was a firm and delicate line imbedded in the shapeless flesh. A group of students passed on their way to the College gate. A handsome boy in a bright green sweater looked back at her fumbling with her bits of string, and smiled.

I never wished to speak a word to that old lady. I try to think that after my first real awareness of her I never wanted to see her again. I could not help it—wheeling myself over to the window. I said to myself: it is to get the morning sun. It was to see the old lady. I have seen people as they ought not to be; I have seen whining monsters with only half a face and I myself am not as I ought to be. That is different. Something will hit you, the will of God, and you're no good for the rest of your life. The old lady was as good as she had ever been; she sagged a little, I think, in her whole being, but like the old house she was, all of her, there, in a kind of perfection that I had not known before. The house stood facing her, not a stick of it changed I am certain for a hundred and fifty years. I can imagine the windows every year getting smaller, sealing up the shadows until at last there will be one great impenetrable shadow within.

'. . . and when the war was over Cousin Anne and her husband moved up from Prince William and took possession of the house. Cousin Anne you see was much older than her brother who'd left her the place, and Mr. Posey was younger than she but still older than his brother-in-law. Their children were all grown up. Mama didn't go much to the house after they came, but I did. I was often in the old garden. On my way home from my music lesson at the Convent I had to pass the garden gate. Cousin Anne would lean out like she'd been waiting: "Come in, child, and have some cake." She would take my hand and give me a sharp look. She was tall and thin and her nose tied her face up in a knot. I remember how the garden looked in the spring. We sat at a rickety little table under the back gallery. Cousin Anne poured half water and half sweet wine into tall glasses. She would say, "Honey, give your Cousin

George some sangaree." Cousin George was Mr. Posey. I took it to him where he sat at the other end of the porch. "Little Nellie, she shakes like jelly," he said, never taking the frown off his face, and that was his way of thanking me . . .'

I am now sure that I never wanted to see the inside of the house. I cannot help feeling for it a certain respect. It carries itself well. All effort is over and it is superior to anything its imagination might teach it to do. But it is, in its composure, a little menacing. Like the island of Sinbad the Sailor it is sudden and angry with an incalculable life of its own. I always take my 'walks' in the afternoon the year round; being down there with the old house, or with the old lady, myself with one of them, I should feel secure; I should have a single problem, and its simplicity would leave open the space between the street and my room. But to be there with them together, the old lady and the old house—that is to be entirely alone, with my watch ticking on my wrist, and arrested in time. I should have my own darkness inside, my own angry perfection, and I should no longer be able to say: the student going into the gate is returning from the movies to his room in Carroll Hall. There would be the student, the gate, and my watch ticking; then my watch ticking alone.

'. . . only I didn't shake because I was frail. That was all I ever heard him say. Old Mr. Posey sat in a big arm-chair with horsehair upholstery, his knees wide apart and the black trousers tight on his heavy limbs. He wore a faded bottle-green coat with tails, and a loose black stock around his neck. There he sat frowning, picking his teeth with a gold toothpick that folded like a knife into a small carved ivory handle. I always wanted to touch it but I was afraid to ask him. Cousin Anne colored a tumbler of water with a little wine for me. We just sat there. She rocked vigorously in her chair, then abruptly stopped, as if she'd thought of something. At the end of the garden by the stables was a big sycamore and along the wall by the street ran a high box hedge—it was dug up and sold years ago. On the other side round the kitchen and the quarters bushes of flowering quince grew in huge clusters. Only there was never any cake and at home we never called him Cousin George. He was Mr. Posey. They say he was in a rage all his life. That was peculiar and there was something else . . .'

I have never believed that anger has anything in it that one can touch and see; it is different from love which is always physical and so knows where to stop, at the end of familiar things. Aunt Charlotte I think never had any feeling about anything; she does not know one person from another; she has felt neither anger nor love. There is anxiety but that is kindness and kindness is not love. This is a neighborhood of strangers. Like me I suppose they have all felt that it is not innocent enough, a place that knows more than we can ever know, knows it all in a way that we cannot understand. It is absurd to say that an old house is angry. We get used to absurdity. To say that of the house seems to me as ordinary as saying that it is placed among unfamiliar things. We make it angry; a new house built in another town makes it angry. It must have once loved familiar things. As I looked down at the old lady making her balls of twine I thought how furious she was, but then she could not know she was furious. With incredible fury she wound up the twine as if it were the last of familiar things; furiously she placed her forefinger against the side of her nose, taking in deep breaths; then she resumed her work with new fury.

'. . . and it was even more peculiar. There was Jane and Sarah Georgiana, or Sally George we called her, and it was Sally George who married Mr. Broadwater and went to the southwest. They took Jane's meals up to her room; she never came out. There were Little George and Uncle Rozier, the two boys,

and I expect Cousin Anne called her son uncle because Little
George had a son; he had married one of old Major Beckitt's
girls and gone out west. I never saw him in my life; he couldn't
get along with his father so he went west. West was a word
you heard all the time. Hundreds of people were going west.
It seemed so far away. The land flowing with milk and honey,
old Major Beckitt said sarcastically, but it did seem to flow
because Little George made money out of that land he and
Mr. Ben Tayloe had bought in the west before the war, and
he sent money home. Then he sent his wife and child, a little
girl, Little Jane we called her, named after her Aunt Jane, he
sent them home to visit. After that visit Little George sent no
more money back home, and before long they shut up the
house, had to I reckon. Went up to Rockville and died there
about the time I was grown. Later Uncle Rozier went west
too. I saw him many times, it's right strange how you remember things. I can see him in the front hall coming down the
wide white stairway in his carpet-slippers—I remember that because he was such a large man, six feet four they said, and he
walked so quietly I noticed his feet. He was different from his
father, had the sanguine temperament, but he swore every
breath no matter who was present. I think it was this same
day. He put his huge hand on my head and shook me. "By
God, she's a pretty young un." Then he gave me a nickel.
Old Aunt Martha who sat in the back hall with a white cap
and apron on—she was too old and fat to work so she answered
the front doorbell that rang about twice a week—she whispered:
"Don't you be scared, honey, they ain't no harm in Marse
Rozier." She laughed and showed her big eye-teeth, and all
she had left, hanging down over her lower lip. The old hall
was always dark. I could never see the faces in the frames on
the wall opposite the stairs. They were Gibsons. You know
the first Gibson was a dwarf. I think of those times, how I'm
the only one of their kin left here. Jane died while Little

George's wife and daughter were here on that visit. Doctor Lacy Beckitt, one of the major's boys, waited on her till she died. They said she just died, but don't crazy people live just as long as other people? Longer. Nobody saw her laid out. She was foolish about her little niece Jane, I reckon because she was her namesake. All morning she sat alone in her room and after dinner she peeped out into the dim hall, and called Little Jane. Little Jane went upstairs for her daily present. Jane cut up old newspapers into strips like ribbons all day long, and laid them in rows and piles. "Here's your present for today, child"—handing her some paper strips. She never spoke above a whisper; no one saw her smile; she was very gentle. When she got a new dress she cut it right up into scraps—"They might come in handy," she'd say. She tied strings round empty boxes, they found hundreds of them in her wardrobe after she died. She saved tinfoil and bits of thread, and made balls of twine. Sometimes I think the old house is waiting to be taken away too, and nobody will ever look inside again who knew what happened there. Not, my dear, that anything really happened . . . '

'That's what I tell my nephew, folks work so hard but don't never get anything out of it. Like carrying water uphill in a leaky bucket.'

When Aunt Charlotte broke the silence I knew that I had heard everything that Mrs. Dulany had said: I was brought up sharply against the innocence of my poor aunt, who had heard not a word of it, I mean really heard it. And yet I was convinced that Mrs. Dulany herself, could the question have entered her mind, would have seen nothing that was not perfectly plain. I knew, however, that as Aunt Charlotte spoke Mrs. Dulany was squinting her eye, and her face was twitching. These mysteries are understood in our bodies, not in the mind. I thought I understood that too: when the umbrella mender cries out in the street I feel restless, even a little exposed, and thinking suddenly that my bureau needs tidying up I wheel myself over to it and find myself brushing my hair.

That, too, must be a kind of anger. I looked out of the window. The old lady was tying up the ends of her string to start a new ball. The air was still and warm and I knew it was almost noon. A coal truck pounded by on the cobblestones, leaving the noonday suspense deeper than before. I had seen into the old house, and there was the old lady, that cavernous bird of passage, across the street. Damnation had read itself out to me. I remembered the elderly gentleman who had come for her in the spattered carriage, and I wanted him to come again today. I found myself saying, Little Jane. There was the solemn negro boy. Good mornin', Miss Jane. I suddenly thought: Doctor Beckitt, who knew the room in which the crazy woman had died. The old doctor whose carriage might have become his grave. I suppose I wanted Miss Jane to die but I found myself wishing for her a distant grave, or perhaps— and I think this was it—a moving grave that would bring her back to the old grey house in Indian summer after the morning light of autumn had begun shaking the leaves. Though I knew it was impossible I could not bear to think of her dying in the old house. I saw her consumed by the rage of the invisible fire within. I kept thinking, foolishly enough, that she might be saved. But she had no place to die. She could neither die nor live.

The young man was coming rapidly down the street. He looked like a tower of new brick. He was all of six feet; his head, arms, legs moved all together. His clothes seemed carefully impersonal and subdued. He must have stepped out of a fashionable hotel. He wore thick glasses and looked occasionally up, then down, to satisfy himself that there was no obstacle in his way. He wore one glove; the other he carried in his bare hand. He walked quickly and deliberately and he scarcely touched the ground.

He was leaning over the old lady, kissing her, his arms at his side. She put both arms around his neck, and kissed him again and again. He withdrew at last. He sat down beside her. Neither spoke. The old lady fumbled with her bag and relaxed with a sigh. He rose, and standing with his legs slightly apart, the backs of his hands on his hips, he looked up at the house.

Still looking up, and I thought gradually tenser and more alert, he rocked on the balls of his feet. He stood suddenly still. He rubbed his bare fist slowly in the palm of his gloved hand. He turned abruptly, as if everything were quite clear, took her by the arm, tenderly, pulling her to her feet. The sun from over the wall lit up her face. I could see that she was in tears. He took her cane, a little awkwardly. She leaned heavily on his arm; they started slowly up the street. He hesitated as if he were about to speak, but thought better of it, smiled, and led the old lady on her way. I never saw her again.

Lawrence Judson Reynolds

THAT GRAND CANYON

All morning flurries had whipped about in the wind, but now the snow was falling in earnest. It laced the brown grass which bordered the road that wound down the hill past the field of junked cars to the clapboard house and the garage covered with the rusting tin signs that advertised Coca Cola, wheel bearings, and radiator stop-leak.

An old-model, black Buick bounced down the road and pulled into the yard in front of the house. It stopped for a moment as gears clashed angrily. Then it moved slowly backwards into the garage.

"Can you have her fixed by tonight?" asked the Negro who had been waiting inside the garage. "I sure would like to have her tonight."

Handel Irby got out of the car and rubbed his hand on the back of his neck the way he always did when talking to a customer. There were quarter moons of grease and dirt beneath his nails. He scratched his thinning hair and rubbed his neck again. He knew damn well he could fix it today. It sounded like a burnt-out wheel bearing. He could fix it in thirty minutes if it were.

"Can't do it," he said. "How the hell you think I can put another rearend in this thing today?"

"Rearend?" The Negro's dark pink lips parted in a tentative smile, showing a flash of teeth. "You kidding, man?"

"Nope."

"You sure it needs a rearend?"

"Yep."

"Man, that's gonna touch my back pocket right hard."

"Sixty bucks."

"Sixty?"

"Yep."

"Man, I don't know 'bout that." The Negro patted the pointed toe of his shoe on the dirt floor of the garage.

Handy stared past him at the falling snow. He hated snow. It was so damn silent you never knew when it was falling and when it wasn't.

"If you don't wanta take my word, you just drive on back where you come from and get one of them city boys to tell you. And see how much he'll charge! I told you, sixty dollars, installed. You ain't gonna find another mechanic that'll do it for that. Them city boys wouldn't even look at it for less'n a hundred."

"I know that, but. . ." The Negro paused and seemed to forget what he was going to say.

"Well, it's up to you," said Handy, walking over to the stove. Every nigger that had ever been in his garage had tried to gyp him. They all wanted something for nothing. Just like those stray dogs that Ida had collected all her life—just waiting for somebody to throw something out to them. And then, half the time they were too lazy to get off their fat bellies and eat it. He ought to kill every damn one of them.

"Well, I s'pose I'll leave her then," said the Negro after a long silence.

Handy kicked open the door of the tin heater and began poking about in the fire with an iron rod.

"Don't make any difference to me. You can drive it away now and let the rearend fall out on the road, or come back next week after I fix it. It's up to you.

"When you think she'll be ready?" asked the Negro, at last putting down the temptation to just drive it away and hope for the best.

"Monday or Tuesday. Soon as I find a junk I can get another rearend out of." Handy turned and looked off up the hill in front of the garage to where the mass of junked cars lay stripped and ugly in the snow.

The Negro nodded and stared at Handy's back as he bent over the fire again.

"Wonder if anybody 'round here is going to town this afternoon?" he asked finally.

"If you walk out to the main road you can make the 'leven o'clock bus," answered Handy. He knew Marshall was going to drive in later for some parts, but why the hell should he tell him. He could catch the bus easy as anybody else.

The Negro turned and started off through the snow. Handy tossed the iron rod beneath the heater and kicked the metal door shut. He watched the dark figure as it moved up the hill past the cluttered field of stripped cars. It'd be just like a damn nigger to come back wanting to borrow a car or something. They all thought they were too good to walk through a little snow.

The Negro moved hurriedly up the road and disappeared over the hill leaving Handy alone in the doorway, leaning against the hood of the Buick. He looked at the dark holes of the empty car windows on the hill. The snow accentuated their darkness and gave them the appearance of eye sockets from which the eyes have been removed. He wondered which one it was. The metal bodies all looked the same through the swirling flakes of snow. Their empty eyes all seemed to accuse him now, and he turned away, somewhat disappointed that the Negro hadn't come back.

"That was my car! My car!"

He was lying beneath a car, and she was talking to his feet, which were sticking out on the other side.

"Your car hell!"

"Well, our car, Handel. Yours and mine. You know where we were going in that car." Her voice softened. *"You know what we've always planned."*

He knew damn well it wasn't the car she cared about. It was that infernal trip. There was something triumphant about lying there, pretending to work and listening to her. He hoped she was looking at that goddamn calendar. He hoped she was seeing how ugly and stupid it really was.

"My two hands worked for it, and kept it running," he said, *shouting up at the underside of the car. It was the first time she'd been in the garage since the year after they were married. He wished he could get out and stick the calendar in her face. Maybe things would be back the way they were then.*

"Where is it, Handel?"

"All you ever did was sit in it and drive. I guess I gotta right to junk it if I want."

"You junked it, Handel? You junked it?" She was crying now, like she hadn't known all along where the damn thing was, like she hadn't walked right by it on her way back from town, like she hadn't seen it—rotting up on the hill with the rest of them.

He could see her feet planted in the dust, the firm, pale flesh of her legs, and the hem of her skirt. He had hoped then that things would be different.

Handy walked back into the garage and kicked the side of

the tin heater. The damn fire wasn't burning right at all. Marshall must have put a goddamn stick of wet wood on it before he left.

He hadn't thought much about her crying though. It was just like a woman to cry, the way she'd cried everytime one of her filthy dogs didn't show up for its free meal. With twenty of them swarming about the back door he didn't see what difference one could make.

"What happened to Blackie, Handel?"

"Blackie who?"

"My dog. Blackie!"

"You got twenty Blackies out there. How the hell do I know? If shells didn't cost so much I'd shoot every damn one of them."

"And you'd never see me again, Handel Irby!" He knew she wasn't kidding about that, and afterwards, he never ventured more than an occasional kick at one or another of the mongrels. But when she stopped crying the silence was frightening. He hadn't known she'd act that way about the car. But it wasn't the car. It was that stupid trip. And he'd known that when he stripped the old '39 Chevy, when he tore it apart piece by piece, and smashed the glass from its windows.

Marshell drove up in the truck, pulling right up to the front of the Buick and revving the motor a couple of time before cutting the ignition and getting out. He walked over to the stove and extended his hands, palms out, toward the heater.

"It's snowing!" he said. He had a young, eager face. His long blond hair was stuffed beneath a red stocking cap, but his bulbous ears loomed from either side of his head.

"Is that what it is?" replied Handy, walking over to where the boy stood. Twenty-five years Ida'd been after him to hire another mechanic, and now she wasn't a year dead and he'd gotten this: A hot-rod kid who didn't know a screwdriver from a pair of pliers, and still thought a rearend was something you sat on.

"Weather man says six inches or more," said Marshall.

"If you listen to that fool you got less sense than I thought, boy, and that ain't much. Now are you gonna get to town before the roads get slick or are you gonna wait and slide in a ditch somewhere?"

"I just wanta get warmed up," said Marshall, rubbing his hands together briskly. "Ain't no heater on that truck, you know. You sold it, remember?"

"That ain't my fault," answered Handy. If he didn't need him to run errands so much he'd fire him right now. But with Ida gone, he had to have somebody to drive to town. He damn well wasn't going there again as long as he lived.

"It'll be after twelve before I get back," said Marshall.

"So what?"

"I thought maybe you'd want me to take the truck on home and just come in Monday."

"So you can hot-rod around in it all weekend?"

Marshall didn't answer. He tucked his ears beneath the stocking cap and turned and moved toward the door.

Handy watched him walk out into the snow.

"Well, if it's a minute before twelve, you come back here. I ain't paying you four hours time this morning for nothing."

"Sure," said Marshall, putting his hand on the door handle of the truck. The wet snow flakes clung to the rough wool of his cap.

The truck left dark tracks on the road as it moved up the hill. Handy could remember the boy's smile through the icy windshield as the truck backed away from the garage. It'd be just like that jackass to throw a rod in it or something. He never did anything right.

Alone in the garage again, Handy walked around to the other side of the Buick and stared at the 1941 calendar that hung in a clear spot on the wall surrounded by a maze of frayed fanbelts and used head gaskets. The first eleven months had been stripped away, but December still remained attached beneath the large color picture of a girl sitting on a rock and looking out over the vast expanses of the Grand Canyon. At the girl's feet one could see into the deep cavity all the way to the faded blue water at its bottom. It was as if the water had sliced through a million years and left this beautiful, ragged wound exposed for this one girl, sequestered from time and held forever in the fashions of the year 1941.

"*This's where we're going. Soon as I get my garage in shape and can hire another mechanic.*"

He unrolled the picture before her slowly, revealing it to her an inch at a time. The blue sky rolled up first, and then a distant opacity that concealed the horizon and blended the sky and earth. Finally, the canyon appeared, unwinding across the picture until it reached the very feet of the young girl.

"*You're talking through the top of your head, Handel Irby. You ain't ever going to get any closer to that place than you're standing right now.*"

"*Aw, I think the '39'll get us out there, don't you?*" *he said.*

"*Huh! You can just leave me outa that, please.*" *She was snappy like that when they were first married, but he knew she'd liked what he said. It was the kind of womanish dreaming she was fond of.*

He cleared a place on the garage wall and hung the calendar that same day. It was as if he had installed a window through which he could look into another world. The rich colors of the canyon offered a vivid contrast to the rust and grease and dirt of the garage. And sometimes, he thought he could see eternity in the picture; he could see the beginning and the end, and he knew that what he was then was not what he would always be.

Handy walked back to the stove and kicked the door open

again. He chunked at the the dying fire with the iron rod and put two new sticks of wood in on the glowing coals. It was just like that damn jackass Marshall to go off without tending to the fire. And him complaining about no heater on the truck. He was just like a nigger, never missed a thing till it wasn't there, and then complained. If he came back today he'd put his bare ass on that stove and show him who built the fires around here.

Handy jacked up the left rear of the Buick and removed the wheel and pulled the bearing. The bearing didn't seem bad when he spun it on his finger, but he replaced it anyway and put the wheel back on. The dull roaring noise was still there when he spun the wheel around. It was just like a nigger to have something else wrong. It might take him the rest of the afternoon to fix the heap of junk. It probably was the rear-end.

He tried to lower the hooks on the chair hoist so that he could hook them to the bumper and lift the entire backend of the car. The chain refused to work properly, however, and soon became so jammed in the casing that he was forced to get a stepladder and unfasten the hoist from the metal beam above the car. He brought it down carelessly, beating the chain against the trunk of the Buick, and threw it on the work bench by the stove. The chain had run off of one of the pulleys and was tightly wedged between the casing and the side of the pulley. The hot-rod jackass didn't even know how to work a simple chain hoist that could work itself if you gave it half a chance.

Handy forced a screwdriver up into the casing and beat on it with a hammer until the plastic handle shattered and the hammer came down full force on his knuckles. Throwing the hoist to the floor, he kicked at it and stalked about the garage cursing.

On the other side of the Buick three Beagle puppies lay

curled against the wall just inside the doorway. Handy cursed vehemently at them, and finally gave each of them a solid kick with the toe of his shoe, sending them flying out through the doorway into the snow. He didn't know why he hadn't killed every damn one of those curs. They ate everything they could get their teeth on, and now they wanted to turn his garage into a dog pen. He ought to throw them all in the trunk of that Buick. Half of them probably belonged to some nigger anyway.

He pulled an empty nail keg up near the stove and sat down on it and spat on his knuckles and rubbed them. He stared at the Buick for a long time. It was just like a nigger to try and fool you. Well, he'd see damn well who got fooled. He'd stuff that rearend so full of sawdust it'd grind out two-by-fours.

He got another jack from beneath the work bench and took two blocks of wood and placed one in front of each front wheel. Lowering the one jack that he had beneath the car, he placed two cinderblocks just behind the rear axle on either side of the car. He worked savagely, throwing the blocks beneath the car and then crawling about on his belly in order to position them.

After placing the jacks on top of the blocks he turned the handle of first one and then the other until the car was raised to a sufficient height for him to remove both rear wheels. He checked the bearings agaih, then the axle and the brake linings. Everything seemed to be in good shape.

"Goddamn snow," he said aloud, looking out the door and seeing that the ground was white now. The tire tracks were gone but the red dirt of the road could still be seen through an inch of snow.

Handy looked across the trunk of the Buick to the wall where the calendar hung. His eyes moved across the first six numbers on the curled, yellow sheet and came to rest on the seventh—the seventh of December, 1941.

"*I hope this won't mean that you'll have to go,*" Ida said when they first heard the news on the radio.

"*Of course I'll go. I'll go tomorrow if they'll let me.*" The words had come out automatically and they seemed strange to him even then, for he had never thought of leaving his garage for more than two or three hours at a time, and then, only to go to town for parts. But now, suddenly, and for no reason it seemed, he had committed himself to something halfway around the world.

The next day he drove into town and went to the post office where the men were standing in a thick, irregular line in the second floor hallway. Listening to their strained, vibrant voices he felt even more uneasy about his commitment. It seemed ridiculous that all these men should be so concerned about something that had happened in another world, and he felt awkward standing there among them. His garage, built with his own hands on the same little farm where he had always lived, and the town, which fulfilled any outside needs he had, all seemed as safe from the enemy as ever, and it seemed a foolish thing to leave what one knew in order to fight for something one cared nothing about. But though Ida would have welcomed him back without question, he knew that he could not go back to her until he had fulfilled his hastily-made promise. He had to prove to her that he meant the things he said.

"*You're talking through the top of your head again, Handel Irby,*" she had told him before he left that morning. "*Just like when you talk about going out to that Grand Canyon. You been talking about it for a year now, and that Chevy still ain't gone no further than town and back since we had it.*" He thought of the canyon again. In his mind he looked on over the girl's shoulder and felt again the aura of mystery that lurked in the length and depth of the great cavity. All that day and the next, he waited and filled out forms and answered *questions, and dreamed of his ultimate task of defending the canyon against the enemy.*

On the third day, they took him, along with the others, to the armory for the physical examination. There, standing in a long line of naked men they culled him—threw him out like a bad ear of corn—because his feet were flat.

"Well, I'm just glad you didn't have to go," Ida said at supper that night. And seeing his bitter, dejected face, she added: "I couldn't have you going off to war. We've got to go out to that Grand Canyon soon, you know."

Handy lay down on his back in the dirt and slid beneath the car. The rearend was caked with grease and dirt and he scraped it away with his fingers until he found a small crack through which the grease was oozing. That nigger had known all along. That rearend probably worked about as well as ten loose bolts in a bucket. He ought to just get out and kick the jacks out from under it and see if that helped any.

He lay in the cold dirt for a while staring up at the rearend. Then he turned his head and looked up past the side of the car where he could see the bottom two rows of numbers on the calendar. Ida had made a real fool of herself that Christmas.

"Don't bother buying me any Christmas present, Handel. We've got to save our money for the trip."

But he no longer wanted any part of it. He no longer felt that it was his to see, or want to see. It belonged to those who fought for it, and all that belonged to him in the world was the oil-soaked ground that was covered by his garage.

More and more, he withdrew into that dirty, mechanical world. He came to have a loathing for the job which he once had chosen over farming, and his only pleasure came to lie in the total destruction of the automobiles he had once so aptly repaired. Whenever he could afford it, he would buy old, junk cars and strip them of every part. Then, he would drag the shells away with the tractor and burn the upholstery from them and leave them with others on the hill above the garage.

In this way he escaped from the fanatical plans that Ida was always proposing about the canyon. She never asked about the calendar again or came into the garage to see it, but as the years passed the dream that it had once sparked in him became an obsession with her. She talked about it continually, and sometimes she would call people on the phone for no other reason than to tell them about it. She even tried to make the plans sound immediate.

"Handel and I are going to drive out to that Grand Canyon this spring—as soon as he gets some more help in the garage."

She would smile at him over the receiver whenever he was within sight, and he would look away, and go outside again and work with new energy on whatever car he happened to be junking at the time. Or sometimes, he would go back to the garage and stare for hours at the calendar until he became so embittered that he stalked about in his small domain and cursed the thick black dust he walked in.

He often thought of tearing the calendar off the wall and burning it, but he never did. He kept it partly because he knew that Ida did not want to see it again—that she was afraid to look at it—and partly because the picture and the month and year that hung beneath it had come to feed a bitterness that grew within him.

Handy put his hands down on the ground beside him and dug the heels of his shoes into the dirt and made one jerky movement back out from under the car. As he moved again, his hand brushed against a brown and white beagle that had curled itself in the soft dirt of the garage floor. The dog yelped and in its confusion managed to get over Handy's legs and scramble out toward the back of the car.

"You sonofabitch!" Handy drew his feet up and tried to lift the dog with his knees and trap it against the chassis, but the dog escaped and he hammered out at it with his left foot, trying to bring the heel of his shoe down on its back. He put his hands up on the chassis and raised himself a little and kicked out again. The car rocked under his weight and suddenly began to roll backwards. The jacks tilted diagonally and their bases ground into the rough cinder blocks. Handy dug his heels into the ground and pushed back against the chassis. The dirty underside of the car came down toward him like a press. Closer and closer it came, until at last he was able to stop it by digging his elbows into the ground and using both his arms as braces against the monstrous press.

"You filthy cur, sonofabitch," he shouted at the beagle as it ran around the car and out into the snow.

For a moment he lay there getting his breath and staring at the underside of the car that was so close upon him. He'd damn well shoot every one of those dogs now. That would have been just dandy if one of Ida's curs had gotten him squashed underneath some nigger's Buick.

He looked at the leaning jacks and at the blue scars their bases had cut into the cinder blocks. If those goddam jacks would hold now till he could get out, he'd kick the sonofabitch down on its ass for good. He started to ease one hand out from under the chassis, but with his slightest movement a groan came from the car above him and he jammed his elbow back into the dirt again.

He waited, his head laying back flat in the dirt, his arms sticking straight up from his sides. Several more times he tried to ease his hands from beneath the chassis, but each time a creaking sound passed through the car making him shudder and press his elbows deeper into the dust.

He lay very still for a while and tried to imagine how the situation would end. Marshall might come back from town before twelve. The little bastard had damn well better. But he'd probably stumble over his own feet and knock the car down on him after he got there. That nigger might get tired of waiting for the bus and come back wanting to borrow a car. It'd be just like a nigger.

Through the space between the front of the car and the ground he could see the snow flakes silently piling up. Far off on the hill the hollow eyes of the junked cars stared down at him through the haze of snow. More than ever he hated the silent falling of the snow.

At times he felt sure that no one would come and that he would be left to die beneath the car. When such thoughts came to him he would draw up his knees and dig his heels into the dirt, determined to thrust his body out so that his head and shoulders would be clear before the car fell. But each time that he looked back over his head and saw the narrow space through which he had to slide, he would feel the weight of the car, like the heel of a shoe on a worm, grinding his body into the dirt, and he would stretch out flat again and wait.

By raising his head a little and looking down between his feet, he could see the legs of the tin heater and the ashes that had sifted through the front draft. All about the garage he could see the faint impressions his shoes had made in the dust. His recent spittle lay drying in little dust-balls about the stove.

Near the door the pointed shape of the Negro's shoes seemed so much clearer than his own more numerous footprints. He wondered how much the Negro had weighed. He tried to imagine the Negro's feet coming down past the car and fitting again into those pointed molds.

The fire cracked in the stove and for a moment he could almost see the shoes patting silently in the dust. But after he realized that it was only the fire, the minutes passed slowly into hours and the weight on his arms became almost unbearable. He lost all track of time. Sometimes, imagining that he had been under the car only a few minutes, he would listen intently for the sound of Marshall returning in the truck. Then, abandoning all hope of Marshall's return, he would think of how many other customers he might have on a Saturday afternoon. Everybody knew he was open, not like those half-ass city garages that closed for Sunday and every two-bit holiday, and then took off at noon on Saturday. It wasn't unlikely that someone else would come.

The snow continued to fall. The logs in the fire cracked spasmodically and finally settled into a bed of coals that gave off no heat that could reach Handy there beneath the car. The desire to yell for help kept gripping him, although he knew there was no one within a mile to hear. He suppressed the desire for a long time, but at last he drew in a deep breath and screamed: "Help! Help! Help!" He screamed until he was exhausted, but the words only rose and disappeared like his frosty breath into the dark underside of the car.

Ida could have heard him at the house if she were still alive. Twenty-five years she'd been there, day in and day out, and he hadn't needed her. And now that he did, she was dead. She probably wouldn't have come in the garage anyway. She'd probably have let him rot underneath the car before she set foot in the garage again. She'd only been in once in twenty-five years.

"Handel, we were going to drive the Chevy out to that Grand Canyon." She sobbed violently like a child. Then suddenly, her crying stopped and he saw her feet moving toward the front of the car and out through the doorway.

She never spoke of the canyon after that. She seldom spoke at all, and inside a year, she was dead.

In the weeks after the funeral, he sometimes would look at the calendar and find the girl sitting at the edge of the canyon to be Ida. Once when he had looked, the girl had disappeared altogether, and he had run to the house and looked through every room before he finally cursed himself, and Ida, and the dogs that got in his way as he walked back to the garage.

The afternoon wore on, but still no one came. Handy's arms became numb, and only a dull ache remained in them. He lifted one foot off the ground, but the feeling in his legs seemed to go no further than his ankles. They were going to freeze now, and rot off. Served the flat, worthless things right. With all his strength, he kept his trembling foot raised above the ground.

"Okay, okay, step over on this paper and put both feet down flat."

The paper was sticky on the bottoms of his bare feet. He had never been naked in front of people before. But everyone was naked—everyone but the two doctors who stood before him.

"Okay, step back."

He stepped back onto the cold floor and stared down at the footprints he had made on the paper.

"Flat as last night's beer," said one of the doctors.

"Yeah," the other grunted, scribbling on the clipboard he held in the crook of his arm. "That's all for you, Irby. You can get dressed." He handed him the paper from the clipboard, and pointed towards the rear of the building. "Report to that office after you're dressed."

The two doctors moved on to the next man. Handy's clothes lay in a pile behind him and he turned and began putting them on. He could feel the eyes of the other men on him as he dressed. They were still watching when he zipped up his jacket and started across the long drill floor. His shoes made hollow, echoing sounds in the quiet hall as he walked away.

Handy let his foot fall back into the dirt.

The last of the heavy snowflakes floated to the ground, and a sharp slanting snow began to fall. Through the new snow the cars on the hill seemed to move closer. Their empty windows became wider and darker while the snow hid their ugly bodies. Handy stared at the exhaust pipe above him, then closed his eyes against even that.

"Handel, the Chevy has a miss in it. I suppose I'll catch the bus to town—would you look at it while I'm gone?" She *was so trusting, almost tempting him. But he didn't think of junking it then.*

She started off up the hill toward the main road. Then she turned, and he knew what she was going to say.

"We'll want it in good shape for the trip, Handel."

She walked away, going past the rotting cars and disappearing over the hill. The old '39 stood alone before the garage door, black and shiny, reflecting the hot July sun. He didn't even look back up the road again.

Handy drew his knees up suddenly and wedged the heels of his shoes into the dirt. With one great heave, he tried to force himself out from under the car. But the strength seemed to be frozen within his legs and his heels only wiggled through the soft ground until his knees lay flat again. The car groaned above him, and he trembled.

Toward nightfall a wind began to stir the snow, pushing it this way and that, and twisting a loose curl of it in through the garage door, scattering the glittering flakes in the dust. Then the wind ceased and night had fallen. Outside, the snow seemed to have retained some of the daylight, but in the garage everything was dark and formless. Handy's arms braced the car now with no more purpose than the two iron jacks which they assisted.

Sometimes his eyelids stayed closed for long periods of time and he seemed to sleep, his only movement being the slow heaving of his chest. It was during one of these periods that the daylight failed and the darkness crept down from the underside of the car and enveloped him. He awoke with a start, looking about him but seeing only the white strip of light in the doorway.

"Ida! Ida!" His voice echoed from the rusting metal of the Buick. He blinked his eyes and looked at the strip of snow. She probably wouldn't come even if she were alive. She'd let him rot first.

He raised his lifeless foot again and let it drop. It seemed to drop for a long time before it finally hit the ground, the same way Ida had gone down for such an eternity before they finally pulled the straps out and shovelled the first spade-full of dirt on top of the casket. *Standing there, looking down into the small cavity in the earth, it seemed that he was standing at the very edge of the canyon. He felt a strange mingling of joy and sadness, and would have stayed longer staring down after Ida, but the spades-full of dirt splattered one on top of another until there was nothing left but a mound, covered by the greens and flowers that the neighbors had sent.*

Another silent hour passed. The only sounds in the darkness were the steady rhythm of his breathing, and occasionally, when he could find the strength to lift one of his legs, the clump of his lifeless foot falling back into the dust.

But then, there came another sound—the slow, padded sound of feet compressing the loose snow. Handy dropped his raised foot and listened. The footsteps were faint, but they seemed very near. He stared at the narrow strip of light in the doorway with a kind of horror and amazement.

"Ida! Ida!" His voice was a hoarse rattle that carried no further than his smoky breath.

For a moment, everything was still and quiet. Then the line of snow across the garage door quivered and burst forth, scattering its whiteness beneath the car. A large black hound slipped beneath the front bumper and shook the snow from its coat.

The dog curled itself up by one of the front wheels and lay motionless. Handy stared at the dark form whose noisy breathing broke the silence to which he had now grown accustomed. He thought of the nights he had lain beside Ida and listened to the whispering sounds of her breathing. Often he had wanted to reach out and touch her, touch her the way they'd touched in that first year before the war. But then she would murmur in her sleep and he would know that she was dreaming of the canyon again, dreaming of its quiet length and depth—its peacefulness. And he would feel the bitterness again, and would take a blanket and leave the bed and sleep in the garage among the worn parts of the junked cars.

Handy tried to raise his foot, but the muscles in his leg only trembled and fell slack. He closed his eyes again and behind his lids everything seemed to bloom with light. It seemed that he was moving along through bright sunlight. All about him a motor hummed peacefully. He recognized the sound as that of the old '39 Chevy. He took pride in its faultlessly throbbing engine. He felt the sun glinting from its black hood—and before the hood, the canyon stretching endlessly and deep.

The old Buick rolled slowly backwards, its front wheels passing the dog without disturbing its sleep. The exhaust pipe was the first thing to touch Handy, coming down against his face and forcing his head to one side, leaving a smear of brown rust across the bridge of his nose. His eyes popped open for an instant but closed again as the chassis pressed against his chest. The air hissed like steam from his lungs.

The hound whined in its sleep and snuggled toward the tire that was no longer beside it.

By midnight the snow had stopped and the moonlight came in through a thin haze of clouds. The blue-white light shone brilliantly on the snow and fell in a block through the open door of the garage, stretching across the hood of the Buick and along the wall of gaskets and belts, and reaching all the way to the faded canyon and the curling leaf of days that hung beneath it.

Hiram Haydn

VIRGIL'S MANUSCRIPT

In the beginning was He, the Great Original. We are all children of His breath, but we know Him not. And we, the multitudinous manifestations of His energy, act out our microcosmic miracle plays, but know ourselves only darkly, as a bar of shuttered light crosses a room and is gone.

Throughout the far-flung galaxies we expend our metaphors, which we call life. Each planet, parasitic itself, carries, or has carried, its own parasites. And there are those who say that every star is complemented by its twin, its dark sister of antimatter particles, those electric charges opposite to the ones we know.

Be all this as it may, there are worlds we live in, but never perceive: dimensions that are as truly our experience as that of a mundane life, yet unknown to most of us most of the time: aspects of reality in which we participate unwittingly.

Ask me not, therefore, whether I write a tale, a fable, an allegory, or history. It is all one: I give you what I can of my vision of how it has been, of the roles I have enacted.

My story begins amidst the whistling of galaxies, the grinding of constellations. I was not, am not a man, yet in some sense I am. Perhaps, as Odysseus would have it, I am No Man. Yet I have been called upon more than once to play a manlike role, and I have obeyed, ever since my primal revolutionary disobedience.

How it fell out that I was discharged from one of the great stations of the universe is like a dream to me. I believe this happened, but even my belief is of another order of reality from that which I am about to recount. Set it down in your mind then, that I, Tod, was once a captain in the sidereal ranks, and understand it as a metaphor.

Metaphors also my disobedience and fall from grace; words cannot suffice to describe the dimensions of that experience. And all this had nothing to do with man.

Man appears in my story only after a second phase, which concerns Abram, his mate, and that elusive female spirit who tiptoes down the legendary corridors of all history.

I use symbol. I personify that which was not human. My first phase was multidimensional, embracing all electric circuits, resolving opposing charges. My second was four-dimensional, surpassing the capacities of man, yet trivial beside the first. So I choose here to translate into human terms, although thereby distorting, grossly simplifying, the actual nature of my experience.

Abram was the most effective, the most potent of us in the second phase. The value of life, on that level of reality, was the accumulation and effective expression of energy. Although the term was not used amongst us, it may clarify what I mean to say simply that Abram generated by far the highest voltage. His mate, whom I shall designate hereafter as She, reveled in obedience to so powerful a creature, and invested me with but little of her output.

I coveted more, but futilely until that fair and fiery one, whom I shall name Her, entered our orbit. Her crackled intermittently in the distance long before we came to know her.

When I say "long before," I am speaking, of course, in light years. But since the tale I would write concerns the third phase of my existence and the origins of the world in which I now reside, I shall here be brief.

Her diverted much of Abram's energy from She. She suffered then from electrical anemia and became more receptive to me. Abram would not relinquish communication with Her, yet repeatedly tried to short-circuit the connection between She and me. Electric confrontation followed: a vast storm, terminated only by my grounding the whole matter with a proposal for a transformation and the establishment of a new power station.

My proposal, if it may be so defined, was that we combine our strengths to generate a new life for all of us, select a planet on which to produce a new play, and assume new forms.

So it was agreed, and man was created. Abram alone was reluctant to relinquish his existing potential and form. But I suggested (the inadequacy of verbs!) that he maintain a double role, leaving himself as the life-giving generator of our new world, while also becoming an actor in our company.

A word about the play itself. Our concept of it was not unlike what has been termed a "happening." We had no plot, consciously devised; no one "wrote" the play, unless Abram's generator-self secretly directed our role and relationships. I suspect that he did, in the early cycles, but as his power slackened, was no longer competent to control events.

THE PLAY

I

The moment of generation was not unlike that depicted in Michelangelo's "Creation of Adam." Only there was no touching of Finger to human finger: rather, a blue electric flame, short-circuit, and Abram the generator had produced Abram the man.

The human bodies the four of us were to wear were lying in marble coffins in a vast Doric hall. When Abram rose from his, a man, we others were aware of him. I cannot say that we *saw* him; we recorded the experience, and all subsequent ones, until each of us was in turn humanly animated. But that was later.

Abram's attention was at first divided between his surroundings and himself, his awe for the one no greater than that for the other. The vast proportions of the hall, its graceful pillars, its elegant simplicity—all these, apparent to us in one dimension, were overwhelming to his new vision.

But his curiosity about himself was insatiable. He felt each muscle as though it were an *objet d'art*. He tested all his extensions, lingering longest and in most bewilderment over the smallest, central one, but returning to each. He probed every crevice, tested all the curvings and frettings, the swellings and dwindlings of his body. Only his face and head were left unexamined. It was as though he was observing *from* them, hence found the rest of his body an object.

Abram conducted his inquiry for a long time without any evident memory of us. But finally, as he paced the great hall, he returned to the coffins.

Long he stood then, studying each of us in turn. I find it difficult, even now, to appraise our reactions—or at least my own. Anticipation, fear, wonder? Yes, but dominant over these, a nostalgia, as much for the new order of life (as though we were to retrieve these bodies from some long-forgotten past rather than newly inhabit them) as for that we were leaving.

And only then, as Abram stood long over She, longer over Her, and briefly over me, did I regret the inordinate power he held: at once the generator of these lives and the first man.

He was in no hurry to animate us. He turned back to the

wonders of the hall, left it to pursue various corridors of the—house? temple? Wherever he went, however long he stayed: of these matters we were aware, but powerless otherwise. Trapped in the passage from one life to another, we were nervous embryos.

At last he returned. There was a new decisiveness in his movements; now his body was fully invested with him. He paused over She, made a gesture of the hand—sadness? dismissal?—and moved to a position near Her. Again the electric birth.

Her stirred, reached up languidly, and accepted Abram's hand. He lifted her from the coffin, and she came to him in a single fluid motion. There they stood, barely separated, gazing raptly at each other. Then each reached a hand to the other; their explorations began.

If it was maddening for me to observe their total absorption in each other, how must it have been for She? Some new element had entered my field of comprehension; there was a different circuit connecting me to She, so that I experienced her shocks, her loss of voltage.

Yet it would be fatuous, as well as inaccurate, to speak of "envy" or "jealousy." She's system, dependent upon whatever Abram's attentive energy had brought her, was sadly disrupted: it was her deprivation to which I was attached. Yet I could not fill it; indeed, as usual, She was hardly aware of me.

Abram and Her were experimenting joyously now, their eyes hot and glazed, their breath strenuous. I observed other changes in them with interest, and various riddles seemed less difficult.

I was also aware of subtle differences in the ways the two experienced their bodies. Abram's joy and excitement were naïve: each contact with Her was patently the first of its sort; his movements had the awkwardness and the fierceness of the untried. Her, however, epitomized a practiced grace: the lingering of her hand here, the responsive movements of her

shoulders, the aggressive ones of her hips—all betrayed a know-
ingness that I could then record, but only much later evaluate.

At last Abram could endure their play no longer. Uttering
a howl, he scooped Her up and carried her off.

Thereafter, She was dormant: her vital energy had dwin-
dled; she seemed scarcely aware of the two human beings. I
was alone, at first a not uninterested observer. I was preparing
myself for my own new life; I would not enter it uninitiated.

That life, as Abram and Her performed it, seemed to have
only four aspects or cycles. The most active was what I
"thought" of as using each other. In this ritual both seemed
to take great pleasure: it was as though an incalculable number
of volts was exchanged—and consumed. For there were inter-
vening periods of flickering exhaustion, of a depletion as radical as that experienced by She.

Nor could I comprehend the purpose of this activity. It
seemed as though the plug-in was the goal, its significance an
end to their separate identities, a fusing into a perfect connection. Yet at conclusion, the plug-in did not hold; they came
apart.

A second cycle was that of what I now know to be sleep.
Then I "thought" of it as a dead circuit: they were burned
out. But my observation of fitful movements, twitchings and
stirrings, made it clear that there was active current present,
though somehow mostly quiescent.

A third phase—one they seemed to enjoy almost as much as
using each other—consisted of placing objects in their mouths
(I can think of no substitute for these words except some awkward circumlocution). At first I found this activity more interesting and puzzling than the plug-in, but eventually my preference reversed.

I had no conception of the purpose of putting objects in
one's mouth, and "mused" on the possible connection between
this act and that of rapidly opening and closing the mouth,

each person facing the other when performing this function, and then attending the other while he took his turn at this curious jaw-wagging.

At first I "believed" that this must be a way to eject those objects, previously taken into the same opening, after having obtained some energy from them. But then I began to observe various squattings and posturings during which objects were emitted from lower parts of the body. These seemed more appropriately an opposite charge to that of ingestion. And so I came finally to the conclusion that jaw-wagging was a primitive sort of signaling. How absurd, even degrading, to one accustomed to electric communication!

The fourth cycle was the most complex, and I awaited it regularly with my equivalent of eager anticipation. The monotonous repetitiveness of the other three cycles would have snapped my circuit, had there not been this recurring fourth. For this they made greater use of their lower extensions, moving from place to place, observing objects, studying them, exchanging signals all the while. (I have not designated signaling a separate cycle, since it clearly was a saturating activity, uninhibited in using each other, intermittently employed even in the quiescent cycle.)

I remained my equivalent of skeptical about the value of the fourth cycle, but without it, I should have felt that we had chosen a far too rudimentary form of life for our new play. . . .

Having no knowledge then of human "time," I cannot even approximate measuring "how long" the life shared by Abram and Her continued in this fashion. But eventually there was an alteration in their pattern.

It originated in Her. I had not, of course, understood Abram's preference. To me She was the most perfect system of my experience. But some premonitory concept of humanness slowly began to convince me that I, too, once newly animated, might find it pleasant to clasp Her in my extensions, to encounter the proximity of her bulges and cavities, and even to plug in to her. Not in preference to She, but *additionally.*

I think I first experienced this projection shortly after I observed an aberration in Her's behavior: occasional absences from contact, a total evasion of our circuits. When this occurred, Abram, too, altered his program; it became statistically impossible not to link these two events. During Her's absence, he would either sit motionless, all his activity limited to his head, or break into wild total activity of some deviant sort, the purpose and meaning of which I could not conceive. The static was most unpleasant.

Once Her was again present, Abram completely changed his current. He used Her, but differently. Employing primarily his upper extensions, he seemed rather intent upon destroying her than on joining her. Her would assume a counter-charge, but it was clear that Abram had the greater energy, and soon Her would become nonresistant. Sometimes then, fully turned on, he would plug in, but the reception had a different quality; the fusion was, as it were, unilateral.

But I have not made clear the relation between Her's absences and returns, and my new conception of Her. Her would come back from these absences altered. Some distortion was evident in Her's "appearance," and each time my charge was strongly positive. Her seemed to have found a source for a different and potent variety of energy.

And now they less and less frequently functioned in the fourth cycle; each would remain alone until united in the third cycle. Often they would not enter the first cycle at all, but move swiftly from the third to the second. And Her's absences became more and more regular. During this period, I was aware of a growing strength in She; her charges were positive.

Then a sustained absence. No Her at all. Abram came to look at us, for the first time since Her had become a human being. On his third visit he activated She. Now I was alone, in an observational vacuum. A chilly realization, even now.

She was radiant energy: the human body became her. Abram the fortunate was more careful with this mate; he nurtured She in a tender storage. They observed the four cycles, but he ordained more attention to the fourth cycle, conducted the first one with a finesse, a—tenderness—that created an even, steady, confident hum. Had I been capable of bitterness (I had never heard of it), I would have eaten my cells out with acid. . . .

No attention was paid my human shell for a considerable interval. But at last they stood before my coffin, and their signals were directed against each other. She, I realized, was reminding Abram of the initial part I had played in the whole venture, and arguing that I, too, must have my turn at playing human. He was reluctant to animate me.

Communication broke down; signaling ceased. It was then that I learned woman's power in human life. For She persuaded him by means of the first cycle. When he rose from her, he sullenly performed the last electric birth.

I became a man with two feelings dominant. The first was relief—a relief that I echo at this moment of writing, freed in this narrative at last to use a human vocabulary. The other feeling was one of wariness. Having experienced the ultimate in impotence before birth, I was a congenital dissembler.

Nor was this natural to me. Until human birth, I had been forthright in essence; indeed, my troubles had always been caused by my radical candor. . . .

"She has persuaded me to this act," Abram said curtly. "But I do not trust you, and you may not live here with us."

My first words were acquiescent, and perhaps prophetic. "Very well," I said. "I will go." But my heart was protesting as I looked upon She's unabashed rosy nakedness, and She smiled at me.

Outside, the sunlight smote me. Then I crossed an open field of tall grasses, bending in silvery waves before a cool breeze, and saw in the distance the brazen sea. I took courage and felt myself a man.

II

I lived alone on the plains of time. I learned to hunt, fish, swim; I built a rude shelter amid the dunes of the coast. I grew dark and strong.

Now and then I would walk the several miles to the Doric temple. Twice I had a glimpse of She bathing in the sea, bright wet body glistening in the salt-splattered light. But each time, as I cautiously approached her, under cover of a dune, Abram appeared in the entrance of the temple, and walked slowly to the beach.

It was his world; Abram the father, the generator, wholly controlled it. This I had not foreseen, and I felt bitterly frustrated. What sort of a play is it, when the characters never meet?

I brooded. Each night, as the sea darkened, I sat on my highest dune, surveying the empty world. And so it was one evening that at last, as the great red disc was slowly sliding behind the sea, I saw in the distance a human figure.

I waited. I was in a strategic position, between this figure and the temple. I waited, feeling a certain exultation that I had rejected the impulse to hide. Clasping my knees and rocking to and fro, I waited in contentment over the knowledge that for once I might be in command of a human situation.

It was Her. I recognized her first by her slightly swaying walk and her long flowing red hair. She had draped around her middle a belt of woven leaves and wore a single white flower in her hair. She was singing softly.

As she passed my dune, she looked up and I cried out, "Her!" my voice cracking rustily.

She stood there, looking at me speculatively, and then moved slowly toward me, to stop a few paces away.

"Well," she said. I did not know whether it was a question or a comment.

"Come."

She shook her head.

"How are they?" she asked. "I didn't believe he'd ever bring you to life."

"He didn't want to." I told her the story.

At last she moved swiftly up the dune and sat beside me. I found it difficult to return her steady, mocking gaze.

"And now," she said softly, "you would like me to entice Abram away."

"Why do you say that?" My voice, to my annoyance, shook a little.

"Because it's true. You want She. It's obvious."

"Where do you go when we can't reach you?"

She shrugged her shoulders; I was reminded of those moments after Abram brought her to life.

"There are other worlds. You know that. Other forms, other dimensions, other—amusements."

By this time, I had recovered some composure, found myself up to the game.

"Tell me about some of them."

Again she smiled mockingly. She stretched out a slender hand and patted me on the head.

"Tod," she said lazily, "you're not very subtle. Let's plan our conspiracy."

I was forced into a reluctant smile. My chagrin made us both laugh.

"There," she said. "Dissembling is so ridiculous. Considering our chief creator, we're all bound to be corrupt in this play."

"Not She," I said angrily.

To my surprise, Her looked thoughtful.

"Perhaps not. And I wouldn't put it past Abram to have taken care of that in advance. He would have me to play with, but should it not work out, then at least he'd always have She, innocent and obedient. All behind his front of great dignity.

"But you see, Tod"—and she suddenly looked very demure— "Abram, even in his other manifestation, was always stupid. He designed me to be the wanton, the woman always ready to please men, and irresistibly alluring to them. But in his greed, he forgot that he must necessarily, at the same time, endow me with real power. He came to need me much more than I needed him."

I considered this statement. It was the more difficult to evaluate for her leaning toward me with a new sweetness of expression. And then Her flung back her long hair and bared herself; she looked at me with that strange expression that had excited me after each of her returns to Abram from an expedition.

I kissed her long, thirstily. Then I thrust her away.

"Yes, I want you too," I said. "But we have things to plan." I stood up. "Why did you and Abram quarrel?"

Those eyes were fiercely animated, but I could not read their meaning.

"Quarrel?" Her finally said with contempt. "Quarrel! He's so stupid. He has no flair, no style. And whenever I baffled him, he'd beat me because he had no other way of retaliating."

"Then why are you coming back to him now?"

Her yawned.

"Boredom. Things can also be too subtle, too fine-edged. One wearies of that too."

"Where do you go?" I demanded heavily, insistently.

Her stretched out beside me. "Tod," she said sleepily, "you're almost as bad as he is. Let's rest. Do you have anything to eat?"

I was studying her short belt-skirt of leaves. I touched it. "That's pretty," I said. "But why do you wear it?"

Her opened her eyes wide.

"That's what you must teach She." Her smiled that half inviting, half contented smile.

I fed her, and when the moon appeared, and the stars, I carried her into my shelter. Through the night, from time to time, Her educated me.

III

In the bright morning we approached the temple. I stopped where a huge boulder would hide me. Her continued on alone, in her swaying walk, and I watched until she reached the entrance and disappeared. Waif, seductive tramp of the sidereal wastes.

I waited long. Had She won Abram from Her? Did Abram suspect our plan? Or had Her beguiled me into a sleepy-headed credulousness, and was she really a counterspy, plotting with Abram against me? The longer I waited, the more uneasy I became and the more distrustful of the secret wisdom Her had taught me, to impart in turn to She.

But at last Her reappeared, followed by Abram. He looked fierce and eager. He caught up to Her and tried to embrace her, but she withheld herself while clearly promising, by words and movements, all that he wanted, once they reached their destination.

About this destination Her had remained mysterious. I knew only that it was that realm to which she often retreated and whence she returned periodically. In persuading him to accompany her, she was to have promised a new order of ecstatic experience, as well as herself.

They were gone, over a hill. Yet I waited, though more relaxedly, partly in awe of my opportunity, partly in distrust. How well Her had completed the process of disillusionment begun when I was helpless before Abram's decision whether to animate me or leave me forever passive in the marble coffin! I, who had once been defiantly honest, was now a wary and tricky dissembler, skeptical, cynical, stained by experience.

The sky had darkened suddenly. A menacing squall line was advancing from the northeast. Trapped between nature and man, I chose man for my adversary. It was possible that Her and Abram would not return; there was no chance that the storm would fail to come.

Inside the temple, all was quiet. The only sound was from without: the preliminary whistling of the wind. On tiptoe I passed the four empty coffins and slowly went down that hall so often paced by Abram. Each beautifully tiled room was empty, but as I approached the end of the corridor I heard the sound of stifled weeping.

In my eagerness now, I forgot to be quiet, and so I saw her first expectantly raised on one elbow, on the pallet she had shared with Abram. The darkening of her expression as she looked upon me, rather than him, was not flattering.

But I was not surprised, not discouraged. Having made sure that there was an emergency egress from the building close to her room, I entered and sat on the floor beside her.

I awaited the end of her weeping, knowing by now that everything human comes to an end. I did not venture to comfort her; I did not want to be repulsed.

At last She took her hands from her face and looked at me.

"You—you know that they've gone?"

I nodded. "I saw them."

"I can't believe it. We were so happy. I have not—failed Abram in any way."

I had chosen to be thoughtful, kindly but a little removed.

"You remember how it was before? Her came between you then, too."

She nodded and fell to weeping again, but more softly.

"What—is it?" she asked at last. "Why does he want Her more than me?"

"He probably doesn't," I said pensively. "He wants both of you. He has made man, and hence himself, a restless wanderer, who cannot be contained within any one pattern. I feel it myself."

She seemed startled.

"You? For as long as I have known you, you have been faithful in your feeling for me, even though I have not encouraged you. Would you too, Tod, go off with Her if she were to ask you?"

I paused judiciously.

"Perhaps. Perhaps," I said and stopped, not to overplay my part.

She pouted, but did not speak. I was encouraged.

"But Her has not asked me," I resumed more briskly.

"Instead, it is you and I who are together—and alone together."

I caught her swift glance of appraisal; she was not sure of my meaning.

"But I am Abram's mate," she said at last, averting my gaze.

"Abram's abandoned mate." I was pleased that I was still able to pitch my tone at a dispassionate level.

She brooded.

"Come," I said decisively. "Let's go down to the sea—"

As though on signal, the rest of my words were lost in a tremendous clap of thunder. With a cry of fear, she flung herself to me and huddled in my arms.

I had thought that I knew the extent of my feeling for She: I realized now that I had not. To hold her thus surpassed my every imagining.

Slowly, with a caution close to impossible in my delight, I began to caress her. For a little, she relaxed in my arms, neither responding nor rejecting.

The storm was massive now, and at each awesome stroke of lightning and the rumbling and crashing that followed, she clung to me.

And then the insistence in me grew; my caresses became more importunate. Suddenly she cried out, "No, No. It's wrong. We mustn't," and threw herself back on the pallet.

"Wrong?" I repeated as quietly as I was able. "Wrong?"

"Yes, wrong. Abram told me that I was never to do that with any other man. He said it was the Father's will, and that if I disobeyed I would lose my innocence."

"But," I answered gently, sitting down beside her, "who is this Father if not Abram himself, in his other manifestation? Abram is concerned only with what he wants for himself. He is a bad father."

She shook her head.

"No. No. He told me he's not. I must obey the Father and keep my innocence."

"What does 'innocence' mean to you?" I asked gently.

She blinked tear-filled eyes.

"Happiness," she whispered. "The way I've been."

"But you were happy just now in my arms," I replied. "If you let me make love to you, you'll be still happier. And you'll be a woman, instead of the girl you are now. You'll be ready and able to decide for yourself whatever you want to do and don't want to do. You'll be free. And all this will happen because in these matters I know more than Abram, and I can teach you. For instance."

She quivered in response to my hands and said, "Oh," forming the word on her lips with a delicate precision. But almost immediately she sat upright and said, half in fear, half in excitement, "A woman! Free . . . But I don't want to have to choose, to be filled with opposites!"

"Yes," I said, and drew her to me. "A woman, a beautiful woman, and free. Free to choose."

IV

The rest of the story is a familiar one, prototypical. Abram returned eventually, to find She a woman, pregnant, and wearing her own garland of leaves. He seemed somewhat dispirited; his adventures had made him even more somber and cranky. He began to study primitive astronomy and biology, and was given to long and lonely bouts of what seemed to be contemplation. Describing them, he would mutter something about theology.

Although his temper was still fiery at times, he bore me no special ill will, tolerated my presence, and never suggested either to She or to me that he suspected us of having been lovers. The baby was born so close to nine months after his departure with Her that he assumed it his own. None of us knows.

I left them. I wandered through the ages of man, preaching total freedom. I was frequently opposed, hated, jailed. Eventually I returned to the Red Windmill. I found both She and Abram astonishingly aged and completely disaffected. I learned that the son, a distasteful lout named Romulus, I think, had long ago murdered his younger brother. Abram could not bear the sight of him.

And although She had grown fat and petulant, something of our old camaraderie returned and we drifted into a partnership that eventually bought Abram out of his holdings in the Red Windmill and The Motel.

And Her? Rumors, insubstantial gossip. But always the word that she is as beautiful and seductive as ever. I wonder. I look at She, gross; at Abram, gaunt; at myself, well worn. Clearly the power has run down and may soon give out. The Great Generator has been failing for a long time. If Her is unchanged, she has been charged elsewhere, transcended our local resources.

Now and then I am nostalgic about the early days. Now and then, adjusting myself for sleep, I conjure up the old visions: Her on the dune, She in my arms and the wild storm without. A twinge of sadness assails me. But I remind myself that its meaning escapes me, and gently propel myself toward oblivion.

Fred Chappell

A PROPERTY OF HOPE

S he used to scream and curse when she was angry, and dash water on the walls and threaten to sell the damned chickens or the two yearling heifers and move to a town. In a town things happened, or at least there was something to look at. But when Johnny got back from the fields for supper, she was calm and quiet. The long, brittle summer afternoons did that to her, to anyone. From the doorway she could see the fields stretching listlessly under the butter-colored sun, a breeze moving among the corn tassels, lifting the leaves of the tobacco. Woods Creek gave up miserly flashes of the sunlight from pockets of shadow under willows and tall weeds.

Over the meal of cold chicken, cold green beans, cold biscuits—she was not going to fire the wood range on a July afternoon—she would tell him quietly how they could move. He used to work in a furniture warehouse down in High Point. Hadn't that been all right? Even if he went back to baseball, wouldn't that be better? She had first met him when he was a third-string catcher for the Browns. It seemed so long past now, that May five years ago. Actually, wasn't anything better than this . . . this—she didn't know what to call it. *Waiting,* she wanted to say.

He ate quickly, but somehow ruminatively too. The big muscles at the corners of his jaws bulged, unknotted, bulged; he chewed slowly but ate quickly. His throat distended with appreciative swallows of buttermilk. "After January is the only time. After the market." His voice was gentle, yet guttural. The tiny silver leaves of dry alfalfa lay in his black, dusty hair. Dust of the hayfield was powdered over his arms.

Another waiting. Tobacco, the one crop which brought in actual cash money, sold in December and January, and now it stood in the field, blackly green, tarry, heavy, the broad ribby leaves furred with a white down. She could see the patch through the doorway; she could not now imagine it cured, ready to grade, with the leaves the color of syrup and spotted here and there with circles like frog eyes. She could not now see the field as she had seen it last January, pale with new rye-grass and splotched with wintering cattle. January was as far as St. Louis. Farther.

"It ain't worth your time, you farmin' on shares like this. You're a pure fool to get caught in it like this. It's always the market time when we'll have money. There wasn't any money last market, after all we counted on it."

He shrugged. He knew better than she that there was no money in it. Maybe he ought to have told her—if it would have done any good. But she always seemed to have this idea that something was going to turn into money for them, and he doubted that anything he said could correct the kind of expectation the certainty of money roused. In his thirty-five years he had seen the attitude often enough to know that it only fed on disappointment, and that continual rebuff to these hopes only represented an eventual guarantee. "Mabel," he said.

She picked at her meal. When she looked up, his hard brown eyes bored against her gaze, but his look was dulled, a bit glazed. Having satisfied one appetite, he had discovered another. She felt a touch of panic, and leaned away from his advanced hand. She took up her cup of cold, pitchy coffee. "I'll heat some water for a tub for you if you want me to," she said.

In the bare yard she could see a pair of metallic-looking chickens futilely fleeing the bantam. The shadow of the spindly oak was long and still; the air was quiet, now settling down to coolness.

He sat back and began to make a cigarette, opening the booklet of OCB papers and blowing into it to separate the leaves. "Last year we had the truck bill to pay off. But this year we ain't owing a penny, so far at least. And I don't plan to get in debt again. I told you before we came up here, if we got in debt share-farming, it'd be hell to pay getting out."

She nodded. She remembered, but then she had never lived on a farm; she had thought it would be pretty and peaceful out in the country. She hadn't thought about dust and flies and being dirt poor. Dropping the plastic-handled fork, she rubbed her cheek with her wrist. It felt dry and feverish.

"Johnny," she said, "let's leave this place. Let's get away." She hadn't planned to say it that way; it sounded as if she were begging. She was satisfied she didn't have to beg.

He licked along the open edge of the cigarette paper and, with a twist of his thumb, rolled the cigarette tight and drew his forefinger along the seam. He went to the stove for a kitchen match. "You know we can't do that," he said.

His voice was low, almost a mumble, and she understood from the sound of it that if she talked any more about leaving he would only become more withdrawn and taciturn. She searched her mind for another beginning point; she wasn't ready to give up. "How much will we get, come market time?"

He sucked at the cigarette. It was hard to say, not knowing how the tobacco would weigh out, and not knowing how prices would run this year. "I figure about fifteen hundred dollars, but I don't know how close it is. Might be more, might be a lot less."

"Fifteen hundred? That's a lot of money."

"Not much, not enough."

She knew what he meant: He wanted a farm for himself, he wanted to own ground. But that was because he had grown up on a farm, and he didn't care about the mud and grit and the mindlessness of the long day when she was alone in the house. What was this house anyway but a shack, a shanty? When it was too hot to bear under the tin roof she stood on the splintery back porch in her white cotton slip, staring across the heaving fields at Ballantine's comfortable white house. It was easy to imagine how cool it must be under the gray shingled roof and how orderly the rooms would be, the large drapes drawn and the softened light nuzzling the furniture. In that house the buzzing of a fly would sound loud as a tractor; in here she didn't even hear them, gathered in clusters to a spot on the wood range or stupidly blundering against the window glass. Johnny hadn't asked her about living on a farm.

"It still sounds like a lot of money. Fifteen hundred." She rolled the big round figure in her mouth.

"It'd be a start, and that's about all. And we ain't got it yet." He shrugged. For him, merely prospective money was boring, having neither weight nor taste. He lifted a lid from the stove and dropped a long ash into the black firebox.

"But it's a *good* start, and we *will* get it." She nodded assertively as she spoke, agreeing with herself. Already she had changed her plan: it was no use talking to Johnny now; he had no foresight. After the market, when the money was solidly in hand, she could talk to him. They could plan together then. She imagined the money, dozens of crisp bills, lying here on the oilcloth, he and she gathered hushed around it in the light of the kerosene lamp.

He took a few sulphur matches from the box and put them

in his shirt pocket, went into the bedroom and returned in a moment carrying the chipped guitar. He bore it with calculated carelessness, almost shyly, and sidled past the back of her chair without looking at her. Out to the small front porch he went, and she heard the scrape of the chair drawn over the worn boards. She heard him striking casually at the strings, then pausing to give the tuning keys minute turns. It always took a long time before he settled down to play a tune; he loved to fuss with the instrument, to peck at disjointed chords, and then just drift into something that came to his mind. He was happier than usual; he never played unless he was happy. Work must have gone well today—there had been no arguments with old man Ballantine, who owned the farm. Oh—she had forgotten—tomorrow was Saturday, and Johnny had the half day off.

She rose and began with some haste to gather the dishes. She piled them on the stove; it would be foolish to waste this time washing dishes.

Without really thinking, she hurried into the back room and looked at herself in the dresser mirror. She wasn't so bad: Her dark hair was perhaps too fine for this long glamour-girl style, but her heart-shaped face was clear—her color rather heightened now—and she had the candid blue eyes of a child. She gave her eyebrows a couple of quick strokes with the pencil.

The first few organized bars, and then Johnny began to sing softly, slurring the words, almost humming.

> *"He courted me fairly, by night and by day,*
> *But now he is loaded and going away."*

She hurried to join him on the porch—it seemed so much like the long courting hours they had spent on other porches in the twilight. And now was a lucky time to have it all come back; it could be almost as if they had begun together again.

It was not to be. Just as she came to the doorway, Ernie

Ballantine streaked down from the road into the yard, his thin figure a pale blur in the twilight. He jumped off the bicycle without braking it and walked toward the porch. The bicycle rolled a few feet and wobbled over on its side. Ernie advanced, showing the palm of his right hand to them, holding it alongside his ear like an Indian in a Western movie. "Howdy," he said.

Johnny grunted and sat forward in his chair. He leaned the guitar against the wall. Mabel went helplessly to sit in the sagging cane-bottomed chair beside Johnny. Ernie plopped himself down in the dirt at the edge of the porch. He always did that, looking for a cheap peek up her skirt.

She held her knees tightly together. Ernie was detestable. He was thirteen years old, a long awkward kid with a thick neck and an uncertain, nerve-racking voice. A lazy kid, Johnny said, but not spoiled. It was hard to think of Emmet Ballantine, bitter-looking and taciturn, being soft enough to spoil anyone.

She knew what was going to happen and, sure enough, in a few minutes Ernie had talked Johnny into going into the house and digging out his old heavy mitt and a baseball. He came back through the door, holding the ball still, the oiled glove dangling by a strap from his ring finger. They went up to the road to play. She watched: it was always the same contest. Ernie wound up, his long body crane-like, and delivered the ball with his whole strength. But Johnny never dropped the ball, though he had to lean and jump in every direction to contend with the kid's vehement wildness. If the pitch was really wild, he waited stolidly while Ernie chased the ball. Occasionally Johnny returned the ball with some force, and Ernie would drop it, cursing. The boy had no consideration for her. Why didn't Johnny shut him up when he talked like that?

Thwuck . . . *thwuck* . . . As Ernie got tired, his pitching got wilder, and he had to keep chasing the ball. It was getting dark, and still he kept throwing: his will never tired of the silly rivalry. At last they gave up and came back to the porch. Johnny dropped the glove and put the ball in it, an egg in a nest, and sat in the chair beside her. Ernie flung himself on the ground again, and Mabel brought her knees together.

"Whoo! I'm all tired out." Ernie's voice wobbled about the edge of a falsetto.

"You ain't done nothin'," Johnny said.

"I worked all day in that hayfield, didn't I?" He rubbed his forearm. "And throwing that ball around is work too."

Johnny began slowly to make another cigarette. "You ain't old enough to get tired. And you don't throw hard enough to hurt a cat."

"When are you going to show me how to throw a curve? You said you would."

"We better wait till you can get one straight across. You ain't got the patience it takes to learn a thing anyway."

"A curve's not so hard to learn, not like a screwball. Anyway, your best pitch is always a good fast ball."

"Where did you learn so much about it?" Johnny seemed still to be amused by this familiar exchange.

It was getting darker, but no stars showed in the profound sky. If any were out yet, they would be to the north, behind the house. The air was quiet and almost cool now, and the mutter of the creek had got louder.

They were talking about baseball, and the discussion soon resolved to a catalogue of unfamiliar names. She tried vainly not to think what might have happened in the twilight if Ernie had not turned up: she knew that wishing like that would make her discontented. She rose and went wordlessly into the kitchen. By doing the dishes now, perhaps she could salvage the rest of the evening. All day she was alone, and when Ernie and Johnny were together she was still starved for company. Clumsily she fired the range and set on it an aluminum pan filled with water. From the bottom of the pan tiny bubbles rose continually, as if the water were carbonated. By the light of the kerosene lamp her eyes yet ached from staring over the sunny fields.

They were still talking outside when she finished drying and stacking the dishes, and now the low words were as unintelligible, as much a mere part of the night sounds as the singing of the crickets. She threw the dish water out the front door, not trying to splash Ernie, but not avoiding him either. Then she refilled the pan and filled two kettles and put them on and added a few lumps of coal to the fire. Because the heat was steamy, it wasn't too bad in the kitchen now. In the storeroom adjoining the kitchen she wrestled with the big galvanized foot tub and finally got it out into the kitchen, banging it heavily against the doorjamb. She sat at the table, drawing idly on the oilcloth with a long red fingernail. Everything was ready for Johnny's bath and he was outside, talking the night away.

At last he came in, carrying the guitar and baseball and mitt.

"You better close the door so you can have your bath in here," she said.

He nodded and nudged it closed with his foot without looking. The wedge of pine that was the doorstop slid across the mottled linoleum. He went on through to the bedroom, and she heard the guitar hum slightly as he hung it on the wall, and heard the creak and slap of the trunk when he put up the ball and glove. She fixed the old bedspread over the nails at the top of the window so that the room seemed much smaller, with the darkness closed away and the light gathered inward. He had already taken his shirt off when he came back, and the black dust was gathered under his collarbones and down the front of his chest in a big Y. His chest was ridged with muscle. His whole squat body was as unyielding as stone.

Breathtaking clouds of steam rose as she poured the pan and kettles of hot water into the tub. Then she poured in cold water and turned back immediately to damp the fire down. Johnny, stripped, dropped one foot gingerly into the water, testing the temperature, and got in and squatted, hunched tightly. With the strong-smelling yellow soap he began to lather his neck and arms.

"You'd never know how good this feels," he said. "Loosens your muscles up."

"I bet it does," she said. "I know you've been looking forward to it. I thought Ernie never would leave." With a faded rag from a flour sack she began to scrub his back.

"Yeah," he said. And then in a lower voice: "Ernie . . ."

There was something premonitory in his voice. She straightened and rubbed her forehead with her wrist. "What's wrong with Ernie?"

"Nothin'." He soaped his belly assiduously. "He was just telling me that his old man is thinking of selling a pretty good piece off of the back acres. It's a good piece of ground back there. Needs getting rid of some scrub pine and a couple of years of liming it down."

"I thought you said it was no good back there."

"Needs building up. So he's got to let it go at a pretty reasonable price. I bet you could satisfy him easy with a thousand dollars' cash payment down on it."

She was wholly confused. A thousand dollars was almost all. She couldn't think how to begin. "Johnny . . ."

He spoke evenly and coolly, as if he were settling an argument. "Well, it's something worth thinking about."

She leaned and wrung out the cloth, trying to plan what she was going to have to say.

Diane Oliver

KEY TO THE CITY

One story . . . two stories . . . five stories . . . Continue counting until the windows become blurred, then add ten. An apartment building . . . Not a very unusual one—Chicago has several housing units designed from this same architectural plan. The early morning sun sparkles on the windows. Hundreds of window panes glisten in the sun, leaving a transparent glow on the building. A chalky white sidewalk juts in and out of green park benches, following the brick contours of the apartment unit.

In another region of the country, the peaches are yellowing on the tree near a small unpainted frame house. In sunlight, the sides of the house are brownish grey. On the side of the yard nearest the peach tree, three thin-necked chickens wander around, scratching the clay. The house and the chickens belong together. They were a part of the farm land when the first tenants moved in a generation ago.

In the smallest bedroom of the white house, the cord belonging to the manila window shade swings back and forth pushed by a slight breeze, making a queer tapping sound on the window ledge. Directly across from the room's single window, a big imitation mahogany bed is set squarely on the floor. Suddenly the next door dog barks at the chickens, and the hens enjoying the excitement, giggle with cackles as they flap across the yard.

At the peak of the noise, a thin brown hand reached out, grasped the sheet, and pulled it tightly toward the top of the bed. The figure on the other side grunted, and turned in the direction of the slowly moving sheet.

"Move over Babycake," a sleepy voice muttered.

Babycake made another peculiar sound, turned over, and was quiet.

The room was still except for the continuous ticking of a big white alarm clock stuck on a table in the crowded corner of the room. A pair of jeans, two tee-shirts, and a baby doll lay on the arm of the chair. A few minutes passed. The same hand crept from under the cover. A pair of dark eyes peeped over the sheet and stared absently at the clock as if counting the tick-tocks.

Only six-thirty. She slid down under the covers and thought about getting up. She knew the alarm would not ring for an half-hour yet. The sheet muffled her yawn but this time the burial was short-lived. On one side of the bed, the cover was thrown back and a small brown-skinned girl sat on the edge of the bed, wrinkling her nose in an effort to wake up.

With her big toe, Nora Murray felt under the edge of the bed trying to find her bedroom slippers. Finding one rubber thong sandal, she slipped it on and rubbed the rough pine floor under the bed until her foot touched its mate. One, maybe two seconds passed. Then found, two blue sandals. She slid off the bed, careful not to wake Babycake, and made her way to the window. Raising the half-lowered shade, she looked past the chickens scratching up the grass, seeing instead the picture of Chicago her father's letters described.

Chicago. She whispered the word. Chicago was on the water front. They had arrived yesterday she decided. And from her father's letters she felt as if she knew this neighborhood. From the tenth floor where their new apartment was located, she watched a Pet Milk truck turn the corner, beginning the early morning milk run. A few minutes later Officer Todd passed McConnell's Grocery and Drug store, completing the first round of his six-thirty A.M. police beat. This section wasn't exactly the nicest part of town, but then she didn't expect it be.

She had known she was going to be a city girl for years now. But this—all those buildings and things down there. She had never dreamed the city would look like this. Back home the county courthouse wasn't even as big as the apartment building she was standing in right now. Why this place made Mayor Dodge's house look like a little chicken farm. Chicken farm? Now why would she think about—Good heavens! She had almost forgotten. It was time to go out and get the eggs. Nora dressed quickly and hurried out the back door.

She was so excited she could hardly count the eggs. After her graduation from high school, they had all planned how they would make the big move. Tomorrow, finally, the family would leave. After saving Mama's egg money, her baby-sitting money, and the few dollars Daddy had sent before he got so busy he didn't have time to write, they had saved enough money for the bus trip. And she was sure her father was saving money in the Chicago bank. He had a good part time job, he said. Tomorrow, she, and Mattie, and Mama, and Babycake planned to ride all the way from Still Creek to Chicago without ever leaving the bus except when they all had to go to the bathroom.

Mama probably would have a time with Babycake. She always got sick whenever she rode for a long time. And they couldn't wash her very well in those bus station bath rooms. But they would get to that later. Her Daddy, she knew, would meet them at the downtown bus station. He would be awfully glad to see them. A lot of people around Little Square said that he'd left them and wasn't going to send for them or even see them again. She had known better. If he said he would send for his family, he would. Besides, when he first married her mama, he promised they'd get away to Chicago. Which was really why Mama took on another job instead of staying with the kids. With both of them working full time, she figured she could save some money.

Nora had so many things to tell him, she could never write down every thing in one letter. She would rather wait until she saw him. Neither one of them was very much for writing letters, and he had missed her graduation program. He hadn't even heard her valedictorian speech. It was a good speech, everybody said it was. And then when the time for the program came, she didn't make a single mistake.

After Mr. Douglas awarded the diplomas, he announced the two members of the class who would go on to college, which was really why they were moving. Her parents said she could go to a branch of the city college practically free and finish up her education. They were moving so she could have a chance to be something better than Mrs. Pringle's maid. Even thinking of that Mrs. Pringle made her mad. Maybe a teacher. Yes, she would like that. History always had been her favorite subject, she could be a history teacher. And then they wouldn't have to live in an apartment, they could afford a real house. Even one with a real yard.

They had planned to move "one of these days" for as long as she could remember. She could repeat their special family formula backwards, frontwards, and even sideways. They had talked about it ever since she was a little girl. Mama and Daddy would get jobs up North, and with the money she could earn, she would eventually get through college. Then she would put Mattie through and Mattie would see to it that

Babycake graduated. And of course if any other sisters or brothers came along, they would do the same thing for them. She waved to Mrs. McAuley who was hanging out clothes next door. Already early morning sounds had begun in the neighborhood. Behind the chicken coop, she could hear the grinding noise of Mr. Johnson's tractor. Yes, a history teacher, she decided definitely. So she could have an electric washing machine and drive a Buick.

She had seen a brand new Buick once, a long time ago. She was walking home with Jimmy Douglas and for some reason the fifth grade let out early that day. When they were halfway home, they saw the lady Mrs. McAuley worked for driving her home. She had taken sick on the job, and the lady had put her right on the front seat. She wondered even then how it felt to ride in a car like that. Later, she told Mama about Mrs. McAuley and the white lady bringing her home. "Why can't we have a car?" she had asked. Her father just laughed and said right now they couldn't even afford a pair of roller skates. How childish she must have sounded. Even then she should have realized their money was always low.

She hadn't thought about Jimmy for weeks. He was at the summer science institute of the Negro branch of the state university. Ever since she won the first prize in biology he hadn't said very much to her. She guessed he wouldn't write her from college in the fall. But if he got angry over a school prize, he wasn't worth worrying about. Still she wondered if he would remember the Buick.

The Edwards, their neighbors three doors up, had been the first people in Little Square to own a car. It was a 1948 Chevrolet. She had ridden in that one lots of times. In fact, they were to be driven to the bus station in the Edwards' car. That was just a day away and even thinking about leaving home made her throat feel a little funny.

Mama and she started packing the day after school was

closed. They had begun very systematically. The little kids' stuff went into the last suitcase. They were to be kept quiet and out of the way with some of their play things. Only it hadn't worked out that way. Every thing went along fine until Mattie decided to help. Oh . . . that Mattie. Even her name almost made Nora drop an egg. Mattie had dumped over a whole cardboard box, which they had to fix up all over again. Trying to pack with two little girls in the house made her nervous. Twice she found herself trying to pack the butter dish with butter still in it.

By the time the eggs were gathered and set up high on top of the ice box, Mama had long since been off to work. Nora made Mattie and Babycake mayonnaise and egg sandwiches for breakfast, and fixed a fried egg for herself. After they were through eating, she tried to persuade the two little girls to play house outside. But in an hour they were tired and wanted to help her.

"Go on, Mattie, go back outdoors and play." She was losing her patience now.

"But we don't got nothing to play with," Mattie said, determined not to leave. "Margie and Tanker-Belle are all packed up and you said we won't see them again until we get there.

Mattie's brown eyes began watering as if she were going to cry. Margie and Tanker-Belle were the two dolls of the family. Tanker-Belle had been one of those fancy toaster cover dolls. Some well-meaning aunt on Mama's side had sent Mama a cover for her toaster as a Christmas gift. Which would have been nice, but they didn't have a toaster.

Mattie had practically confiscated the doll and for reasons known only to Mattie had named her Tanker-Belle. She had spent most of her time since Christmas in the Pretend House back of the pecan tree. Tanker-Belle was rather frayed now, after having spent several nights in the rain.

Now Nora explained to the little girls that at last she was going to have a nice long rest. She had packed the doll immediately after breakfast while Mattie was busy with something else. Tanker-Belle was now inside of the big roasting pan with the dictionary and the kitchen forks. But Mattie insisted that she knew Tanker-Belle was lonesome inside of the turkey pan.

"I'll tell you what, Mattie," Nora said as she tried to comfort the sobbing child. "Look on my dresser and get a nickel out of the blue bag. You go find Babycake and you all walk up to Mr. Jame's store for a double orange popsicle. Then go play in the Pretend House until lunch time."

"Can I, Nora? Oh, can I?" Mattie's smile stopped the tears running down her cheeks. She raced out of the little hall way jumping over boxes and through the bedroom for a nickel. In a second she was calling Babycake and the two little girls started up the road.

Five dollars and ninety-five cents worth of graduation money was left. Nora kept a mental record of her savings since June. Well, it was worth the money to get them out of the house. They would never be ready to leave at this rate.

She stooped down and began cramming some books in another cardboard box, in a hurry to move on to something else. By the time the little girls were finished with the popsicle, it would be time for their naps. Nora tied a string around the box and made a double knot. If she could just have an hour by herself, she could finish the packing.

She sat down on the floor and reached up to the table for the sugar can. Mrs. Pringle wouldn't let Mama off early from work. And because they needed all the money she could earn, Mama wouldn't just walk out. She emptied the sugar from the can into a brown paper bag. In fact, Mrs. Pringle had acted really nasty about the trip. The least Mama could have done was to help her find another cook. Well, Mama had tried, but with the new factory hiring colored help now, nobody much wanted an all day job like that with the Pringles. Nora stood up and downed the can in a pot of dish water. She picked up the dish rag and began scrubbing.

A noise that sounded like a rock hitting the wire of the chicken coop made Nora drop the rag and step out of the back door.

"Babycake you and Mattie stop bothering the chickens. We won't get any eggs if you keep on. What's wrong with you anyway?"

"Babycake wants all the popsicle, Nora. And you gave it to me, didn't you Nora?"

By the time Mattie explained about the popsicle and how Babycake had gotten angry and thrown a rock at the chickens, Babycake was crying. Mattie, upon seeing Babycake's tears, had begun to cry herself. Nora stood there outdone. Faced with two squealing little girls and her with all that work to do.

"I can tell," Nora said firmly, "that it's time for two naps. Give me the popsicle and you can eat it after you've had a nap." She marched her sisters through the back door, stopped to deposit the ice cream on the kitchen table, and continued toward the bedroom. While she undressed the little girls, the popsicle lay forgotten.

Fifteen minutes passed. Babycake was asleep. Mattie who was ready to get up again decided she was not sleepy and began singing to herself. Nora had to stop packing again and tell her to be quiet. She didn't notice the popsicle until she saw the sticky orange drops on the floor. Oh, not on her clean floor. . . . She took a rag from under the sink and dunked it in water. While she was sprinkling soap powder on the cloth, she ate a bite of popsicle. Mama didn't believe in letting anything go to waste. The melted popsicle came up without scrubbing; she took another bite. Nora rinsed the rag in the water and wiped the spot again. She would have to spend another nickel for some more ice cream. She wiped up the

table and swallowed what was left of the dripping orange popsicle.

Nora worked all evening, sorting clothes, folding linen, and
packing kitchen utensils. Finally, the boxes were ready to go.

In the morning the smell of freshly fried chicken lingered
throughout the house. The two friers Mama killed last night
plus the one Mrs. McAuley brought over would last them the
time the trip would take. In the bottom of the lunch basket
were three sweet potato pies and a brown bag full of the
Georgia peaches that grew wild in their back yard.

In an half-hour, according to the schedule propped on an
empty milk bottle on the kitchen table, everybody would be
ready to pile in the Edwards' car for the bus station. She was
glad they didn't have to move everything. The Edwards were
going to keep all the house pieces in their barn until they sent
for the furniture.

The two big beds already had been dismantled and Mattie's
roll-away cot was folded up near the front door. Nora walked
from the hall into the living room. The whole house looked
so empty. Even the mantel Daddy built over the fireplace
looked bare without the pine cones and greenery. The gold
pine cones Mattie painted at school had been packed away. All
of the window shades were down and rolled up on the floor.
Even the woodwork was clean.

All summer the neighbors had been saving newspapers for
the Murrays. The papers certainly came in handy now. Nora
covered the living room sofa with sheets of the *Still Creek
Bugle*. Suddenly she smiled. Even covered with newspapers the
sofa cushions sagged. She decided to leave the newspapers in
the hall. Mrs. Edwards might need them for house cleaning.

By seven-thirty Babycake had been freshly washed and
ironed for the trip. She was commanded to sit still on the
front stoop and announce the Edwards' arrival. Mattie who
also had been dared to get dirty, kept her company. The two

little girls sat on the first step, facing the swing tied to the pine tree. Their sliding feet had trampled the little bits of grass growing beneath the rope swing. Scattered in the yard were a few green weeds the chickens had not pecked away. Babycake reached over and gave the potted Christmas cactus a goodbye pat. The leaves were shiny because she had poured water over them this morning. Mama wanted the plant to be clean when Mrs. Edwards took home the pot.

All at once there was a honk from the horn and a long lanky boy, the oldest of the Edwards' boys, was running up the steps.

"Pop says are y'all ready yet?" Without giving them a chance to answer he started piling boxes in the trunk of the car. Babycake and Mattie were so scared they would get dirty and get left they did everything Nora told them to do.

"Mattie, pick up the little shoe box . . . Babycake, make sure we got the lunch. No, I'll take care of the lunch, you grab the hat box over there."

Their little house had never been so cluttered and then so empty. Come to think of it, their neighborhood seldom had seen such excitement.

Everybody in Little Square was at the bus station to see the Murrays off. There was no need to ask how they'd gotten there. Those few people who had cars drove down and piled in as many neighbors as they could. Uncle Ben, Aunt Mabel's husband, was one of those who had walked the three quarters of a mile to the bus station. Mabel had caught a ride. Anyway, they were all there. A mass of black people overflowed the little waiting room marked "Colored."

In one corner of one-half of Still Creek Bus Terminal, Mattie sat on an upright box as Aunt Mabel gave her pigtails a quick brushing. When she had tied each end with a bright yellow ribbon, Mabel thumped Mattie on the neck and pushed her off the box toward her Mama's voice that attempted to round up the family.

Nora saw Aunt Mabel trying to catch Uncle Ben's eye. Mabel tried to speak above the noise in the room.

"Haven't been this many people here since they brought that Jackson boy's body home," she said. "You know the one who was killed overseas three years ago."

While Uncle Ben and Aunt Mabel discussed the community gatherings at the station during the last five years, Mama was getting ready to buy their tickets. Somebody got up so she could sit down and count out the money for four one-way tickets to Chicago.

Mattie was hanging over her shoulders wide-eyed. "Mama," she breathed, "are we rich?"

"Hush child, I'm trying to count." When she had counted out the correct amount of money four times, she tied what was left into a handkerchief and put it in the blue denim purse which in turn went into her genuine imitation leather cowhide bag. Still counting silently, she made her way to the ticket window. When the man had given her the tickets and counted out the change, Nora felt like giving a glorious hallelujah of relief. At times like this she always felt something wrong was going to happen. She could imagine the fare going up and then without enough money having to go back home.

With Mama talking to Aunt Mabel, Nora slipped out of the side door for a final look at her home town. The Georgia landscape was shallow and dull, and to her eyes that had seen no other part of the country, beautiful. Even this early in the morning a thickness had settled over the countryside, covering everything with a film of fine red dust. She fingered the purse inside of her pocket. Six dollars even she had now. Mrs. Edwards had given her a dime to buy some candy or something in case she got hungry on the way.

The sound of voices inside the waiting room reached her

ears. She could hear Aunt Mabel crying, louder and louder. The voices seemed to reach out and carry her with them. The bus—the bus must have come. Quickly she shut her purse and ran back toward the waiting room.

Sure enough there was her mother frantically hugging and kissing everybody and thanking them for all the good things they had done for the Murrays. Mattie was pulling Mama's hand and begging her to hurry up before they got left. Seeing Nora, her mother beckoned her to come and get Mattie and Babycake for a final trip to the bathroom.

By the time everybody had been pushed out of the waiting room, the men had most of the luggage stored underneath the bus. Then began the last minute hugging and kissing and gift-giving all over again. Nora felt a dollar bill pressed into her hand. She couldn't help the tears; she knew Uncle Ben really didn't have any money to spare. She bent over and kissed the old man on his cheek.

The bus driver checked his watch and in a dry matter-of-fact voice announced that anybody who was leaving with him had better hurry up and get on because he was leaving in exactly two shakes. Finally the steel door closed. In the rear of the bus, their noses pressed against the window panes, the four Murrays waved good-bye to friends and neighbors and to Still Creek, Georgia, "the original home of fine Georgia peaches."

After hours of riding, Nora lost track of the towns they passed. The slight jogging of the bus didn't even make her head hurt any more. Still Creek seemed so far away. She had never been a long way from home before. Except once when she was five, they made a trip to Atlanta. She spent the whole morning almost kneeling in her seat, counting the split-level houses. What would all those people in the cars think, she wondered, if they looked up and saw her staring down at them. Heavens knows what they did was none of her business.

At the next rest stop, Nora decided to stretch her legs in

the bus aisle. Mama herself took the little girls inside for a glass of milk and a trip to the bathroom. When the bus started again, she began telling a fairy tale to Mattie. But she didn't have very long to think about stories. A few minutes after the rest stop the accident happened. Little Babycake stuffed herself with too much sweet potato custard and lost all of her dinner on the back seat of the bus. They tried to clear up the seat with some old waxed paper, but they couldn't clean and pay attention to Babycake too.

Babycake started crying. Her stomach hurt and she wanted to go home. Mama tried to hush her, but the more she patted, the more Babycake cried. By the time the odor had spread throughout the bus, Mama sent Nora up to the bus driver to ask him if he would stop and let Babycake get her stomach settled.

Nora stood up and held on to the seat, cautiously walking up the aisle. She wished the bus had a ceiling rail, then she could keep her balance. She looked at the back of the bus driver's grayish blue suit. After hours of riding, the jacket still looked freshly pressed. He didn't even turn around when she approached the driver's seat. He looked into the mirror instead of glancing at her.

"My little sister's sick," she explained. "If she could get some air, my mother said she might feel better." She held on to the pole near the front steps facing the back of the driver's gray head.

Muttering something unintelligible, he said No. He had lost enough time and would be stopping soon anyway. They would just have to wait like everybody else.

While she was standing in the aisle, the bus picked up speed and turned a sharp curve. Nora felt herself fall against two elderly women who were sitting with pastel handkerchiefs to their noses. And although the bus was airconditioned, one was struggling trying to raise the window. Glaring at her, the other woman helped Nora get her balance by elbowing her in the ribs.

"Dirty nigger," she whispered.

Nora was not certain she had heard the woman speak, but even thinking of the words hurt her ears. Nobody'd ever called her a nigger to her face before. At least not like that. She travelled the rest of the trip hearing nothing but the woman's words. When she looked up the bus had pulled into a station and after a few minutes she felt the wheels moving again. She didn't know how many rest stops the bus made. Once, as she turned toward the window she realized the daylight had changed into darkness. Nora even forgot to watch for the sign telling them they had crossed the Illinois state line.

Mattie wanted her to play Grampa Bear, but Nora did not feel like playing games. She sat at the back of the bus, making up things to think about trying not to remember the words. She was almost asleep when the bus turned into an entrance, pulled up to the curb and stopped.

Because there were so many bundles to carry out, they were the last people getting off the bus. Babycake was the first to see him. She caught hold of Mama's hand yelling, "Here we are, Here we are," and started to run across the terminal to the man in the tweed overcoat. Nora had to hold her back. The man Babycake saw was not her father. He was a little too tall, and when he passed the family, he just looked at them strangely.

They stood outside the big glass door with the little packages, waiting and looking through each crowd of people, but no one came. After fifteen minutes and two "May I Help You's" Mama guided them through the revolving door and to a bench in the middle of the station. "That way he can see us when he comes," she explained. They sat down on the bench and Nora again braided Mattie and Babycake's hair. And then there was nothing to do but wait.

He was supposed to be here. They had sent the letter last Friday telling him the exact time of their arrival. Babycake was getting sleepy again, "Where's Daddy?" she asked. "Aren't we there now?" Mama told her to hush up and motioned for Nora to get up. "Maybe he can't find us," she whispered.

An hour had passed, Nora stood up. "Where are you going, Nora?" Mattie asked.

"To check the luggage." Nora began walking down the side of the terminal, near the shiny cigarette machine and past the magazine rack. Everything glittered with a metallic glow, but the fluorescent lighting only emphasized the emptiness inside her. She looked up and saw an overhead panel advertising a course in speedwriting—gt—gd—jb . . . Then she met Elizabeth Taylor's gaze beneath the sign pointing to the telephone booth.

At once she was aware of what had happened. He was working overtime, and had overslept. She had the apartment building's telephone number from one of her first letters. She would call. Nora slipped into the booth and loosened a dime from her money collection. With sticky fingers, she lifted the receiver and dialed the number. The phone rang once, and a voice answered: "McConnell's Drug Store—Hello? This is McConnell's Drug Store."

"Please," Nora whispered, "could I speak with Mr. Joseph Murray."

"Sorry Miss, but no Joe Murray works here."

"But don't you know him?"

"No, but I'll check the list of people working in the building." In two minutes he was back and he was sorry, but no Murray was ever listed there.

Nora emerged from the booth and stood at the lockers, wondering if she should look outside when she felt someone bump into her. She turned around quickly, but it was only a woman tugging on a little boy who murmured, "Excuse me." Nora abruptly pulled away and ran toward the doors out to the walk-way into the darkness.

She tried to brush the hair from her face, but when she removed her fingers they were damp. She stood outside until her eyes were dry.

Nora went back to the station bench and whispered to her mother who was sitting down quietly. She and Mama agreed—they would spend the night in the terminal, just in case. She watched her mother cover Babycake with a coat, her face turned from Nora as if afraid she might cry. Nora wondered if she had known all the time. Strange that it was morning already, outside the sky was still dark. Later they would call the welfare people, something they'd never done before, and they would find them a place to stay.

Stepping over the suitcases piled near the bench holding Babycake, Nora began sorting out bundles. She'd probably have to babysit for a while, until Mama found a job and a place to leave the little girls during the day. She began fingering the boxes. Today was Saturday and Mattie and Babycake's Sunday dresses would need ironing, but she'd worry about that later. Their ribbons didn't have to be pressed, if she could ever remember where they were.

Slowly Nora put down the box. Her shoulders slid down the back of the bench. She couldn't press anything, she couldn't even remember where they had packed the iron.

Robie Macauley

LEGEND OF
THE TWO SWIMMERS

Everyone must have a worthless uncle; it is a part of life. At ten I knew all there was to know about remittance men and black-sheep younger sons shipped off to Australia. It seemed significant that no one in the family ever mentioned such a thing and I was certain that, if I watched carefully enough, one morning I would find a letter dropped through the slot onto the faded blue of the hall carpet, addressed in an unfamiliar hand and carrying a foreign postmark.

I was certain then that I would discern a strained look on my grandmother's face, or a trace of tears. My father would upset his coffee cup at the table and shout for no reason. I had begun to read the indecent language of signs, a child's first corruption.

There would be tense consultations behind closed doors. One day I would come across a picture in an album, the face cut out, or a silk hat in the attic, marked with unknown initials.

The months passed and letters with a foreign postmark

came—but only from a friend of my father's vacationing in England. I never found the picture in the album nor the silk hat in the attic. The front door never opened to the sudden sight of a tall man in dark clothes with a wicked familiar-un-familiar face. By the end of that year I had finished the shelf of old paperback novels in the basement and had begun to forget all about that uncle.

In dull truth I did have an uncle—he lived only four blocks away and owned half interest in a small, failing drygoods store in a bad neighborhood. Under the shadeless bulbs hanging from the tin ceiling, he fussed around among the counters piled with Big Yank and Oshkosh B'Gosh boys' corduroy knickers, caps stuffed with tissue paper—marked down from $1.98—and canvas gloves. The air in that place was a weight on the lungs, loaded with the smell of cheap new cloth. The shadows in the rear hid only bareness and a roll-top desk, for everything Mr. Rood and my uncle had in stock was piled on the front counters. "Come in out of the rain, boy," Uncle would say as I stood reluctantly in the doorway on my way home from school on a Friday afternoon.

My mother was dead three years; my father was, most likely, on one of his business trips; and Mrs. Fahey, my grandmother's iron nurse, had said at least three times this morning, "I won't have them kids underfoot around the house this week-end." My grandmother ruled, but Mrs. Fahey made the common law in the house.

It was not so much that I would be bored and lonely. As I opened the door to the jangle of the brass bell above it, I knew that I entered the world of worn linoleum on kitchen floors, sooty front porches, smells of cabbage cooking, back yards full of washing, darned socks, pinched pennies, overdue rent, angry protests and angry silences—the gravelly downhill slide of the poor.

In my grandmother's house I felt rich and good. In the

cold persistent mist of my aunt and uncle's company, I felt sad and pauperized. I had begun to divide things clearly not so much between good and evil, but between good and bad.

A year or two ago I would have gone along willingly enough, squabbled with the Polish neighbor's two boys, contentedly mooned over an old picture book in the living room while the clock hands slowly drifted towards Sunday night. Going there now seemed like the act of becoming my uncle's son. What was it like to be dumpy, ineffective, getting bald, needing money? I knew. I felt it already in myself.

My mother had lain complaining and bedridden in the little house on Jefferson Street for over two years. When she was gone, my sister and I cried at the funeral, but it was more of an exorcism than a death. We moved in with my grandmother—with her temper and her money. My father seemed to work longer and was away more often. We seldom saw him and when we did it was like too much candy all at once. "He is becoming a very successful man," my grandmother told us. "Like your grandfather. You should be proud of him." We sensed a secret reproach to my mother and our fading loyalty stiffened for a moment. But Mother had always been a reproach to *us*—she suffered so much and we were so selfish. It was often brought home to us how selfish we were. Her painful smile had seemed to live in the room long after she disappeared.

My grandmother was the colonel of the family; she assumed we had a regimental duty to live up to, not unpayable debts of tears. She was the drillmaster of our ideas; our silly feelings she conceded us and left alone. One Sunday a few months after we had come to live in her house, she made my father take me to the "upstairs parlor" to explain, in a way, what she meant.

It was by far the pleasantest room in the house and, though dusted daily, almost never used. Long windows the whole length of the north wall made it a reservoir of sunlight. Beneath them were oblong wicker baskets of ferns, a tame jungle two feet high. To the left of the hearth was the glass showcase with all its trophies.

On its shelves silver divers poised gracefully for the double jackknife that would never follow. Crossed oars that would never touch the water lay on polished plaques; medals of different shapes and sizes glinted at my eyes out of silk-lined boxes. Obscurer mementos filled the lower shelf—a copper pocket-piece, a pipe and pouch, seashells, a leather-bound picture album, a framed sketch of gulls, a box with a silver dolphin on the lid. To me it was an undistinguished hoard. On the center shelf there was a black silk object of some kind, lying there like a small discolored puddle.

Abruptly my father said, "Over here. Come look at them." The spirits of the room, the two champions life-sized and piratical, posed above the fireplace.

Their bare arms were folded on their chests, like great oars momentarily shipped. There was an impressive curve of chest muscle under the short-sleeved swimming jerseys. Their heads were tipped back at the same slightly scornful angle and their black eyes, even through the dull filter of time and the lens, showed total confidence, like a lost trait of man, the sense of absolute monarchy. It persisted for a few moments. Then, like one of those trick geometrical drawings that will change before the eye, the picture would change and you saw only two young men in striped swimming suits staring dourly.

They had identical moustaches like startling pairs of wings, thick eyebrows, my grandmother's heavy cheekbones and her Welsh head; they were, I heard, her dead brothers, Owen and Lloyd.

My father shuffled reverently through the pile of picture postcards from the table drawer. Tebb's Beach, Florida, 1902. A million dollars has changed the name and the landscape since then. A ramshackle boarding house-hotel on a fine beach, backed by scrub jungle. *A splendid place,* my father said, quoting, *a mite lonesome. Just fishermen and a few boarders. Wonderful sunshine.*

Yesterday we saw an Indian ninety-eight years old. Still smokes seven cigars a day—he fought in the Seminole war and they left him for dead in the swamp. Big pink shells here, most beautiful you ever saw. We gathered some, are sending a basketful. Is it snowing in Michigan? We hear there is ice and snow. Sometimes we go out with the fishermen. Owen is getting wonderfully good at the Trudgen stroke. Yesterday we swam for three hours. We had our picture made and we shall send it to you. Give our love to Nettie and Mama.

There wasn't much more to the story, just a glimpse in a letter of the two sunburnt young men on the beach one morning, taking off shoes and robes and preparing to go into the water. Owen, who was the younger, must have tired after a while, it said, and came in to sit on the beach. Someone saw him there for a moment, wringing out the little black silk skullcap he always wore while swimming. Evidently Lloyd stayed out in the water and evidently after a little while Owen looked up to see a shark-blade cutting near him and then his brother must have been gone.

Owen must not have waited, my father said. When the man from the hotel happened along the beach a half hour or so later, the beach was empty and the sea was empty too. Owen must not have hesitated for a moment.

That was not quite the end, he said, because they found the skullcap. It was lying in the sand in the afternoon sun, quite dry by this time.

My father said I was always to remember how Owen had never paused or waited. It may not seem like anything very much to you at your age because you are so young. And it may sound very simple, but it isn't at all simple and you should think about what I'm telling you. There will be times when you yourself will be called just as Uncle Owen was and then you must remember him. When you are older you will understand.

In his voice there was a terrible undertow of pride and I felt it dragging me down. I tried to think of just what it was that had happened and I thought that two young men had gone swimming in the ocean twenty-five years ago and had disappeared. My father stood in the sunlight in his gray suit and tried to tell me about sharks and oceans in a place where he had never been. But I could hear the urgency in his voice and I felt that he was really talking about something that had to be paid back, a strange debt not of money which would keep us poor all of our lives.

"Do you understand?" he demanded, unsatisfied.

I felt shameful and small because, try as I would, I could think of no answer. What kept coming into my head was a warning sign that said, "Watch out for sharks!" and finally I just hung my head and lied, "Yes."

As time went on I began to understand, or thought I did, and I strove to make up for my failure by covering the swimmers in imagination with doubled glory. I would spend hours in the room, lying on the windowseat in the sun reading or idly examining the souvenirs.

"Come in out of the rain, boy," my live uncle said again and I stopped in the doorway. It was not raining. The late afternoon sun, half-tangled in long rags of clouds, shone momentarily down on the street. With his poor joke dropping from his lips, my uncle stood in the middle of his shop and life gathered dust around him.

One day he had confessed why he made jokes like this. "I found out in the army I wasn't strong enough to fight and I was too fat to run, so I took up telling jokes." It was the truth; I had never heard a grown man say anything so spineless. When he was nineteen, he said, he ran away and joined the army.

First they taught him to take care of horses and then they taught him to cook. The World War was just one pan of hash after the other. He came home, borrowed money from my grandmother, lost it, borrowed again to go halves in the shop, was losing it again.

Grandmother's soldierly kindness was qualified by her high blood pressure and occasional tempers that glowed and smoked like a coal fire and sent off poisonous fumes. There were times when she could not bear the thought of children in her house; her own had betrayed her so. Annette, her daughter, a beautiful girl by family standards, had turned traitor at the age of nine and died. My father's older brother Will, a pale figure not easily recalled, had got himself killed at Belleau Wood. My Uncle Clinton turned money into dry goods and dry goods into debts, and there it was. My father, who was at least getting somewhere, went completely out of his mind. On those days my sister had to stay in her room and not make any noise and I was sent off to my uncle with $1.75 for board.

I played with the Wisnewski boys down the street until we fought bitterly. Thereafter I moped around the house. My aunt urged me to read the Bible and my uncle took me for walks in the woods. We walked along the river road, which began on the other side of the railway tracks, and he showed me how to make a willow whistle. I said, "What good's a willow whistle? That's for little kids." He told me some army stories and I took interest; then I was bored. They had no gunpowder in them. They were all about what the first sergeant said to the chief cook about the stew. He liked to potter around the woods, with a city man's interest in birds' eggs that had fallen out of trees and the sight of a rabbit. He had a noisy little dog named Butch who sometimes went with us.

The one thing I liked to do was to go fishing with him and during the summer, when I was pawned off on Aunt and Uncle for weeks at a time, we would often go out for an afternoon on the river. We used bamboo poles and angleworms for bait. He dropped things in the water, rocked the boat, then went to sleep while his line slowly wound around an oar. Still he had marvelous luck. He caught many fish—mostly bullheads and catfish that had to be thrown back again.

I liked those somnolent afternoons when I had nothing at all to live up to. I could see French cliffs rise up on the far side of the river as I lay with my arms over the gunwale. I thought we drifted past the estuary of the Tagus and there was Africa on the horizon. I dozed and saw a blue sea with a black fin splitting the water a long way out and came to myself with a shock, asking myself if I wouldn't hesitate, wouldn't wait a minute until it was too late.

The trouble was, I felt, that this very instant was traveling in me like an air bubble in a vein and I could never foretell the moment it would reach the heart. When my father had talked to me, for the first time in my life I had doubted him and thus had doubted myself. I wondered if when Owen was a boy my great-grandfather had told him one day he would see a fin in the water and that he mustn't hesitate or wait even a second. I tried to imagine him telling Owen that. Boys die young and become their fathers.

I looked at my uncle, asleep on the back seat of the rowboat, his face sagging peacefully under his sagging hat. I wondered if he had ever heard the story, or if it meant anything to him.

Then one day I brought the subject up. He fixed the angleworm carefully on the hook and yawned. "Mother never did get over the death of those two darn fools," he said.

"Fools?" I said, shocked. "They were as brave as anybody can be and Owen went to save . . ."

"I know, I know," he said. "That's the way people talked. I say it was lack of good sense. Hadn't got brains enough to stay on dry land or a boat at least. Then go swimming around in shark waters. One got himself eat up, then the other one got himself eat up, too. Darn fools, I say."

At first I was too angry to speak, then when I looked again I saw it was only sluggish Uncle Clint bending over his bait pail and I realized it wasn't even necessary to forgive him.

When the cold water in the bottom of the boat would reach his foot, he would wake up. "Bail for dear life, men," he would say, "the ship is going down." The boat was an old one, paintless and splintery. He had found it one day half submerged in some rocky shallows down the river. He had dragged it ashore, nailed tin strips over the most obvious holes, caulked it, had given the bottom a coat of tar. He loved it in the same way he loved my aunt, who sustained him on the muddy waters of day to day, but who might sometime disappear and leave him to drown.

He was very much afraid of deep water. It must have been the earliest thing that set him apart from the rest of the family, of which Owen and Lloyd had been natural products. Almost all of the men had been skillful swimmers. My father, who never let me have such a dangerous thing as a bicycle, would point out the deepest part of the lake and dare me to swim to it. When I told my uncle about the swimming lessons I was taking from a professional, he pinched his nose and cast his eyes up, as if he were sinking hopelessly among the fish.

Our slow leak he regarded as a monster of the deep. Sometimes he would give up an hour's fishing and drifting because of an extra inch in the bottom of the boat.

"I couldn't be expected to save you," he would say, rowing for the shore.

"*I* can swim pretty well," I would say defiantly. The phlegmatic old Grand River seemed safe as a sidewalk—safer.

He had no very good place to tie the boat and so we just pulled it up on a sandy strip where he had put down a stake with a chain. Then we took our basket and our poles and started back along the river road.

The most agreeable spot in the world, I thought, with woods on one hand and an outpost line of huge trees along the waterside, a great green arcade in summer, it had been claimed by squatters and their shacks. Once it was fashionable to have a boat and a cottage down here, but now people went north or west to the lakes. Bristly mongrel dogs stood by the doors of mimic chalets with sinking roofs and crumbling lines of gingerbread. Four—five—six children's faces were piled in a pyramid inside a window. A man in a ragged leather jacket refused to answer hello, just took another swing with his axe. Some of the places were recently built huts, actually projecting over the riverside slope and supported there by a crazywork of long poles. Underneath them, like the droppings of a tethered animal, were tin cans, newspapers, ash piles, old tires, broken bottles.

Darkness dropped out of the air; it had already dimmed the city by the time we reached our street. My uncle hummed a tune. I walked pigeon-toed and lagged behind, nursing a wish like a bruise. A hundred seventeen steps from the corner, ten steps down the walk, four steps up to the porch; he reached for the knob.

I hung back, kicking the risers. The thought of that house with its long bare hours between bed and bed stunned me. In the hall, my uncle gave a three-note whistle and Butch came running. "Angel, we're home!" he shouted.

At dinner—fried mush and boiled cabbage were nearly inevitable—he talked about our afternoon as if remembering the striking events of history—"Just then a grand trout jumped in the air about fifteen feet away from us. Oh, it was a thrilling moment." He discussed manners and morals—"Six kids, a hound dog and an old car. No curtains on the windows, no running water but the river and still enough money to buy gas for an old car . . ."

Mute and unimpressed, Aunt finished her food and poured the coffee. When he had drunk his cup dry, my uncle began to rise, but it was only a poor habitual try. My aunt raised her eyes and stared at him. Saturday night meant prayers and bath for all good Christians. We bowed our heads.

"Forgive us for what we have left undone . . . guide our steps in the right pathways . . . make us better and stronger to withstand temptation in the week to come . . ." As she worked into the substance of her appeal, she became more fervent, more obscure, more biting. She referred obliquely to those who, though not unblessed by the hand of the Lord and having plenty of the goods of this earth—though how they expected to get through the eye of the needle she wouldn't presume to say—refused to help others needier than themselves and acted as if water was just as thick as blood. She worked around to those who sometimes through pure chuckle-headedness neglected to do certain unspecified things they ought to do while their nearest and dearest suffered as a result. My uncle dozed.

Ordinarily she did not scold or complain but went silently on with her work, her mouth like a seam; she was a different woman when she prayed. I listened and was scared at her tone. It came from a hollow distance. Even though its mixture of sarcasm, anger, bitterness, and sorrow confused me, I could recognize it. It was low and muffled through the thickness of many walls, but it came unmistakably from the torture chamber itself.

When she was silent again, Uncle raised his head, yawned, and said, "That was fine, Angel." He went into the living room and she began gathering up the plates.

That summer, the summer of which I am speaking, approached. My sister in a white dress played in the piano recital in the school auditorium and all remarked that she didn't make one mistake. I practiced my curve at the playground and pinned a picture of Lefty Grove over my dresser. My father went to Kansas City on business. My grandmother began to feel the heat approaching and predicted it would be the worst summer on record. School let out. I was banished to my uncle's. Uncle came home at night, slumped, and my aunt put a dishpan full of cool water next to his chair for him to soak his feet. He stared at the water and said, "We can't do it, Angel. It's no use." A man came to see him in the evening and they sat out on the porch for a long time. When I was in bed, I could hear their voices rise occasionally above the ziz-ziz-ziz of the tree toads and I heard my uncle ask, "Foreclosure?"

The summer clouds piled high over the river like marble monuments. I tried my crawl stroke in the river (this was forbidden) and watched the grainy water slide over my arms. On the bank one of the river kids, a solemn child in a patched dress, stood and stared.

My uncle hadn't the heart to go fishing much. Aunt's Saturday-night prayers increased in violence and developed in mystery. June turned into July. The lawns burned brown and crisp like shredded breakfast food. My friends were away at camps or cottages and I no longer wanted to go down to the river alone. From the swing on my uncle's porch I watched the clouds transform themselves and move away. I longed for fall, school, a disaster, anything.

In the course of time, it became Sunday morning of the first week in August. My father was home again, my grandmother was in a fit of well-being, and my exile was over. I was to go back to the other house the same day. Belly down, among the comic strips, I lay in squalid comfort on the worn rug. There was, thank God, no Sunday school in summer. My uncle lolled in his plump chair and surveyed the world as it came, printed, before his eyes. He muttered comments on it. The clock struck nine, shortly ten.

Aunt came home from church with a queer look. We heard her feet on the porch and then she came into the room and stood looking at us. "I'm going to see Mrs. Banning this afternoon," she finally said, but it wasn't what she was thinking. Slowly she began to pull off one of her gloves, staring in apparent pain at her hand, exactly as if she were in the process of stripping the whole skin from it.

"You must ask today," she said in the voice of her prayers. Uncle was alarmed. He looked up at her with a deserter's look. His glance roved to the window; he tried to raise the newspaper in front of his face again, but the inexorable skinning stopped him.

The glove came off at last with a final little snap and he jumped—it was as if we had all expected to see white bone. He said hurriedly, "I'll try. Yes, today's the day and I certainly will consider going to ask. They can't refuse me, can they, Angel?" He sighed. The newspaper began to cut him off again. Aunt stood quietly and began on the left hand. For some long-drawn minutes we could hear the same soft stripping sound. Only her fingers worked.

At last my uncle jumped out of his chair and yelled. "Stop!" He was breathing heavily and his thready hair was flying. He yelled, "Don't get so excited!" and rushed upstairs where we could hear him crashing his dresser drawers. He reappeared in a coat and tie and hooked his straw hat off the hall rack as he hit the bottom of the stairs. "Come on, son," he said, grabbing my arm and pulling me, protesting, to the door. As we went stumbling down the steps, I looked back and saw my aunt sitting in a chair with wet eyes and her hands buried in her dress. She looked beaten.

On the way over we marched and did not speak. When we came into the cool living room, I saw my father and shouted, "Dad!" In a cold voice he said, "Go upstairs and play. We've got business." Then I noticed my grandmother, Mr. Rood, and a stranger in a dark suit. The men were sitting in the shadow on the far side of the room while my grandmother, all by herself, garrisoned the nearer end. Her hand opened and closed on a little ivory stick.

I resented it, but my only choice was to go through the glass doors into the parlor—a room overfurnished with a stupefying taste. I went upstairs, wandered in and out of rooms and finally found myself in the swimmers' room. I stood before the fireplace looking up at them. Nothing had changed. "Play the game! Keep the faith! Grasp the nettle!" they said silently. It was all very easy, all very well, I thought. It was in their bones and muscles. It was only in my head. I was frightened. Then I thought—times change. For all I knew sharks were killed by some kind of machine nowadays. It didn't help. I stood in despair for a long time.

When I heard a clock striking in the hall, I finally went slowly downstairs. I crept through the parlor, up to the glass doors and looked in. They were still talking. My father stood in front of the fireplace, his arms half extended in his usual gesture of irritation. My grandmother's face had petrified—the horrible calm before she opened her mouth. She must have said something to Mr. Rood already because he sat heaped in his chair like a pile of worn-out clothes. Only the stranger seemed detached. With one eye in a squint, he calmly looked across the room at a china figurine of a camel perched on the whatnot. He looked as if he might be ready to take a shot at it.

My uncle looked as if he had been boiled. His face was red and puffed with his eyes bubbled, his mouth sunken. On the other side of the glass, my grandmother was saying, "Last time was really the last time, Clinton; you know it."

"Mother, just think what you're saying," Uncle pled.

"We have thought," said my father harshly. "We have thought and we can't do it." I saw him turn his back.

And he was right to do so because my uncle was crying. In

his horrible little fat-man way he was crying and tears ran down his cheeks. It was unbearable for me and I had to go into the room to distract their attention, even though it might make my grandmother angry. I had to stop the beating. But I would never be seen with my uncle again. I would run away and get a job as a cabin boy on a ship.

"Well," said my father pleasantly. "you're back. Now why don't you go for a walk with your Uncle Clint? He hasn't been feeling well, you see. He'll bring you back in time for dinner." It was the last thing I had expected.

"I won't go with him," I said.

My father came over and took me by the shoulder with a strong hand. "You will go," he said abruptly. "We've had enough trouble for one day." He did not say this as if it were meant for me, but to all in general. As we were going out, I heard him say to my uncle in a confidential tone. "Don't worry, Clint. I'll do the best I can." I couldn't understand what was happening.

When we were outside, Uncle stood on the walk and looked back at the front windows of the house while words seemed to thaw in his throat. "So that's the way the land lies, hm? So that's it? For your own good, they say. Well, if you ask me . . ." I didn't know what to expect. I stood and listened to him mutter.

He looked down at me and said, "You got some better place to go?"

I shook my head. He looked queer and choked and we walked along with very slow steps.

Finally he laughed and said. "Let's go down by the river. Yes, the river's the place for me today." He suddenly started to stride and I had to half run to keep up with him.

The streets were quiet; in the heat of Sunday afternoon the houses dozed behind their screens of trees. We crossed the railroad tracks and finally got to the river road, which was cool and deserted. The sun through the leaves made yellow sketches and signatures in the dust of it. My uncle looked anxiously around and I felt his desperation. He broke off a willow twig and made a few random slashes at it with his knife, looked at me, dropped it.

We walked some more. Abruptly he said, "Do you want to take the boat out on the river?"

I nodded. He said in the same voice, "It may be the last time."

"Why is it the last time?" I said. "Why the last time, Uncle Clint?" but he didn't answer. We turned around the bend in the road by the big willow and started down the little track that led to our mooring place.

When we had gone about twenty yards, we began to hear a woman's voice in shrill ups and downs beyond the bushes. We could not hear what she was saying. I ran ahead to see what it was. In a minute I burst through the bushes and saw her. She was calmly sitting on the middle thwart of *our* boat.

Worse than that, she was holding an oar and awkwardly trying to pole the boat away from shore while a girl about my age, but small, like a skinny monkey, had just finished untying the rope. My uncle gasped behind me. "Robbers!" I said. "Look, Uncle Clint."

The woman turned quickly; she had long rusty hair and a rusty face with chipped features—like notches in an axe blade. She was wearing some plaid thing that looked as if it had been torn off a table and hastily stitched around her. The girl swiftly hopped around, twisted over the side into the boat, crouched behind the gunwale and gave us a look out of the same face, though younger, more furtive, and even more ignorant.

My uncle stood gaping as his ship was stolen. I could have counted ten. I yelled, "That's our boat. Come back here, you." I knew I would have to do it myself. I jumped for the trailing rope at the bow. He came along behind me with undecided steps.

As I reached, I saw something happening. Slowly, out of six inches of mushy bottom, out of the shallow water, high into the air in a great trailing slimy arc, the oar was rising. The wide-eyed woman seemed to be clinging to it rather than propelling it. I scrambled sidewise as fast as I could.

Such ponderous soggy haymakers are too futile to hit anything in this world—except Uncle, who was fated. He had come up behind me; I said, "Duck," but as always, he did not fail to fail.

The end of the oar smacked him squarely on the chin, filled the air with a great burst of slime, pitched him backward three feet into a clump of rushes, and buried itself with a spout in the river bottom again. He put his hand up experimentally to his eyes.

I was scrabbling for a stone; "A fast one low and inside, just like Lefty's," I prayed as it left my hand. Not very fast, low and outside, it merely hit a tin plate we'd nailed over a leak in the side of the boat. It hit with a loud *clack!*

They were out in the stream, already gathering a sluggish momentum from the current. My uncle said feebly, "That's enough. Stop." Reluctantly I gave up the idea of clearing the decks with my high hard one, and went over to him. It occurred to me then that he was probably badly wounded.

He groaned and got to his knees, while over his face I splashed some water, which ran in red and black ribbons down his white shirt front. "Oh God," he said. "Is my nose still there?" It was. "Count my eyes," he directed.

"You've only got some blood on your chin," I said. "The rest is just mud. Open your mouth. You've got one, no, I think two front teeth out." He groaned again. I put my hands under his arm and tried to help him as he got to his feet.

"You're all right," I said anxiously. "It's only one or two teeth."

"One," he said grimly, and spat it out.

While he was splashing some more water on his face, I recovered the oar and hid it in the bushes. I was already beginning to think about pursuit, recovery, revenge. They couldn't get far with one oar. If we worked carefully along the shore—but just beyond us the trees came right down to the river and it was beyond them that the boat had now disappeared. Uncle responded to my schemes with a weak "Ehh, uh," and attended to his face. He was holding his jaw and his lower lip had begun to rise into a purplish sausage.

He followed me aimlessly as I made a way through the bushes. Over my shoulder, I kept saying things to make him come on—"If you'd only pulled back just half a foot . . . they can't row, they can't get far . . ." He didn't answer.

We went on for about twenty or thirty minutes and it seemed hopeless. There was nobody in the woods and the river was empty; the bushes tore at my trouser legs. At last I knew that we had lost them. Uncle came up alongside me, nursing his hurt mouth in his handkerchief. "I'm going home and put some ice on this. We'll have to give up." He said it almost pleadingly.

"But the boat," I said. "We'll never get it back again, you know that." I was perfectly detached and not selfish. I had just decided that I was through with him and the boat and the river forever, but I was trying to save something abstract. I could not see him ruined completely in one short day. I could not stand to think of him sitting at the table tonight while my aunt was praying and he thought, The boat is gone for good. He shook his head feebly at me and I knew I had lost.

So we trudged back up to the road again while I thought bitterly of running ahead and leaving him alone. Just as I was deciding, we came opposite the place where the old pilings from a former landing dock stuck up in the river. I heard a yell and a sound of splashing. I knew and I began to run.

I cut through the bushes quickly and got down to the river bank again. When I got there, I saw what I knew I was going to see—it was the unexpectedness of the completely expected. Out from the shore about fifteen feet was our boat with the rusty woman and the girl in it. They had evidently hit against one of the stumps and, as Uncle had always predicted, the boat was at last stubbornly sinking.

She was thrashing around frantically in her wet tablecloth, trying to scoop water over the side, trying to push with the remaining oar, slapping at the girl, screaming directions. When she saw me, she wailed, "We can't swim!" Then she yelled, "Your damn boat's full of leaks."

I was so winded I could only stand and watch with a feeling that this contemptible day had finally justified itself. I *had* wanted something terrible to happen. Everybody who involved himself with Uncle, even to steal from him, was going to suffer. I was getting out.

The boat lurched; the woman screamed again; Uncle arrived, running like a car on two cylinders.

He didn't ask anything, but pushed by me to see better. The next thing I saw was his clumsy lunge into the river, knees pumping, heels skidding on the slippery mud; then brown sprays of water shooting up over his pants legs. His mind had gone—I knew it, but what could I do?

"Come back! Come back! Where're you going?" I said, but he sloshed on with surprising speed. He caught the nearest black pier stump in the crook of his arm and grabbed for the next one further out; he was doing a comic swim, half out of the water. He sank to the level of his belt, then to his shoulders and the water bounced furiously around him. Then all at once I was thoroughly frightened—because he was not frightened. "Come back!" I yelled frantically. "Uncle, *you can't swim.*"

He had his arm hooked around the last old piling and he was reaching out to grab the gunwale of the boat. It lurched just then and he caught it; he managed to drag it towards him a few inches. His chin dipped under water and he let go of the boat as he reared his head backwards. I saw his eyes open, white and wide, and I knew that I was wrong. He was strangling with fear.

I started forward alarmed, but at the same moment Uncle had succeeded in grasping the woman's wrist in one hand and pulling her toward him. She was holding the girl in one arm and Uncle inched them over the side of the boat as they weakly fought against each other and him. They hung for a moment on the slanting gunwale, then disappeared together in a great spew of water and plaid cloth.

But in a moment his head emerged, an uncertain island around which they wrapped their arms. But underneath the panicky mess of grasping hands, wet hair, muddy faces, and cloth, a slow dogged engine was bringing them in to shore.

There was a slopping sound from behind them and I looked up. The boat gave a last pitch in the lazy current, slid sideways, and vanished.

And here my uncle, too, vanishes from my recollections. He ceased to take any place in my memory the moment he stepped on shore, as if my mind let him sink at the exact moment of his success. I do not remember if he was triumphant or cast down. We must have walked home together, but I cannot remember it and we must have said something or other about what had happened, but nothing remains.

Nothing remains of him except a few hearsay memories—I walked by his shop some weeks later and saw the windows plastered with signs advertising a sale. A fat man with curly black hair stood in the doorway cleaning out his ear with his little finger. My father did speak of his brother Clint sometimes and, I believe, sent him money after he had moved away.

That is all, or would have been all if it had not been for my father, who never lost his taste for moral fancies and noble illustrations.

Years later, in October, 1943, to be exact, I was a member of a regiment specially trained for amphibious operations. We were waiting at an east coast port of embarkation. The bleak barracks town lay under a gray sky and the days went by in a routine of preparation, apprehension and boredom.

There was nothing to do except line up for inoculations, play cards, check your equipment over again, lie on your bunk for hours tracing the water stains on the beaverboard ceiling. The water stains on those ceilings are remarkable because many of them look like drawings of ships going down, men struggling in the water, or figures suddenly disemboweled. All of the worst deaths known to the world are painted there.

On the Saturday before we were to leave, our last mail arrived, forwarded from our former camp. All I had was a letter from my father and a small package.

The letter began with his usual cheerful sententiousness. On the second page, it went on to say ". . . now I am sending you a memento of your uncle, who, as you remember, was a most courageous man. You might wish to have it with you both as a kind of family souvenir and as a reminder of someone who . . ." I stopped reading and the day came back.

I saw vividly the brown sluggish waters of the river with my uncle's terrified face bucking up and down in them, just as he reached for the gunwale of the foundering rowboat, the ridiculous sputtering, swollen face that against all the probabilities of nature was going forward.

But as far as I knew, my father had never known much of anything about this, or, if he had known, would have dismissed it. It seemed impossible that he could have found anything he could call a "memento." I knew that I now had the only memento of that day. I spent some time recalling it.

At last I opened the package he had sent. In it there lay a small half circle of faded black silk. I took it out and handled it and for a long time I sat turning it over in my fingers, unable to connect it with anything. It was only after some minutes that I recognized it as a small, faded silk skullcap, of course.

Bertha Harris

CATCHING SARADOVE

Outside, the street was covered with snow. At the window, Saradove watched the tenement doors open like sores for the tenants to dribble out, stagger through the slush for a piece of meat, some sugar, some smelly Puerto Rican fish. She sat, stroking the bulge in her belly where the baby lived, to keep from stroking the head lying below the baby in her lap. Her boredom was immense. She was captured in a cold room, stilled by a baby, pinned beneath a head that did not move her heart.

In a corner of the room, they had cleared and swept a place for a Christmas tree. They were waiting for the friend, Price, to come with his car and take them to the woods to cut it down. From the corner of her eye, Saradove saw three Hassidic Jewish boys, their heads and forelocks bent to the street, march past in a tight row. The boys looked at nothing but their own feet; only their huge oversized overcoats seemed to move, propelling them after the father who strode, black-hatted, black-bearded, ahead, watching only the space in front of him. The boys' overcoats would have fit their father; but the father's coat fit him as neatly as a uniform.

The pregnant maiden, thought Saradove, remembering the Saradove who had sat in Johnson's hot kitchen, trapping him. Johnson the unicorn, who put his head in her lap; waited for his chain of flowers. The trouble with life, she thought, is that it moves. The maiden's perfect moment—trapping the fabulous beast—is over the moment its head lies in her lap. Pinned beneath the head, she is no longer the maiden; and the beast has trapped her.

Today, she must gather Christmas trees, not chains of flowers. Johnson held and squeezed her legs.

"I don't know how to say this," said Johnson, thinking of only one way.

"Try," said Saradove, and said it for him. "You want to leave me, don't you?"

"Yes," said Johnson, squeezing his eyes together to keep out the sight of her. Saradove stroked his head then, to thank him. It was over; she was complete, and now it could all disappear; and it all did. She concentrated on the vacancy spreading over her, and she shared it with Johnson, to comfort him. It was the vacancy that belonged to a house, abandoned, rejected by the tenants. The vacancy felt like luxury; she was wrapped in it, the only one home.

She sat still in the livingroom until she heard Duncan turn the car into another street. Safe then, she turned off all the lights but one and knelt on her heels in his chair, fitting her own head into his grease spot. When she had completely replaced him, she got up and struck one note on the piano. The sound was like the noise of a brass band beneath her finger. She lifted her hand quickly. If she were careless, the sound would travel through the walls, across the row of green bushes and into the neighbors' ears like an alarm. She ran the same finger down the rough green surface of the hymnal, propped open forever on the music-stand. Secretly and by heart, she knew all the tunes and words to the hymns. If she wanted to, she could sit down now, pound them out, sing them, stretching her lungs to their fullest. She opened the book and turned the slippery pages, crinkling and bending them in her haste to find "There Is a Fountain Filled with Blood." She played it through, her fingers barely hitting the cold keys. She whispered the words and ignored all of them except for the ones that meant, over and over, there is a fountain filled with blood. Redeemers were not her meat. "Flows from Redeemer's side" was a lie. The fountains filled with blood were not Redeemer's; they were Saradove's and Olympia's.

The small lamp on the marble-topped table cut through more and more darkness. Outside there was winter afternoon light, but in the cramped, over-filled livingroom, it could have been midnight. Saradove slid her thumbnail down the keyboard, feeling it click; then folded her hands in her lap and watched the music. Only the year before, she remembered, she spent nearly all her time dreaming herself into the body of Frederic Chopin. She had curved her shoulders forward to remind herself of his enchanting consumption; she had pretended to hack blood all over the ivories. All during the summer, she had prayed for—no, demanded—rain, so that she could play "The Raindrop Prelude" and cough and long for the sound of carriage wheels bringing George Sand home to her. Saradove giggled and slapped the hymnal shut. Her stomach sank with embarrassment: the nonsense of pretending to be Chopin! Being Chopin had landed her in a ruffled dress beating out "From a Faery's Garden" in the church parlor, a big girl with breasts and shaved armpits playing a baby piece and bringing shame on her head. She hadn't had to play first—it was not that bad—but a girl five years younger had played last, played genuine music, something hard and loud by Tchai-kovsky, and had sent the audience home with sweet disposi-tions.

Saradove shut the piano and went behind the fireplace fan for her hidden store of cigarettes. She lay on the couch and smoked and considered the horror of being sixteen, and the horror of being sixteen and becoming the duplicate of Olympia. She saw it going on forever: the both of them batting about a mean contrary man who gave the mockingbirds that sang in the front yard names like Pete and Sam and got mad as hell when the two bleeding fountains didn't go out on the front porch and listen to them, Pete and Sam, with him. She flicked ashes behind the couch. It was clear that there had never been any real hope of slicing off Olympia's breasts that grew bigger every year on her own chest, or of healing the wound inside her that made blood spout every month, that made her helpless in the company of the boys in geometry class. She had planned other ways, but the great leap from "In a Faery's Garden" to performing something hard and long in New York City was possible only in her head before she went to sleep at night; and the visiting art teacher had got rich from her paint-ings of flattened-out persimmons, vicious-looking Irises before he had packed up and left town.

Saradove rubbed out the cigarette on the sole of her shoe, shoved the butt and ashes behind a cushion. She began to count the folds in the organdy curtains, then went back and counted all the shadows between the folds. What am I going to be? What is me? she had nagged at her mother when the art lessons were over. Olympia had smiled, her face beaming in a rare expression of security. "Why just like me," she had answered. "You'll be a mother and look just like me; that's why you don't need no art lessons, just to look like me."

Between the mattress and springs of her bed lay the George Sand outfit, imprinted with little squares and circles from the pressure of Saradove's sleeping body. When she had it on, she broke into a sweat of fear, but it was the roar of the hall heater coming on, not the car turning into the driveway, that alarmed her. She watched herself in the long mirror on the door, imagining that the levis from Sears-Roebuck were black velvet pants, loose in the crotch, skin-tight in the legs. Duncan's white shirt that scratched her neck was really silk, the color of egg-shell and Byronic. She tied a pink sash beneath the collar and it became a black scarf knotted to flow freely. She pushed her hair behind her ears and pulled up her long white socks to make riding boots. She clenched a cigarette between her teeth and spoke to the mirror.

"Stop sniveling, Freedrik. Get up off your knees before I slap you one. You knew I was coming home, and now . . . You force me to! Slap-slap. Ah no! Poor mon enfant! Ah no, never . . . nevair!" Saradove held an imaginary head cupped in her hands. Chopin knelt before her, his tears beating on her hands like raindrops.

"Listen to you, just listen to you, mon Freedrik." Saradove snorted, began coughing from the cigarette smoke. "You sit up all night in the drafty ballroom at the piano, and it's me that's got to break my neck nursing you." Saradove dropped Chopin's head and stepped into him, consumptive lungs and all. She squeezed tears from her own eyes. I sound just like her, she thought. Mama says, All right for you, Saradove Racepath, it's not you that's got to sit up all night trying to get you on your feet again after you run around without a coat or sit up all night long straining your eyes in a cold house. It's not you, it's me! Now listen to me, standing here saying the same thing to Chopin.

Saradove dropped to her knees and put her arms around Chopin.

"O, listen, listen, mon cher! Did you really write that beautiful Raindrop Prelude just for me, because you were sitting here so agonized about me getting home last night? O, mon cher, mon cher, I love you so much and am so grateful, you wonderful, talented Freedrik! Come on in here to the ballroom and play it again for me. I can't get enough of it!"

Saradove went blindly back to the piano and started pounding through the music. She longed to shut her eyes and rear her head back the way Jose Iturbi did in the movies, but it was hard enough getting the notes right with eyes open. But just the same, wrong notes and all, a summer sun was being turned on inside her; and George Sand's arm was around her shoulder (thin, bony shoulder). And George Sand was whispering, through all the coughing:

O, you're so wonderful, you're so special, unlike other girls! I could just eat you up! O, I'm taking you this very minute to a place fit for you, away from here where nobody appreciates how different, how wonderful you are! My big car, my enormous car, is going to drive right up to the front door for you, going to drive all over your mama's bed of Sweet William, and I'm going to open the door and say, Just step in, sit back and relax here on my handmade silk embroidered car seat while my white chauffeur drives us swiftly north! Yes, north! In New York City, my big house is right between Carnegie Hall and the Metropolitan Museum of Art. The opera house is right across the street, and how they all want you, how they're all waiting for you! And listen! In the morning we'll walk down street and buy you new clothes, silk and wool and lovely; why do they put you in these ugly clothes here, you're so beautiful! And while my white chauffeur pulls out of the yard, so smoothly, I'll hand you a crystal glass of champagne, and you'll drink it all the way to New York City, north! without spilling a drop. I have shades on my car windows, we can pull them down so that no one can see when you lean over and kiss me on the mouth. As we leave, you can look out the window and see all of them sweating on the hot streets, coming out of the picture show, waiting for the bus in front of the drug store, going in Sears-Roebuck to buy ugly clothes. But inside my car, it will be cold because my car is from the north, where I am taking you. Olympia and Duncan will come out on the front porch and yell, pinch up their faces, say, O please come back, where're you going? We'll love you if you just come back. O, your mama will say, if you just come back I'll let you kiss me. But you won't go back, you'll stay snuggled in the cold with me. They had their chance, now I'll love you best, I'll show you how you won't have to be like Olympia, how you can stay free, free and running fast!

The doorbell rang. The summer sun inside Saradove melted her down from an iceberg to a small sweat of anxiety. She thought, they came back, and I didn't hear them coming. They've been standing out there all this while listening to what I've been thinking. She saw herself in the ridiculous outfit.

"I'm coming," she shouted at the door. She ran for her bedroom. The piano bench thudded to the floor, the ashtrays clinked on the marble-topped table. "I was just taking a nap," she whispered to herself in the housecoat, hiding everything but the tall socks, and ran for the door. The whole house vibrated, she was so heavy when she ran. The door stuck; it slammed against her head. For a moment, there were two Mrs. Bagleys standing in the door.

"You shouldn't run like that, Saradove," said Mrs. Bagley. "Stop that kicking, Madeline Bagley."

Madeline, who came up to her mother's shoulder with a head of frizzy permanent curls, was kicking the doorframe with her saddle shoe and sneering at Saradove. It was Madeline who played last in the church parlor, who played something long and hard by Tchaikovsky. In the summers, the whole neighborhood could sit outdoors and listen to Madeline practicing wonderfully.

"The last time you ran like that to the front door, you could hear your mama's china shepherdess fall and break clear across the street."

"They aren't here," said Saradove, squeezing the doorknob, wishing it were Madeline's neck. "They've gone visiting at the hospital, then to the store."

Madeline got past Sardove, yanking open the housecoat with her strong, sneaky fingers. Mrs. Bagley snickered.

"What've you got that crazy outfit on for, Saradove? That there looks like the sash to your recital dress." Saradove stared hard at the pine tree rising up behind Mrs. Bagley's head outside. If it would just bend a little forward, she could grab it and jam Mrs. Bagley's face into the pine cones, scratch out her eyes, stick pine straws up her nose.

"Huh?" said Mrs. Bagley. "You still playing dress-up at your age?" She followed Madeline inside. Mrs. Bagley was square and tall, the shape of a fat, blown-up automobile if it were stood up on its rear wheels.

"You want to come in, sit down? They ought to be back any minute." Mrs. Bagley had already sat down on the couch, next to Madeline. Madeline had already found the cigarette butt. She was holding it in her fingers, looking hard at it and Saradove, acting as if she'd found a dollar in the street. Madeline stood up and started wandering around the room, the cigarette butt an inch from her nose.

"I'm only going to stay a minute. You must be hot with that housecoat on top of all that." Mrs. Bagley giggled. Saradove laughed, rolled her eyes at the two naked girls, princesses, over the mantelpiece. Who would save her now? She yanked at the pink sash, nearly choked getting it off.

"If you don't sit down this minute, Madeline Bagley, I'm going to have a fit. You sit down, Saradove, then maybe she will." Madeline put the butt in her pocket and sat. Saradove fell into Duncan's chair.

Sitting, Mrs. Bagley was all mashed together in the white uniform she wore to work at the Sweet Time Bakery. Next to her, Madeline was not her mother's daughter, was thin and undersized, would not eat, had long, strong fingers that were beyond her age, that played Tchaikovsky. Madeline started kicking the coffee table leg in time to Alexander's Rag Time Band; and she sang it, loudly.

"What?" Saradove yelled above the noise.

"I said," said Mrs. Bagley, "that your mama is a good woman."

"Why?" asked Saradove. "I mean, what?"

Mrs. Bagley's face, concerned, was like pinched fluted pastry crust. It meant, A good daughter of a good woman wouldn't have asked, What? Mrs. Bagley rolled to one side of the uniform, pulled out a Lucky Strike and lighted it. Saradove tried to suck in some of the smoke from across the room.

"Well, Saradove, who else would've come in and waxed my kitchen floor after they had to take poor Desmond away? And bring a chocolate layer cake with her? That's why I'm here. Madeline Bagley, where's the cake plate?"

"Come on and hear!" Thump, thump! "Come on and hear!" Thump, thump! Madeline kept shouting and thumping. "Oh. What, mama? Don't cry, mama!" Madeline said it twice, quickly, automatically the way she said, "Now I lay me" every night.

Mrs. Bagley reached over and cuffed her on the shoulder.

"That's all over now, Madeline," she said. "When are you going to learn some sense? I'm not crying any more. I said, where's the cake plate? That's what we're here for."

Madeline shook her head, the permanent frizz remaining perfectly still. "I don't know," she said. "I left it on the front porch when I had to go back to the bathroom."

Mrs. Bagley closed her eyes, smoked; possibly prayed.

"You don't know about trials yet, Saradove," she said, "but the Lord Jesus Christ willing, some day you will."

Madeline said, "Don't cry, Mama!"

Mrs. Bagley hit her on the shoulder again.

"Then go and get it!" she said.

Madeline ran out, banging the door behind her; and the room did not give the slightest quiver. Saradove felt the sweat soak deeper through her father's shirt every minute. She started to pull the housecoat off, but remembered the front zipper in the levis just in time. She gritted her teeth.

"How's Mr. Bagley, Mrs. Bagley?" she asked. Just as the room had been filled up with the beautiful smell of Lucky Strike, Madeline had had to open the door and let it out. Mrs. Bagley snuffed out her cigarette and buried her face in her hand.

"No change, no change, and there never will be. He just sits there all the time and laughs. He don't take no notice of anything, didn't your mama tell you? And after we make that long trip to Raleigh every Sunday after Sunday School, he just sits there and laughs at us. We can't even stay for church service any more because we got that long trip ahead of us just to sit there and see Desmond laugh at us."

Mrs. Bagley sighed and looked out the window toward her own house. Saradove felt like crossing herself the way she did so freely and frequently in front of the sisters at the Catholic school.

"Well," she said. "I'm glad he's so happy, even if you do have to go to Raleigh all the time."

Mrs. Bagley came up out of her sigh.

"That's not happy by a long shot, Saradove," she said sharply. "You ought to know what's happy and what's not by this time, and I've known you since you were a baby. You ought to hear some of the things poor Desmond does when he's not laughing! What the doctor tells me about, then you wouldn't think he was so happy."

Saradove forgot to wish that Mrs. Bagley would light another cigarette.

"What?" she asked instantly. "What things does he do?"

"O, now. Well." Mrs. Bagley took out another Lucky Strike. "I can't think why I'm sitting here jawing on when I've got enough for a mule over there." She smiled and blew smoke through her nose. "A little bird's going around telling about how Oriental isn't good enough for you, how you're going to go *north* any old time, New York City, and break your mama's and daddy's heart. It's not for me to say, I know your mama's said it enough times for you, you don't appreciate what a good mama and daddy are until they're dead and laid out in their coffins. Then you know, but then it's too late. Besides you don't have to leave town. Let me tell you, just look at me, it don't take being beautiful to get married. You don't have to worry about that in the long run. There's other things."

Saradove fixed an idiot grin on her face and thought about sticking lighted Lucky Strikes up Mrs. Bagley's nose, and then setting the rest of the pack on fire and shoving it up between her legs if she could only find the hole in all that fat.

"I'm not going to get married," she said. "Besides, I have to go to college first."

Mrs. Bagley smiled, knowing better. Her answer came out in a long sigh of smoke.

"Well, I wouldn't know about all that, you know. Jones Business College was good enough for me, and I'd like to see Madeline Bagley in some nice-looking insurance office or something before she settles down like I did."

Saradove felt herself turning into a lunatic from the heat of all the clothing: God's punishment for pretending to be George Sand or Chopin; one.

Mrs. Bagley went and opened the door, letting in the cool

November air. The skirt of her uniform, because she wasn't wearing underpants, got stuck between the cleft of her buttocks. She called, "Hoo hoo, Madeline! Hoo hoo!" and pulled gently at her skirt, trying to release it without notice. Madeline didn't answer and the skirt did not free itself. Mrs. Bagley looked hard at the pine tree outside and used two fingers, before Saradove's eyes, to reach in and yank the skirt out. Saradove grew hotter, from shame, or from her clothes, and prayed for her mother to come home. That was just the kind of thing grown women were always doing in front of one another, and then laughing about it. If Olympia were here, she and Mrs. Bagley would be laughing about it right now.

Saradove wrapped the housecoat tight around her and thought about poor Desmond. Give me Desmond any day, she thought. He's the only person in this whole town I'll sent a post card to when I get to New York.

"Madeline!" shouted Mrs. Bagley across the yard. "You answer me this minute!"

Saradove had adored Desmond ever since the August Sunday last year, when it was so bad that the heat swirled in and out of your brain, and you couldn't move because your brain was sweating too hard to let you. Desmond had strolled out of his house to watch his wife and daughter come home from church. Madeline had been rummaging in the back seat of the car, Mrs. Bagley in the front, getting out their gloves and pocketbooks and Sunday School lessons. They had already set the big bag of two dozen cream puffs, that they always picked up at the bakery after church, on the steps. The altar flowers they would take to Mrs. Bagley's daddy's grave that afternoon leaned against the bag. Desmond had sat down on the steps, his left leg crushing all the Baby's Breath; and he had opened the bag. Saradove, watching him, had wondered how he could eat on a day like that. But Desmond couldn't eat. He opened the bag wide, stood up, unzipped his fly, and pissed lengthily and with perfect aim straight into the cream puffs. They caught him before he could run around the house. He was too little to be a match for his big puffed wife and his strong-fingered daughter. They got him inside through the kitchen door, but it was all day before one of them got back outside to move the bag and wash the steps. The flowers were all wilted by that time.

Saradove had told her mother about it, but her mother had said she must have dreamed it all. That night, Saradove did dream about Desmond running around and around his house, stuffing himself all the while with disgusting cream puffs and waving to Saradove every time he circled the front. It must have been a nightmare all the time.

"Here comes Madeline now," said Mrs. Bagley. "What I meant about Desmond is you'll have to get your mama to tell you after you're a grown married woman."

Saradove got up to watch Madeline shoot into the front yard with the cake plate. Zaaaaap! thought Saradove. I have paralyzed you with my ray gun, Madeline Bagley, so you can't run another inch until she tells me what it is about Desmond.

"I know the nurses are Christian women with crosses to bear just like me, but I wear my dresses longer," said Mrs. Bagley. "And there are some things I could tell you about the colored boys, the help, up there and poor Desmond that I didn't even *know* about ahead of time!"

Madeline rushed up the front steps.

"I could tell you too!" she said breathlessly. "Don't cry, mama. Here's the cake plate."

"Here's the cake plate, Saradove; I can't wait any longer. Tell your mama I said Thank you. I could just hit you, Madeline Bagley, for the things you say!"

Saradove held the big green plate in front of her face and watched them leave her yard, Madeline sailing and leaping; Mrs. Bagley rocking her flesh apart with every step.

Through a glass, darkly, said Saradove's mouth, against the plate. Through a glass, greenly, Saradove rolled through the town, beyond big and little Bagley, losing one relative after another, shaking the rest off her ankles; prizing only one friend at a time, shaking the rest off her ankles. She marched, ten years old, in the Confederacy Day Parade wearing a skimpy Girl Scout uniform, enclosed by withered, tattered, tatty old ladies uniformed in purple and hats; behind the mayor who rode like a beauty queen on the back of a convertible. She sneaked, at twelve years old, the dirtiest book she could find in the library to a friend waiting beneath the library window. "Oh honey," the book moaned, "Doris moaned, do it do it DO IT, go on do it hard, and they wallowed in the black lace of underwear, he tearing and biting, she sucking on his tongue, twirling her thighs, First you bitch he said, when he had her where he wanted her, Why did you go out with Jimmy last night? Oh, honey, Doris moaned," the book moaned. Saradove posed, seven years old, on the front porch across the street, Desmond's porch, with five other little girls (no boys born on that street since the Depression, the funniest thing) all in white or pink or blue, skirts stuck out with starch; the sun, the world, the termites beneath the house, all pausing dead still to hear the happy birthday song from five little girls' mouths, all waiting for little two-year-old Madeline, wobbly big-eyed Madeline, nearly bald little Madeline Bagley to blow out her candles. And the six mamas, round in the hips, round in the chest, round in the arms that crossed and hugged the chests, stood in the yard, frowning or smiling at it all—don't pick your nose, stop holding yourself: do you have to go to the bathroom? Don't Madeline look pretty (wobbly, bald Madeline), just like a little girl—the strong odor of woman and mothers rising up in a mushroom cloud above them, stinking or sweeter than roses, one; the smell each little girl learned and nestled to. The women and mamas, they didn't want to do a single thing but get on home after the cake and ice cream and shell them butter beans, set the food on the table and eat last of all, with the sun going down behind the back porch; and get to bed, last of all, after the socks were washed out, the shoes polished, his shirt ironed and hung on the icebox handle. They didn't want to do a single thing but get up in the morning in their torn nightgowns and love their little girls: You'll be just like me, you'll see, you're mine, aren't you? And the women and mamas, they didn't want to do a single thing but wait, wait all day, running the washing machine, sweeping the porch, digging around the rose bushes, tying up the broken branches that had been crushed down. And: Let's go down street on the bus and see about new patent leathers for you; let's dig up those bushes before they choke up the bathroom plumbing; let's hear you say yes ma'm and no ma'm get your feet off the coffee table. One day, a week before the bleeding started, Saradove got up with the sun and took over the house, moving a broom over rugs, under rugs, squeezing Duncan's undershirt, oil-soaked, against the carved legs of all the tables, getting wild-eyed at the sight of dust-curls in organdy ruffles, throwing Old Dutch with a free hand into the sinks. She'd never lifted a hand before, content to give a puff to the piano lid before she opened it; enjoying the feel of toast crumbs beneath her bare feet on the kitchen floor. Olympia watched her that day, moving silently from room to room, always one room ahead of Saradove's frantic cleaning, sucking on a fingernail, chewing the skin around her thumbs, waiting to see the end. Even then she did not tell her why. It was hard only to wait, to suffer for poor Saradove. It was so hard to be so shy about things. It turned a mother gray; the poor little thing.

Saradove lowered the glass plate. Big Bagley and little Bagley were holding hands at the edge of the street, trying to decide if anything was coming. All of a sudden, something was coming. A green Ford, the Racepath Ford! Saradove saw.

It came slowly down the hill, traveling in a curving line; and at the wheel, Olympia, deliberately twisting the steering wheel extreme right, then extreme left. Two dogs chased the crazy car, barking with delight. This time they'd get it! Mrs. Bagley ran, chased it, too. She was a big ball bouncing. She hit the pavement and went back up, straight for Heaven. When she got hold of the Ford's door handle, Olympia had braked in Desmond's front yard. Desmond's azalea bush was directly beneath the right rear wheel, as though he had planted it, planned it that way.

Saradove stood stock still and raised the green glass before her eyes again. Through the blackened screen door, through the glass, the entire scene across the street convulsed into a jumble of fat fishes and thin fishes, swimming and playing it all out beneath green swimming-pool water. And Saradove was catching them all with a net, a green glass net woven into a pattern of roses.

She put the glass plate on the floor and stepped on the porch. The car sat still on the azalea bush. Mrs. Bagley was looking through one of its windows, Madeline through another. Olympia was going home, crossing the street with her shoulders thrown back as stiff as broom handles, looking thin. In one hand she carried a box of powder; in the other, a lipstick.

"Sit down there on that step, Saradove," she said, "I know this is going to hit you like a thunderbolt, but you got to take the bitter with the sweet. Just a minute." With enormous care, she opened the powder and the lipstick and began to make her face up, copying some memory she had of the face of Gloria Swanson. Saradove could not look at her. Something was still in the front seat of the Ford, something she hadn't seen yet. The Bagleys were looking at it; and Duncan was not here at home with them. Was this the way she planned to go on shelling butter beans and worrying about the porch light attracting bugs? Like this? Looking like Gloria Swanson?

"That's better," said Olympia to her face, and snapped the powder box shut. She grasped her knees and began rocking back and forth on her spine, like a little girl sitting on a step.

"How do I look?" Saradove looked.

"Like Gloria Swanson," she answered. It was a little bit true. There were old movie magazine photographs of Gloria Swanson pasted into a dime store scrap book that Olympia kept on her bedside table along with the Bible.

"About time," said Olympia. "That's all right for you, missy. Right after we left the hospital, he pulled over and said, You take the wheel, and so I started driving, and then before you could say Jack Rabbit, he just keeled over in the seat and dropped dead. And that's just the way I got him home, dead. There's a lot to be said for me, Saradove."

Olympia rocked; the Bagleys went into their house to telephone. Finally, Saradove began to scream.

"You can't do this to me! I'm just a little girl, what are you doing to your little girl, you never, never love me, and it'll be no time before I go away north!"

Olympia rocked and rocked, her spine creaking. Death crawled through the brown November yard, through the sky pumping out little gray clouds, into the body where the organs were straining to grow up, to grow old before Death could get them, could make them shudder to a stop. Saradove watched her own hands rise with purple veins, grow chalky and dry in the skin. Her hair began to crinkle and gray against her skull; her heart faltered, needed medicine; her legs trembled, needing a wheelchair.

Olympia got up, smoothing her legs, straightening her stockings.

"Are the seams correct, Saradove? Listen to me, are the seams correct?" Her voice was the soft, romantic whisper that swept off a movie screen, a whisper that hundreds of people could sit and hear and sigh to; could take for their very own.

Saradove's voice, cracked with old age, asked, "What are you going to do with him? You can't leave him over there, Desmond might come home."

Some neighbor women started coming from their houses, their arms crossed over their breasts. Already, one of them carried a covered dish. They all went straight for the Bagleys without a look at the silent Ford. Their side-glances saw what was happening across the street. When would the ambulance come?

Saradove stood beside Olympia, her hand reaching for an invisible baby's hand, her eyes hunting for lost toys and socks, wondering with her whole mind where the money for a baby's new shoes would come from.

"Things get taken care of," said Olympia. "Your fancy notions you can just take with you to that biggity old north you want so much, but I'll see you off at the train if I have the time. You take your part of the insurance money and go on off to school if that's what you want so much; and I'll take my part and go I don't know where. Now it don't matter any more about big sister Lila and all her big house and rich husband and those girls with natural curly hair. A thing or two. We'll show her a thing or two. Sit up straight now, Saradove, and try to see without your glasses. You can if you try. This is the last time I'm telling you. The very last time. Now, are my seams correct?"

The ambulance came clanging down the street, in a big hurry over nothing. Madeline Bagley stood in the middle of the street waving her arms at it. Then she sat up on the Ford's back fender and sucked at a Coca-Cola. She rolled her eyeballs at the two very black colored boys who jumped out with a stretcher and started wrestling with something in the front seat of the car. One rolled his eyes back at Madeline; then he had Duncan by the arms.

Duncan seemed to weigh an enormous amount beneath the

white tablecloth. Two polished brown shoes, two navy-blue socks stuck out from beneath the white sheet; it was not a tablecloth. Who in the world would place a felt fedora in the center of a white *tablecloth?* Working as neatly as two mules, the black boys got him in the ambulance, and without looking at anything or at each other, sprinted into the front seats and clanged away, in a big hurry over nothing.

Olympia stood dead center on her porch and watched. Her arms stretched out in a gesture she would use to welcome to her body a child running for her. The child was not there, but Olympia looked for it, across the yard, across the street, across the past to some point where, at that very moment, the poor orphan girl was being revealed to the world as a changeling princess. Her white face glistened above her pink dress and sweater, made her look like some big rose caught by the early frost.

In easy, straggling lines, the neighbor women began to come into the yard carrying the suppers meant for their own families. They went straight for Olympia's wide-open arms, saluting death with well-cooked food.

Hunched inside herself like a jackknife, Saradove sat on the bottom step and wept to a stray worm that coiled itself around her shoe, "You brute, I am the wicked fairy, brute brute! I was the uninvited guest at the wedding. Her long sleep, her wrong life is all my fault. Where can I find her again and start all over? Where can I be good?"

Thomas W. Molyneux

BEFORE, ONCE

Around him, the stadium still was thinly filled. The row behind him still was empty, and he leaned back against it. He put the case with his fieldglasses in it on the bench plank beside him, unbuttoned his jacket, and let it slide open across his chest in the November sun.

He wished that he had arrived in time to see the teams warm up. He would have liked to see this boy Jaker. But, instead, he had stopped to buy the tie; he had taken ten minutes to buy the tie. *Something college boy,* he thought in words, and looking down at the red and cream swirled tie, glossy in the sun's defining brilliance, he exhaled a thin, derisive snort. His face, in the quick moment of the snort, seemed that of an older brother indulging a child, but unable to resist some occasional sign to the world that he, anyhow, knew better.

When the face straightened, its skin and the lines in it were thin and hard, and it was closed beyond prying. Once, the man's face had been so handsome that people forgave him things. His head was large, his black hair thick and slick in heavy waves. He wore a white shirt and a blue blazer and the swirled tie which he had stopped to buy in Cambridge, in the gesture he had mocked even as he performed it, from a feeling he had not mocked so as not to acknowledge, toward a ritual he did not even suspect.

He sat forward. For a second, he considered going down to the Princeton dressing room and identifying himself. He would have liked to talk to this Jaker boy. Then again he snorted softly. What would he have to talk to Jaker about? Princeton clubs? Girls? Nonny? Why he'd chosen Princeton? Kirby had chosen it because only Princeton of all the Ivy League schools retained stripes down the length of the sleeves on its football jerseys. And because that was where Bix Beiderbecke had been so popular. Now, how would you say that to Jaker, who probably had never heard of Bix Beiderbecke? How ask him to believe that? In Kirby's own undergraduate years, Beiderbecke had been already nearly forgotten. And what would Jaker say to him? Calling him mister or even sir. That he was sorry about all those records? Sorry that in all these places Princeton's record book had read Andrew Kirby, it was soon going to read David Jaker? And what would he say then: *Oh, I don't mind?*

But it wasn't that, he knew. He would have liked to see and talk to Jaker, and there would have been something to talk about. But identifying himself would have set terms and conditions on the day. And he was just a businessman visiting a city on business and going alone to see his old school play an old rival. He needed, he knew, to be only that today—factually, ostensibly, anonymously.

Eight undergraduates had filled the row three before him. On one, he recognized a Cottage Club tie. That would have been an all-right sort of gesture, hint. Better anyhow than the swirled thing he had just 'paid four dollars for and already smirked to know he would not wear again.

Across the field, he could see the small spots of color and

movement as the Harvard people began to arrive. The day was still and the sun warm for November, coming into him and spreading upon him, so that effort seemed something alien and far away and now purposeless. The growing crowd's curr came to him, as from some irrelevant distance, speckled now and again by the hawking voices of the white-coated concession salesmen or by other louder, nearer, realer sounds. On the Harvard side, the busy brilliances of the sun dartled among the colors, seemed to sink into the distant gashes of the concession salesmen moving there, to become a part of the white and shine out through the jackets like snaps. That was where Nonny would be, somewhere there, some one of those spots.

Behind him, he heard a woman's voice going hoarsely on. He turned then and saw her, newly seated, still moving about on the plank, two rows behind him. She wore a suit of thin tweed, a houndstooth pattern, blue and tan and maroon. At her neck, a silk maroon ascot arched. Looking at her, he knew that from his own clothes, from the shoes he wore, she would know that she might know him, as she would not know some of the others round them. But too, he knew that, looking at him again, she would know that she did not know him, and would dismiss him as wholly and finally as he would dismiss those others neither of them would know.

Nonny had said to him once, "I have only gone out two times in my whole life with a boy whose shoes I didn't like, and each time he was awful." Kirby looked now at his own wing-tipped shoes on his short feet, golden as though worked with neat's-foot oil. He knew that then they would have been shoes Nonny didn't like; but he knew, too, that Alfred probably had a pair like them today.

Already, the man who was with the girl was reascending the broad steps of the stadium. For a second, Kirby watched the other man's long back; and then he looked to the girl. She was a girl, and not a woman, and the other man had been, really, a boy. She could have been anywhere from eighteen to twenty-eight. Someone else would know, he thought; Nonny would know; and the girl's date. But for him, as he watched her place the leather flask on the coarse cement at her feet, sense his attention, look to him, page through her program, pull down her skirt, uncross and recross her legs, there persisted an old consciousness of not knowing. Undeniably, she was young, was a girl. Yet, too, there had been something once done and tired in the matter-of-fact line of her hoarse voice, there was something premature in the largeness and finality of her features, and something past touch in the brittle sere brown streaks of her hair.

He thought that once he would have known her, or anyhow could have known her, would have known someone who could introduce them. Once he would have known her date. And once, this surely, her date would have known him. He looked away from her and back across the field. Once he had known Nonny.

More now, people were arriving. The spots of color across the field stood now one against the other, and, especially in the center, the white concrete had largely disappeared. That was where Nonny would be, somewhere in the center, some one of the bright moments. Alfred would have good seats.

Twice before Nonny had sat there—with Alfred even then, he thought, and snorted to himself—in less choice undergraduate seats, and watched him play in this game.

But that had been before, once. And then, in words, he thought, *Ten years is not such a long time.* But immediately he knew that for him it was. For him the first year had been such a long, too long time. And all the later nine had only shored the distance of that first. He had been seventeen when he entered Princeton, eighteen when he met Nonny, twenty-two when he saw her last. And for him that all was once, one time, one moment out of his time.

Across the field, still, the Harvard people were arriving, from club luncheons, he knew, and others from less decorous festivities, for with Yale away, Princeton was always the important pomp game for Harvard. Even with his naked eye, he could discern in the small and single speckles of color, the gregarious gestures, the elaborate and demonstrative and inconsequential business of their movements. Nonny would be there, one of them, with Alfred in one of the club sections—he could not recall which had been Alfred's club—for Alfred would not miss a home Princeton game or a club luncheon.

The stands around him now were filling. He stood again to let a couple pass. Passing, the girl looked at him as though she might know him, and again he thought that once he would have, could have known her. He smiled and she looked away. Once more he snorted and smiled shortly at himself. Something about the girl's date struck him, so that he thought perhaps he had known the boy's older brother, uncle, cousin. Perhaps he had.

Across the field, on the front row, he saw a thin stroke of sun rebound yellow from a blonde head. Around him, the voices played, scattered, gay, and always somehow mock. He took up the fieldglasses, ducked his head through the strap of the case, unsnapped the case, lifted and focussed the glasses. The girl with the blonde hair wore it long. Her suit was pink, and her head, he saw, was small. Like Nonny, Nonny's colors. Before her, the man cavorted, lifted his glass to someone in the stands, and then the bottle in his other hand also above his head. He could be Alfred. Again, Kirby turned the glasses to the woman, and his long heavy fingers adjusted the focus. But he could not see the features, could not tell whether it was Nonny, though there was something undecided, something partial in the way she moved that made him think *perhaps*.

Then, as he watched, the other man came up behind her and put his hand, holding the glass, across her shoulder. She

turned her head, and Kirby thought he recognized the movement of the smile—like his own, removed and indulging, but
never excusing. But he was not sure even then that it was
Nonny. He could discern only the moment of the movement,
only the colors.

The Harvard team came onto the field. He saw the man
with the woman across the field turn and point, turn back
toward the stands and make a long slowed sweep of his arm,
like that of a Hollywood cavalry officer. Hearing the cheering
and, behind him, the scattered calls, he looked to the Harvard
team on the field. They ran a straight dive perfunctorily and
trotted to the sidelines. When he looked again at the stands
across the field, the girl in pink had moved. He found her
again moving up the concrete steps, and he watched till she
reached her seat and settled. Then he looked back, through
the glasses, across the conglomerate colors of the crowd, just
looking. Each of the single brightnesses seemed cheering, calling, drinking individually. Then he saw a second blonde head,
pale and single and somehow frail in the sparkle of definition
the sun's glare provided, and he hesitated, watching. This girl
looked straight before her. Her hands sat together on her lap,
like those of a schoolgirl. She, too, might be Nonny. He
watched her sitting as though isolated from the activity round
her. He looked back to the girl in pink, then back again to
the new girl; but he could not see enough.

The stands around him cheered then. As the call moved
away from him, it seemed to merge, to unify, and its core,
somewhere far behind him, struck him as vaguely threatening
and vaguely exhilarating, so that he shivered for just a moment.
Before, he hadn't given a damn for the cheering; sometimes,
had not heard it at all. And he laughed that now, when the
cheering was for someone else, it could move him. He wanted
himself to cheer, but, aware of the younger people around him,
knew he could not. Why, even they felt foolish at it. How

would they feel to hear him calling "Go Tiger"? Today, he was just to watch; that was part of the thing. Once more he laughed, more coldly even now, thinking of the swirled necktie it had taken ten minutes to choose.

He looked to the field, where the Princeton team was gathered on the sidelines. They wore white jerseys, with black numerals and black sleeves, and still, ringed down the sleeves, orange stripes.

"Which one's Jaker?" he asked the boy beside him.

"Twenty-four."

The boy had a soft unmarked face. He wore a tan plaid suit and a pink shirt, the collar of which rolled just so. Kirby had heard him, as he came to his seat, stop and talk with the hoarse-voiced girl in the houndstooth suit.

The boy said, "You won't need Davy's number, though."

"Oh," said Kirby.

"No, not once the game starts. You'll know who he is without any number."

After a minute, the boy said, "Wouldn't know him off the field though. Wouldn't spot him as any jock. Davy's a smooth boy."

"Do you know him?" said Kirby.

"Sure I know him. Know him well. We think alike. Know it's all a lark. It's all just how much you can fool the next guy; that's what everybody is up to." His tone had changed. He was not talking any longer about Jaker. "It's all just a game, and we know that. Sure I know Davy."

The boy looked at Kirby till Kirby looked away from him to the field.

Then, again after a minute, the boy said, "People say Davy's arrogant. They're just the ones think everybody doesn't have time for them is arrogant. Davy's smooth. Smart. You wouldn't really expect it with his background and all. But he is. A good man."

Kirby heard the explaining voice, sure of its rightness and anxious to be heard, glad to assist, saw the young face, unmarked, and the eyes dartling like butterflies. As he once would have, could have known the girl in the houndstooth suit, he knew that he once would have known this boy. He once would have been able to talk to this boy, to say the simple yes the boy demanded.

He looked again to the field and found Jaker. Seeing him, his helmet off, the black streaks of charcoal beneath his eyes like some fine warpaint, he wished again that he had gone to the dressing room and talked. Perhaps they would have asked him to sit on the bench with them. But then Nonny would have seen him. Well, that might not have been so wrong. She would only have seen him. And he longed for that, from the safe seat in the stands, the safe time past the moment of possibility. He wondered whether Nonny too was looking now at Jaker. Did she sense the boy's tight young physical knowledge of his own violent possibility? And if so, was she thinking now of him? And what of Alfred?

Behind him, someone said, "If Davy scores twice today, he breaks old Kirby's record. Once, he ties." And someone else, "Hell, they've lasted long enough."

The boy beside him said, "There's no if about it. No if at all. What Davy wants, Davy gets."

Princeton received the kickoff. Standing with all the others, Kirby watched Jaker. The boy touched his toes once and snapped his arms like flexing wings behind him, spit in his hands. With him, for him, Kirby felt the fear. In his own stomach and then behind his eyes, he felt the juices rush. He thought for the boy, *Hit into the goalpost, start the numbness now.* Still watching Jaker, he heard the long trill of the refree's whistle, knew the ball turning bright and dark in the sun's day, traced by the long hollow ceremonial stridor from the Harvard stands. Jaker moved to his right, in front of the other safety, to receive the kick. *The sideline, the sideline,* Kirby thought. But the boy moved up the center of the field, running at about three-quarters speed. *It's on the left,* thought Kirby. And then the boy saw and cut. *Hard now.* The easy roll of his shoulders, the threatening supple flexing of the stripes of his sleeves, which had made Kirby a second before for a brief second think again of Nonny, ceased. It was all tight and fast now. Watching the blockers, Kirby felt inside him the draining rush at the possibility. "Left," he called out. Then he heard himself; then the urging of the crowd around him. And he knew he was just one of them now, and Jaker didn't hear him. He didn't know any more. He didn't do it any more. At the thirty, three Harvard boys closed on Jaker, and Kirby saw him slow, looking for a hole. *Inside, inside,* he thought, though knowing better. But Jaker saw no hole, and started again at full speed, his colors bunched and thick now, trying to angle into them, his head still up and watching. The first of them hit him high about his thighs. *Go down,* Kirby called to himself. The boy tried to lunge forward, but the other held him, and then a second maroon body slammed into his trapped upper body, able only to dance like the cocked head of a snake, and slammed him backwards, down. Now, the numbness would be there, the confidence. But still in Kirby the scattered juices rushed, unfulfilled.

Someone behind him said, "Not bad. But he's better than that."

Kirby thought, *Yes, yes, he is good,* and wished again, in words now, that he had talked to Jaker.

Once, in his sophomore year, he had returned a kickoff eighty yards against Harvard. And been caught from behind at the ten. That was the first day he met Nonny, after that game. She was with Alfred even then, and with some people from Princeton who had gone to St. Mark's with Alfred.

She had been with Alfred always for all the times you

dressed up for and saw people at. Even at David Harrow's wedding, where Kirby had been an usher and she a bridesmaid,
Alfred had been her escort. Even though she had gone with
Kirby out the front door of the hotel and across the night
street and through the park, and stopped in the park with him
and kissed him twice, and held to him, her small hands inside
his tuxedo jacket on his back, letting his hands slide on her
buttocks, standing, straining on her toes, saying, "We're crazy,
we're crazy," and then, "Alfred will know," she had gone home
with Alfred. When he was with her then, he felt and credited
the guilt she would have, and was grateful to her. But as he
drove home alone, the guilt seemed unreal and inconsequential.

Two nights later, when he took her to a restaurant—as all
that year and all the next she met him in such ways—he went
with a speech in mind. He was going to tell her about the
fatuousness of the guilt she sought to make him share. He was
going to tell her about the needs he had. But he did not; he
never had. He began. And even as the first recited words came,
as he sat across the table fixing her with his even then narrowed eyes, holding his jaw clamped, consciously looking his
best in the squared commanding strength of his youth, she
stopped him, made him feel once more that he demanded too
much and was ungrateful. She made him believe the cloying
thrill of her guilt. And he thought, *The time will come; I
must wait, be patient.* And again that night she kissed him
twice, and made him credit and share her fatuous guilt.

The young boy beside Kirby said, "Would you like one?"

Kirby looked to him and saw between his long open knees
a quart container of Bloody Marys. Kirby hesitated, watching
the long-wristed movement of the boy pouring, then said, "Yes,
thank you," smiling to the boy and, already, some at himself.

On the field, Princeton made a first down. Again, Kirby
remarked the heterogeneous bruiting of the crowd. Again, from

higher in the stands, he heard the unified core of a cheer. But that seemed a dull distant sound, only little more concentrated than the cheering from the Harvard stands across the field or the sometime droning of advertising airplanes above. More real seemed the noises near him, and these seemed all addressed to no one, except that some form demanded some noise and, for that, all the surface lines of all the talk and cheers round him were for every one of the other makers of such noise. More real than any of it seemed the snatching loudspeaker voice from the press box: "Jaker was tackled by White and Amstag." But when you played, you didn't care even for that. Though he had cared in his senior year, knowing that Nonny too heard it, and thought of him, compared him perhaps with Alfred beside her. Now, it was Jaker's name. He wondered did she ever still think, ever still compare. Had she ever compared?

"Well, here," said the boy.

"Thank you," said Kirby.

He took the drink and sipped at it.

"Okay?" said the boy.

"Fine."

"Don't I know you?" said the boy.

"No, you wouldn't know me, I don't think."

The loudspeaker voice said, "Princeton: Third down and four."

"They'll pass," said the boy. "Moving on the ground and now they'll pass. You know why we have such room? Know why we're so comfortable here?"

Kirby looked shortly to the boy. He wanted to see Jaker pass. Or anyhow, see what he did now. He wondered why the man had given him tickets in the student section and thought, in words, smiling outright, *It must be because of the tie.*

"It's because I've got two seats," said the boy. "You're sitting partly on one of my seats."

Again, Kirby looked to him. As he looked, his face retained the thin remains of his thin smile at his thought about the tie. The boy's face, too, held an unso smile, a smile thinned by knowing too much.

"I got stood up," said the boy.

Then, the crowd's noise changed, and, signalled, the boy's face turned to the field and Kirby's turned too. The linemen were scattered and sprawled. Jaker moved, loping with that sense of imminent brutality, toward the far sideline. His arm cocked, and two Harvard defenders fell back, and Jaker cut inside them, then veered again, his legs seeming short as they canted beneath him, running full now.

Beside Kirby, the boy was standing. "Go Davy, go," he called.

Kirby became aware of the boy cheering, then aware of his own fist tight and hopping forward at his side. He watched Jaker get trapped and knocked out of bounds in front of the Harvard bench. He felt the energy come live inside him; and more again he wished he'd talked to Jaker. He would have liked to sit on the bench today, with the people who were play-ing, where the paraphernalia and the game plans were. He would have liked to have been asked. He would have liked to be there where all the crowd was watching, to have been seen by Nonny.

"All the way from Princeton," said the boy, "and no show. You know what I like to drink? Bourbon. Plain bourbon. And here I am with two quarts of these things all mixed just for her. Just to get drunk with her. And no show. Know where she is? She's at the Groton-St. Mark's game. A prep school game. Stood up for a little Grotty."

He paused and looked to the field.

"Jaker'll run the same thing again. He always comes back that way. I know him. He told me he always will come back with what works. The Grotty's my cousin. My cousin and that's where she is. No show."

Kirby continued to watch the field, not knowing what sort of response the boy sought. Princeton huddled shortly, snapped out as a unit, and—the boy was right—Jaker did run the same thing again, though this time it did not gain so well. Across the field, the Harvard stands were full. Bright colors speckled through the crowd, particularized by the sun's still brilliance. Their cheering straggled across to Kirby's ears. Looking again to the section where before he had seen the girls who might be Nonny, he found the blonde head, yellow and bright-faceted from the sun, of the girl in the pink suit. Then below and to the left of her, he found the other. Her hair was thin, worn in a twist. But he could not describe the features and he could not tell, though with the fieldglasses he could differentiate between the two.

If he had asked to watch from the Princeton bench, Nonny might still not have recognized him. But she would have. And, down there, he'd have sensed that recognition and been something other for it. That would have asked too much. He was past performing. Even for Nonny, he was past performing. He had been for ten years now, ten years, away from New York and Boston and Philadelphia. What he did now was service advertising accounts. And if he came to a town—even Boston—on a weekend and if his old school was playing an old rival, it was fine for him to see the game. It was fine even for him to buy a tie he wouldn't wear ever again and accept a drink from a stood-up undergraduate boy he had no answer for. But he was past performing. He was a businessman with a day free and only that could be so. Once before he had performed, and after that, after a bit, he became a businessman.

Yes, once he had performed. Once, here, he had performed for Nonny. For though the cheering was a distant irrelevant thing, something you heard once while you warmed up and then forgot, you could know who was up there, know who was aware of you especially. Nonny never cheered for him; without her ever saying so, he knew that. But she had been aware of him and aware, he had felt even then, that what he did was some for her. And he had known, too, that this was something Alfred could not do for her. He had known that all the time he was on the field. He, Kirby, could perform for Nonny, and Alfred could not.

Then he remembered once seeing Alfred perform for Nonny.

"Alfred can do back flips," she said. "Do one, Alfred."

Six of them stood ringed, several steps before the bar at the bridal dinner for David Harrow's wedding. They seemed small and outlined starkly in their black under the high-away lights of the hotel, and Nonny in blue, the only girl among them, seemed still smaller and still more precisely outlined. Almost directly above them, but seeming far high, Kirby recalled the pure bulk of the large-faceted chandelier. He had looked at Nonny and then to Alfred, and when Alfred looked and saw his stare, had snapped his head upward and stared at the springing thin strokes of yellow light piercing from the facets of that chandelier. Immediately, he had felt foolish first before Alfred and then before Nonny, and reached behind him for a fresh drink. He had tried to look coldly to Nonny, clamping his jaw. As she stood across the circle from him, perfectly, softly erect as always, her lids came down some over her eyes and the eyes held on something past him, did not dart about as they did normally. Kirby recalled the slowed unwatched sliding of her finger inside the rim of her glass. Nonny's eyes were large, but Kirby could not recall their color. Looking past him still, Nonny had said flatly, "Alfred can do back flips. Do one, Alfred."

Alfred said, "Let's go outside."

"No," she said. "You can do it here. No one will mind if you do it here."

For a second, they all were quiet. Then Alfred handed his drink to Nonny, took off his jacket and pumps. He bent in one false start, a thin boy inside the too full shirt, his weskit cinching the material on his torso. Then he jumped into the air, snapped round himself, and landed again on his feet.

"You can do better than that," said Nonny. "Alfred's wonderful at this. Do another." Still, her voice stayed flat and she looked somewhere past Kirby.

Standing coatless in his sock feet, Alfred hesitated, alone with the other five of them, and, behind them, the others who approached now. Then again he jumped, and his legs kicked up before him, over his head, and he snapped round himself, and landed on his feet, his arms folded behind his back, straining on his toes to balance.

For a minute, they all stood there while Alfred put on his coat again and slipped on his pumps and pressed his hair with his hands. Then they moved away, Kirby last, leaving Alfred and Nonny together in the cleared space before the bar.

"Hey, have another," said the boy beside him.

Kirby looked again at the young face, approximating eagerness, beside him. He handed the boy his cup and watched the boy fill it.

On the field, Harvard had the ball now. Jaker stood on the sideline before the Princeton bench, his helmet off, talking to the coach.

"You know," said the boy, "I don't care about getting stood up. Women, they come, they go. I really came to see this game. I want to see Davy set the records. When you know a guy and he's gonna do something, you want to see it. But women, they come, they go. This one, she's pulled this before. But I do the same stuff to her. All the time. Tonight, I'll just snake somebody else's woman. And next week, or the next, she'll call me. She'll call me, and I'll just tell her, it doesn't matter. They come, they go."

At halftime, Kirby sat for a time quietly beside the boy. Once, the boy told him he had another little thing at Vassar the girl who had stood him up didn't even know about. And then, the boy told him that when he travelled, he travelled hard and light, and didn't let things bother him because things always changed, like women, they came, they went. Above, the loudspeaker announced scores of other games and invited the Harvard class of 1940 to a reception after the game.

Then Kirby got up and walked up the long stadium steps to the portal, and down through that into the dank and muffling tunnel. As he passed the girl in the houndstooth suit, he saw that her date had once more left her, and he stared at her until she looked away from his gaze. He stood at the bottom of the steps from the portal on the damp packed ground of the tunnel, hearing the sounds all distant around him. He put his hands into his pants pockets, and, after a second, he drew them out again. Then, he started walking around the tunnel toward the Harvard side. In the highness and dankness of the tunnel, the people seemed small and slow. Kirby hurried past them, his head tucked on his neck, his body hurrying with bare motion.

When he reached the Harvard sections, he stopped. If Nonny saw him now, what would he say to her? But he wanted her to see him. He knew in words that that was why he had come. He walked up the steps, and stood in the opening of a portal. As he stepped into the opening, the sun hit him, as though it shone only on him. He turned sideways to let a man carrying sodas and hot dogs in a cardboard box pass by him. Close up now, the people in the Harvard stands seemed more merged and single than they had from across the field. Kirby looked along them from behind, watching for the small insistence of yellow that would be Nonny. It would be best if he could just see her and she him. And maybe he would smile to her as he passed by.

He walked down the stadium steps, feeling the awkwardness of the long strides they necessitated, feeling and fighting the accelerating, control-grasping effect of the unnaturally stepped descent. When he reached the bottom, he stood for a second, squeezing with both hands on the bar of the iron railing, before turning and staring back into the conglomerate faces of the crowd. If Nonny saw him, he wondered, would she call to him? Several rows above him, squeezed in the middle of a row, he found the girl with her hair in a twist. Though he knew immediately she was not Nonny, he stared nonetheless. She was too young, the man with her too young. And, this near, he could see her features were larger, more striking, but less fine than Nonny's. But still he stared, holding his face impassive. Then he sensed the girl's date or husband staring back at him. He looked then to the man, met his stare, still holding his face so that it did not care. When the stranger caught Kirby's eye, he opened his eyes wide, arched his eyebrows, opened his mouth in a mocking little "o", cocked his head. Kirby looked away.

Then Kirby smiled outright at himself. He looked along the slope of the crowd. He saw a girl in pink and his gaze hesitated, but only briefly, for she had dark honey hair.

Then he saw, standing at the railing on the other side of the section of crowd, the girl in the pink suit. She stood talking to someone seated, her head tilted barely to acknowledge his location. She was frailly erect and softly precise, and above the smile of her mouth, her eyes darted about. As she stood, she moved her head two or three times, and the sun moved along the blonde of her hair, painted the gracile glitter of her head.

First, Kirby thought *yes.* He took a step along the long concrete of the stadium steps, as though to leave. Then he was not sure. He could not remember Nonny ever wearing her hair curled out as this girl did. Staring still, he stood at the railing, his left leg long before him.

When the girl stopped talking, she looked about her explicitly and she saw him watching. For a second, she returned his stare. He looked at her as though he believed she would not cease looking. His lip moved, but he did not speak. Looking at her, he did not know whether it was Nonny. He wanted to be handsome for her, for whoever it was, as though if it were not Nonny, Nonny would anyhow know; and he stood straight and clamped his jaw. And then, she looked away and started up the stadium steps, taking full strides, fuller he thought than Nonny's, her hair throwing blonde behind her. For a time, Kirby still stood by the railing at the bottom of the Harvard section. And still he did not know whether the girl in the pink suit had been Nonny. He thought to himself that he would have known, but he did not know.

He stood for a time watching the dark oblong of the portal above him, thinking perhaps she would come through it and smile at him, thinking that something definite would come. But it did not, and when he saw that it would not, he reascended the long awkward steps and went through the portal himself.

As he returned along the tunnel to his seat, he heard the noise, made huge and distant in the hollowness, of the cheering which signalled the second-half kickoff. But he did not hurry now.

He tried to think. He tried to make himself believe that ten years ago he had learned something and gone away from somewhere because of it. He had been an usher in David Harrow's wedding, and for ten years now he had not seen David Harrow.

A few lone people hurried past him in the littered, high tunnel. But Kirby walked slowly, because he did not care who won. Jaker would care, and then, later, Jaker would not care. Jaker would break Kirby's record.

He tried to regain the picture of the girl in the pink suit, as though perhaps now, away from her, he could tell if she was Nonny. But only the brightness, only the gracile sheen would return.

He was an advertising executive who lived in St. Louis and was single and moderately successful. Once, he had played football for Princeton. And then he had taken a job in St. Louis. He had not much ceremony in him.

There had been a girl once. But she did not matter. She was married to someone else now. Perhaps sometimes she thought about Kirby, perhaps she regretted something that had not been done, but that did not matter. He would not know her any more. And it did not matter that she might think him handsome if he did. It would not matter even for her.

Kirby came to the steps of his section. He mounted them, and came down the steps to his seat, not fighting the acceleration and gracelessness of the long steps now. He stopped in the aisle and asked the young boy who had sat beside him for his fieldglasses.

"You moving?" asked the boy. On the plank beside the boy, Kirby saw the two containers of Bloody Marys, covered in brown bags, and the cup he had used, its lip beaded with dried red remains from the drink.

"I'm leaving," said Kirby.

"You're not going to see Davy set the record?" said the boy, incredulous.

"No," said Kirby, "I can't."

"Too bad," said the boy, nodding his head extravagantly. "Too bad."

He looked up at Kirby, and his tongue came out and cleaned some tomato juice from his upper lip. In his lap, in one hand, he held his drink; in the other, he held Kirby's fieldglasses.

Kirby saw a long spot, dark-rimmed, where the boy had spilled some drink on his tie.

"He'll set it without me," said Kirby.

Someone above them in the stands called, "Sit down," and Kirby swung his head to look angrily up across the crowd.

"Just hold your horses," said the boy. Without looking around, he waved the hand holding Kirby's fieldglasses to the side.

"I've got to go," said Kirby.

"Oh, sure," said the boy, handing the glasses out to Kirby. "Well, too bad you'll miss Davy, too bad."

The boy's head snapped around then and Kirby turned, too, to watch the play being run on the field. Harvard had the ball, and the play ran off-tackle, but gained nothing. When Kirby looked again to the boy, he was refilling his cup. Kirby looked back then to the field. Jaker stood talking to a coach at the sideline. Kirby could see the streaked charcoal beneath his right eye.

"C'mon, sit down," someone called again.

After a second, Kirby turned and, smiling, started again up the stadium steps. He wished he had bumped into Alfred, though surely they would not have recognized each other. When he passed the girl in the houndstooth suit, he said "Hi," and she smiled shortly in return.

Sloping about him, the crowd roared then, and he stopped and looked back in time to see Jaker cut to the far sideline in the field, open among the players scattered for punt coverage. He watched while Jaker let a blocker get the last Harvard defender, cut inside the crumpled pair, and outran a futile lunging pursuer. Looking then to the spot where he had sat, he saw the boy jumping in the air, brandishing a bag-covered bottle in one hand, and patting the girl beside him with the other.

Kirby stood until the crowd had resettled, and its tone had

again turned conversational. But something startled persisted now in that tone. He watched the extra point. Then he removed his tie and opened his collar, went back and gave the tie to the young undergraduate boy.

"He did it," called the boy. "What'd I tell you?"

"I saw," said Kirby. He paused, watching the boy's face, open and triumphant, young and looking to him. The boy's eyes were dark and cleanly outlined like a girl's. Kirby saw how curtly they hurried. "Tell Jaker I said he was very good," he said.

"Sure. Why don't you stay? We can go talk to Davy after. I can arrange it. I thought we might do something later anyhow."

"No, I can't, thank you," said Kirby.

"What's this for?" said the boy. He held up the tie.

"You spilled something on yours," said Kirby.

He walked back up the steps, smiling again at the girl in the houndstooth suit, and hearing behind him the boy's sure young voice calling, "Thanks," and "I'll tell him," went out of the stadium, and took a taxi to his hotel.

Caroline Gordon

THE CAPTIVE

We were up long before day and were loading the horses at first dawn streak. Even then Tom didn't want to go.

"This ginseng don't have to go to the station," he said, "and as for the money it'll bring, we can get along without that."

"We've been without salt for three weeks now," I told him.

"There's worse things than doing without salt," Tom said.

I knew if he got to studying about it he wouldn't go and I was bound he should make the trip, Indians or no Indians. I slapped the lead horse on the rump. "Go along," I said. "I'd as soon be scalped now and have done with it as keep on thinking about it all the time."

Tom rode off without saying anything more, and I went on in the house and set about my morning work. The children were all stirring by that time. Joe felt mighty big to be the only man on the place. He was telling them what he'd do if Indians came.

"You'd better hush that up," I said. "Can't you get your mind off Indians a minute?"

All that morning, though, I was thinking about what Tom

had said and wishing he hadn't had to go. It seemed like I
was riding with him most of the day.

"Now he's at West Fork," I'd say to myself, and then after
I'd done some more chores, "He'll be about at the crossroads
now or maybe Sayler's Tavern." I knew, though, it wasn't
much use to be following him that way in my mind. It'd be
good dark before he could get home, and my thinking about
it wouldn't hurry him.

It was around ten o'clock that I heard the first owl hoot-
ing. Over on the mountain, it seemed. Joe was in the yard
feeding the chickens and he stopped stock still and threw his
head back.

"You hear that, Mammy?" he asked.

I knew then that there must be something wrong with the
call, or a boy like Joe wouldn't have noticed it.

I spoke up sharp, though. "I heard it," I said, "and I could
hear a heap of other things if I had time to stand around with
my ears open. How long you reckon it's going to take you to
get those chickens fed?"

We both went on about our business without more talk,
but all the time I was saying to myself that if I could get
through this and see Tom Wiley riding in at the gate one more
time I'd be content to bide without salt the rest of my natural
life. I knew it wouldn't do to let down before the children,
though, and I kept them busy doing one thing and another till
dinner time. It began to rain while we were eating and it
rained a long time. After it stopped raining the fog settled
down, so thick you could hardly see your hand before you. And
all the time the owls were calling. Calling back and forth from
one mountain to another. My little girl, Martha, got scared,
so I made all the children stay in the house and play by the
fire whilst I started in on a piece of cloth I'd had in the loom
a long time and never could seem to finish. I'd put a stripe

through it and I was going to dye it red and make both the girls a dress out of that piece before the winter set in.

By that time the fog had risen as high as the top of the ridges and the whole house was swallowed up in it. The children kept teasing, saying it was good dark now and couldn't they have a candle.

"Yes," I said, "we're here all by ourselves and you want to go lighting candles, so they can't help finding the house."

One of the girls got to crying. "Who's coming?" she said. "Mammy, who you think's coming?"

I saw I'd got them stirred up and I'd have to settle them, for I couldn't stand to be worrying like I was and have the children crying. I gave them all a lump of sugar around and got them started on a play-party. I made out that I had the headache and if they were going to sing they'd have to sing low. It was "Hog Drovers" they were playing.

"Hog-drovers, hog-drovers, hog-drovers we air,
A-courtin' your daughter so sweet and so fair.
Kin we git lodgin' here, O here,
Kin we git lodgin' here?"

I got them started to frolicking and went back to my work. But I couldn't get my mind off something a man said to me once when we were out hunting on the Hurricane, and I made him to go right in on a bear without waiting for the other menfolks to come up.

"You're brash, Jinny," he said, "and you always been lucky, but one of these times you going to be too brash."

Sitting there listening to them owls calling, and wondering how much longer it would be before Tom got home, I got to thinking that maybe this was the time I was too brash. For I knew well there wasn't another woman in the settlements would have undertaken to stay on that place all day with nothing but a parcel of children. Still, I said to myself, it's done now and there's no undoing it. And the first thing I know, Tom will be back, and tomorrow morning it'll fair up, and I'll be thinking what a goose I was to get scared over nothing.

The children were still singing:

"Oh, this is my daughter that sets by my lap.
No pig-stealing drover kin git her from Pap.
You can't git lodgin' here, O here,
You can't git lodgin' here."

I got up and looked out of the window. It seemed to me that the fog was lifting a little. A man was coming up the path. I knew it was a white man by the walk, but I didn't know it was John Borders till he stepped up to the door.

The first thing he asked was where was Tom.

"Gone to the station with a load of ginseng," I told him. "I'm looking for him back now any minute."

He stood there looking off towards the mountain. "How long them owls been calling?" he asked.

"Off and on all evening," I said, "but owls'll hoot, dark days like this."

"Yes," he said, "and some owls'll holler like wolves and gobble like turkeys and every other kind of varmint. Jinny, you better git them children and come over to our house. Ain't no telling when Tom'll be back."

Just then an owl hooted and another one answered him from somewhere on top of the ridge. We both listened hard. It sounded like a real owl calling to his mate, but I was good and scared by that time and I thought I'd best go over to the Borderses'. It was my judgment, though, that there wasn't any hurry. Indians hardly ever come round before nightfall.

I told John that if he'd wait till I'd fastened up the stock I'd go back with him. He said that while I was doing that he'd walk out in the woods a little way. He'd been looking all day for some strayed sheep and hadn't found trace of them, but he thought they might be herded up in that gully by the spring. He went off down the path and I fastened the front door and went out the back way. I didn't fasten the back door, but I kept my eye on it all the time I was worrying with the cattle. Joe was along helping me. The cow was standing there at the pen; so I stopped and milked her while Joe went up in the triangle to look for the heifer. He found her and brought her up to the cowpen just as I finished milking. We fastened both cows up in the stable and Joe went over and saw that all the chickens were up and fastened the door on them. Then we started back to the house with the milk.

We were halfway up the path when we heard the Indians holler. We started for the house on a dead run. I could see Indians in the yard, and one Indian was coming around the house to the back door. I ran faster and slipped in the door ahead of him. Joe was right behind me. The room was so full of Indians that at first I couldn't see any of my children. The Indians was dancing around and hollering and hacking with their tomahawks. I heard one of the children screaming but I didn't know which one it was. An Indian caught me around the waist but I got away from him. I thought, I had got to do something. I fell down on my knees and crawled around between the Indians' legs, they striking at me all the time, till I found Martha, my littlest one, in the corner by the loom. She was dead and I crawled on a little way and found Sadie. She was dead, too, with her skull split open. The baby was just sitting there holding on to the bar of the loom. I caught him in my bosom and held him up to me tight; then I got to my feet. Joe was right behind me all the time and he stood up when I did. But an Indian come up and brained him with a tomahawk. I saw him go down and I knew I couldn't get any more help from him. I couldn't think of anything to do; so I worked my way over towards the door, but there was two or three Indians standing on the porch and

I knew there was no use running for it. I just stood there holding the baby while the Indians pulled burning logs out of the fire onto the floor. When the blaze had sprung up they all come out onto the porch.

I made a break and got some way down the path, but an Indian run after me and caught me. He stood there, holding me tight till the other Indians come up; then he laid his hand on my head and he touched the baby too. It seemed he was claiming me for his prisoner. He had rings on his arms and ankles, and trinkets in his ear. I knew he was a chief and I thought he must be a Shawnee. I could understand some of what he said.

He was telling them they better hurry and get away before Tice Harman came home. Another Indian stepped up. I knew him—a Cherokee that come sometimes to the station. Mad Dog they called him. Tice Harman had killed his son. It come to me that they had been thinking all along that they was at Tice Harman's. I jerked my arm away from the Shawnee chief.

"You think you're burning Tice Harman's house," I said. "This ain't Tice Harman's house. It's Tom Wiley's. Tom Wiley. Tom Wiley never killed any Indians."

They looked at each other and I think they was feared. Feared because they had burned the wrong house, but feared too of Tice Harman. Mad Dog said something and laid his hand on his tomahawk, but the old chief shook his head and took hold of my arm again. He spoke, too, but so fast I couldn't tell what he was saying. The Cherokee looked mad but he turned around after a minute and called to the other Indians, and they all left the house and started off through the woods. Mad Dog went first and half a dozen young Indians after him. The old chief and I came last. He had hold of my arm and was hurrying me along, and all the time he kept talking, telling me that he had saved my life, that I was to go with him to his town to be a daughter to him to take the place of a daughter that had died.

I didn't take in much that he was saying. I kept looking back towards the burning house, thinking maybe they wasn't all dead before the Indians set fire to it. Finally I couldn't stand it no longer and I asked the old Shawnee. He pointed to one of the young Indians who was going up the ridge ahead of us. I saw something dangling from his belt and I looked away quick. I knew it was the scalps of my children.

II

We went up over the ridge and then struck north through the woods. I didn't take much notice of where we was going. I had all I could do to keep Dinny quiet—he warn't but ten months old. I let him suck all the way but it didn't do much good. We went so fast it'd jolt out of his mouth and he'd cry louder than ever. The Shawnee would grab my arm and say the other Indians would kill him sure if he kept that up. Finally I got his head down inside the waist of my dress and I held him up against me so tight he couldn't cry, and then I was scared he'd smother, but the Shawnee wouldn't let me stop to find out.

We went on, up one valley and down another, till finally we come out on level land at the foot of a mountain. The old chief made me go first, right up the mountainside. It was worse there than it was in the woods. The laurel and the ivy was so thick that sometimes he'd have to reach ahead of me and break a way through. My arms got numb and wouldn't hold the baby up. It was lucky for me I was crawling up a mountain. I would put him up ahead of me and then crawl to him, and in this way my arms would get a little ease of the burden. The old chief didn't like this, though, and every time it happened he'd slap me and tell me to go faster, go faster or they would surely kill the baby.

We got to the top of the mountain, somehow, and started down. My legs were hurting me now worse than my arms. It was going so straight down the mountainside. The back of my legs got stiff and would jerk me up every time I set my foot down, what they call stifled in a horse. I got on, somehow, though, all through that night and for most of the next day. It was near sundown when we stopped, in a rockhouse[1] at the head of a creek. The Indians must have thought they were too far for any white men to follow them. They made up a big fire and walked around it pretty careless. Two of the young Indians went off in the woods. I heard a shot and they come back dragging a little deer. They butchered it and sliced it down the middle, and slung the two haunches over the fire on forked sticks. The tenderer parts they broiled on rocks that they heated red-hot in the coals. A young buck squatted down by the fire and kept the venison turning. Soon the smell of rich meat cooking rose up in the air. The juices began dripping down into the blaze and I thought it was a shame for all that gravy to go to waste. I asked the Shawnee to lend me a little kettle he had, and I hung it on a forked stick and caught the juices as they fell, and then poured them back over the meat. When they turned brown and rich I caught the gravy in the little kettle and sopped my fingers in it and let the baby suck them.

The old chief, Crowmocker, smiled like he thought a lot of me. "White woman know," he said. "White woman teach Indian women. You make rum?"

I said I didn't know how to make rum, but there was plenty in the settlements and if he would take me back, take me just within a mile or two of the clearing, I'd undertake to furnish him and his men with all the rum they could drink.

[1] A rockhouse is not a cave, but a place sheltered by an overhanging ledge of rock.

He laughed. "White people promise," he said. "You in your cabin you forget poor Indian."

The Cherokee, Mad Dog, had been sitting there broiling the deer nose on a rock that he had got red-hot in the flames. When it was brown he brought it over and gave it to me. Then he went back and sat down, sullen like, not saying anything. The fire shone on his black eyes and on his long beak of a nose. When he moved, you could see the muscles moving, too, in his big chest and up and down his naked legs. An Indian woman would have thought him a fine-looking man, tall and well formed in every way, but it frightened me to look at him. I was glad it was the old chief and not him that had taken me prisoner. I was glad, too, that the chief was old. I'd heard tell how particular the Indians are about things like that. I thought the old chief would likely do what he said and keep me for his daughter, but if it was Mad Dog he would have me for his wife.

I thought the meat never would get done, but it finally did. The Indians gave me a good-size piece off the haunch and I ate it all, except a little piece I put in Dinny's mouth. He spit it out, but I kept putting it back till he got some good of it. Then I took him down to the creek and scooped up water in my hands for him. He'd been fretting because my milk was giving out, but the water and the juice from the meat quieted him a little. After we'd both had all the water we could drink I went back up the hill and sat down on a log with Dinny laying across my knees. It felt good to have his weight off my arms, but I was afraid to take my hands off him. I was feared one of them might come up and snatch him away from me any minute.

He laid there a while a-fretting and then he put his little hand up and felt my face.

"Sadie . . . ," he said. "Sadie . . ."

Sadie was the oldest girl. She played with him a lot and fondled him. He'd go to her any time out of my arms.

I hugged him up close and sang him the song Sadie used to get him to sleep by. "Lord Lovell, he stood at the castle gate," I sang and the tears a-running down my face.

"Hush, my pretty," I said, "hush. Sadie's gone, but Mammy's here. Mammy's here with Baby."

He cried, though, for Sadie and wouldn't nothing I could do comfort him. He cried himself hoarse and then he'd keep opening his little mouth but wouldn't no sound come. I felt him and he was hot to the touch. I was feared he'd fret himself into a fever, but there wasn't nothing I could do. I held his arms and legs to the blaze and got him as warm as I could, and then I went off from the fire a little way and laid down with him in my arms.

The Indians kept putting fresh wood to the fire till it blazed up and lit the whole hollow. They squatted around it, talking. After a while half a dozen of them got up and went off in the woods. The light fell far out through the trees. I could see their naked legs moving between the black trunks. Some of them was dragging up down timber for the fire and some kept reaching up and tearing boughs off the trees. They came back trailing the green boughs behind them. Two or three other Indians come over and they all squatted down and begun stripping the leaves off the switches and binding them into hoops. An Indian took one of the scalps off his belt—Sadie's light hair, curling a little at the ends and speckled now all over with blood. I watched it fall across the bough of maple. I watched till they began stretching the scalp on the hoop and then I shut my eyes.

After a while Crowmocker come over and tied me with some rawhide thongs that he took off his belt. He tied me up tight and it felt good to have the keen thongs cutting into me. I strained against them for a while and then I must have dropped off to sleep. I woke myself up hollering. I thought at first it was the Indians hollering, and then I knew it was me. I tried to stop but I couldn't. It would start way down inside me and I would fight to hold it in, but before I knew it my mouth would be wide open and as soon as I'd loose one shriek another would start working its way up and there wasn't nothing I could do to hold it back. I was shaking, too, so hard that the baby rolled out of my arms and started crying.

The old chief got up from where he was sleeping and come over. He stood there looking down at me and then he lighted a torch and went off in the woods a little way. He brought some leaves back with him and he put them to boil in his little kettle. He made me drink some tea from the leaves and he gave the baby some too, and after a while we both went off to sleep.

III

I woke with the old chief shaking me by the arm and telling me it was time to get up. I was still sort of lightheaded and for a minute I didn't know where I was. It was raining hard and so dark you couldn't tell whether it was good day. The Indians had built a fire up under the ledge and were broiling the rest of the venison. I laid there and I saw the light shine on their naked legs and the tomahawks hanging from their belts, and I knew where I was and all that had happened.

The old chief untied the thongs and I stood up with Dinny in my arms. They gave me a little piece of venison and some parched corn. My lips were so swelled I couldn't chew, but I swallowed the corn and I put the meat in my mouth and sucked it till it went away. I felt milk in my breast and I was glad for the baby. I gave him his dinny but he wouldn't suck. He wouldn't hardly open his eyes. I thought that was from the tea the old Indian had given us and I feared he'd got too much. He was still hot to the touch and I thought he might have got a fever from laying out all night in the rain. I tore off part of my top skirt and I made a sort of sling that I put around my shoulders to carry him in; and I made a cover, too, out of part of the cloth to keep the rain off his little face.

Soon as we had finished eating, the Indians stomped out the fire and scattered the ashes so you couldn't have told there had ever been a camp there; and we started off through the woods.

We hadn't gone far before two of the young Indians left us. I thought they was most likely going back over the trail to watch if anybody was following us. I heard them saying that the folks at the settlement would be sure to send out a party. Some of the Indians thought it wouldn't do no good because the heavy rains had washed out the trail so nobody could find it. But Mad Dog said Tice Harman could follow any trail. I never knew before the Indians was so feared of Harman. They said he was the best hunter among the Long Knives, that he could go as far and stand as much as any Indian, and that they would like for him to come and live with them and be one of their warriors. Mad Dog said now that the only thing was to go so fast and go so far that even Tice Harman couldn't come up with us. He said "O-hi-yo" several times and I judged they meant to make for one of the towns on the river.

It stopped raining after a while but it didn't do much good. It was level ground we was traveling over and the water was standing everywhere, so that half the time you was wading. I knew we was some place high up in the hills, but afterwards I couldn't have told what country I had passed over. I went with my head down most of the time, not seeing anything but the black trunks of the trees going by and the yellow leaves floating in the puddles. Beech woods we must have been in because the leaves was all yellow and little.

We went on like that all day, not stopping to eat anything except some parched corn that the old chief took out of his bag and handed around to us still traveling. Late that evening we come to a water hole. One of the Indians shot a bear and we stopped and built a fire under a cliff. The Indians hadn't no more'n butchered the meat when two scouts come running into camp. They said that white men were following us, on horseback. The Indians all looked scared at this. Crowmocker stood there talking to Mad Dog about what we had best do. I went over and stood by them. Mad Dog said that they ought to kill the child and change the course, that they would have to go faster than ever now and I couldn't keep up, carrying the baby. Crowmocker showed him the sling I had made and said the baby wasn't no burden to me now. He said he had brought me this far and was going to carry me on to his town to teach his women how to weave cloth like the dress I had on.

He told Mad Dog that and then he motioned to me and said, "Go!" I started off, top speed, through the trees. Behind me I could hear the Indians stomping around in the leaves to cover up the signs of the fire. I went on as fast as I could, but every now and then an Indian would shoot past me. Pretty soon they was all ahead except the old chief.

We went down hill towards a hollow that had a little branch running through it. Mad Dog was in the lead, the other Indians right on his heels, jumping over down logs and bushes quick as cats. The old chief stayed by me, and when I'd slow up getting over a log or fall down in the bushes he'd jerk me onto my feet again.

The branch was narrow but running deep with the rains. Mad Dog started wading downstream and the other Indians after him, single file. They hadn't slowed up much and water splashed high. I could see their legs moving through the splashing water. The old chief by my side was breathing hard. I knew he was winded but I thought he would wind quicker than the others. I thought I would keep moving as long as I saw the Indians' legs going on.

The Indian that was in front of me stepped in a hole up to his waist. When he come out of it he took two, three steps and stood still. I knew then that Mad Dog had stopped and I knew he would be coming back down the line. I looked up, but the sides of the gully was too steep. I turned and ran back upstream fast as I could. I heard the breathing close behind me and I knew it was the old chief, and then there was a big splash. Mad Dog was after me.

I left the water and ran sideways up the gully. The breathing was closer now. I tried to run faster and I caught my foot in a root. They were on me as soon as I went down. Mad Dog grabbed me by both arms. Crowmocker got there a second after, but Mad Dog already had hold of Dinny. I caught at his legs and tried to push them out from under him but he kicked me away. I got up and went at him again but he kicked me down. He kicked me again and then he went on up the side of the gully till he came to a big tree and he held the baby by the feet and dashed his brains out.

I rolled over on my face and I laid there flat on the ground till the old chief come up. He pulled me to my feet and said we would have to run on fast, that the white men were following us on horses. I said no, I wouldn't go, I would stay there with my baby; but he and another Indian took me by the arms and drug me down the stream spite of all I could do.

We went on down the branch a good way. Towards dark we came out on the banks of a river. Water was standing halfway up the trunks of big trees. I saw the current, running fast and covered with black drift, and I didn't believe even an Indian could get across that raging river. But they didn't stop a minute. Crowmocker fell back and two young Indians took hold of my arms and carried me out into the water. The current caught us and swept us off our feet. I couldn't swim much on account of my clothes, but the two young Indians held on to my wrists and carried me on between them. The other Indians come right in after us. They held their guns up high over their heads and swum like boys treading water. I could see their heads bobbing all round me through the black drift and I couldn't see nothing to keep all of us from drowning. They managed to keep out of the drift somehow, though, and all the time they were working towards the other bank till finally we come out in dead water at the mouth of a creek. The Indians that were holding me up stopped swimming all of a sudden, and I knew that we must have got across. It was so dark by that time I couldn't see anything. I got out of the water as best I could and a little way up the creek bank, I fell down there 'mongst some willows. I saw the Indians come up out of the water shaking themselves like dogs, and I saw them falling down all around me, and then my eyes went shut.

IV

The old chief woke me up at the first dawn streak. I heard him and I felt him shaking me, but I didn't get up. As soon as I opened my eyes the pain in my feet started up. I touched one foot to the ground and it throbbed worse'n toothache. I knew I couldn't travel any that day and I didn't care. I turned over on my back and laid there looking up at the sky. It had cleared off during the night and the stars was shining. The sky was all a pale gray except for one long sulphur-colored streak where day was getting ready to break. Behind me the Indians was looking to their guns and settling their tomahawks in their belts. I watched their heads and shoulders moving against that yellow light, and I saw one of them take his tomahawk out and heft it and then try the blade with his finger. I thought that if I just kept on laying there that maybe he would be the one to finish me off, and then I thought Mad Dog was quicker and would beat him to it.

The old chief was still shaking me. "Get up, Jinny. Day come."

"No," I said, "I ain't going to get up."

He took me by the shoulders and tried to pull me to my feet but I slumped back on the ground. I spoke to him in Shawnee.

"My feet bleed and I cannot travel. Let me die."

He leaned over and looked at my feet and then he called to one of the young Indians to bring him some white oak bark. When the bark come he boiled it over the fire and then he took the liquid from the bark and cooled it with more water and poured it over my feet.

The other Indians had finished scattering the fire and was starting out through the willows, but Crowmocker just sat there pouring that stuff on my feet. I could feel the swelling going down and after a while I touched my feet to the ground. It didn't hurt like it had, and I got up and we started off. He give me some parched corn and I ate it, walking. He said we would have to travel fast to catch up with the other Indians. I asked him if the white people were still following us and he laughed and said no white man could get across that river. I owned to myself that they couldn't, and I didn't think any more about them coming after me. I thought the Indians would probably take me so far away that I'd never again see a white face.

We caught up with the other Indians towards dark. That night we slept in a canebreak by a little river. A buffalo was wallowing in the river as we come up. One of the Indians shot him. They butchered him there in the water and drug big slabs of the meat up the bank with ropes cut from the hide. We must have been in Indian country by this time. They didn't seem to think it made any difference how much noise they made. They made up a big fire to one side of the brake and they were half the night cooking the meat and eating.

I went to sleep under a tree with them singing and yelling all around me.

When I woke up the next morning they were having a council. They talked till the sun was high and then they split up into two parties. Mad Dog and three of the young bucks left us and swum across the river. The rest of us kept on up the bank. We traveled all that day through the cane and then we struck a divide and followed it into another valley. We had run out of everything to eat by this time except the strings of jerked meat that they all carried slung around their necks. We stayed two, three days at a buffalo lick, hoping to kill some game, but none came and we went on.

Most of the leaves were off the trees by this time and the nights were cold. I knew it was some time in October that the Indians come and burned our house, but I didn't know how long we'd been on the trail and I didn't have any idea what country we were in.

One morning we come out in some deep narrows just above where two creeks flowed together. A wild-looking place with tumbling falls and big rocks laying around everywhere. I looked up at the cliffs over our heads and I couldn't believe my eyes. They were *painted:* deer and buffalo and turtles big as a man, painted in red and in black on the rock. Some of the young Indians acted like they had never been there before either. They would keep walking around looking at things and sometimes stand and stare at the pictures of wild beasts that were painted everywhere on the smooth rock.

The old chief took a way up the side of the cliffs, the rest of us following. The young Indians went up like deer, but I had to pull myself up by the laurel that grew down in between the rocks. We walked along a narrow ledge and come to a rockhouse. It was the biggest rockhouse ever I saw, run all along one side of the cliff. The old chief uncovered an iron pot from where it was hid in a lot of trash in one corner of the cave and showed me how to set it up on forked sticks. He said that I would have to do all the work around the camp from now on, the way Indian women did, and when the spring rains come and melted the snow he would take me to his town on the Tenassee and I would learn more about Indian ways and be adopted into the tribe in place of his dead daughter.

I thought if he took me there I would never get away and I had it in mind to make a break for it first chance I got. I got hold of two strings of jerked meat and I kept them tied around my waist so I'd be ready when the time came. I thought I would wait, though, and maybe I would find out how far it was to the settlements. I would lie there in my corner of the cave at night, making out I was asleep, and listen to them talking around the fire. I heard them call the names of the creeks that flowed through that valley—Big Paint and Little Mudlick; and further off was another creek, Big Mudlick, where they went sometimes to hunt. The names were strange to me and I never could tell from their talk how far it was to the settlements or even which way to go. I had an idea that the place I was in was secret to the Indians, for it was a wonder to see and yet I had never heard any white body tell of it. I asked Crowmocker what the pictures of deer and buffalo and bear were for and he said they were the Indians' fathers and that I would learn about them when I was adopted into the tribe. Once he pointed some mounds out to me and said they were graves. He said that he and his people always stopped when they come this way to visit the graves of their fathers that was all over the valley.

A spell of fine weather come, late in the fall. Indian summer they call it. We looked out one day and bees were swarming on the cliffside. Crowmocker was mad when he saw them. He said it meant that the white people were coming; that when bees swarmed out of season they were running away from the white people who had scared all the game out of the country and made it so that even bees couldn't live in it. I asked would the white people find their way into this valley and he said they couldn't—that it was a way known only to Indians; that if a white man ever set foot in it the great bear would come down off the wall and crush him in his paws. He said, though, that there would be fighting soon over all the land and a lot of bloodshed.

I knew that was all foolishness about the bear, but I thought likely as not there would be fighting and I wanted to get away worse than ever. One morning I was down in the hollow by myself, gathering wood, and I thought that was the time. Three of the Indians had gone off hunting and I knew the others were laying up in the cave asleep. I didn't think anybody would be following me, for a while, anyhow. I started off, slipping from tree to tree, and I got quite a way up the hollow. I knew nobody was following me, but I would keep looking back over my shoulder all the time. I got to thinking. I didn't have any way to kill game, and nothing to eat but two strings of jerked meat. I didn't even know how far I'd have to go before I came to any settlement. Worst of all, I didn't even know which way to take. Likely as not I'd starve to death in the woods, or freeze if the weather turned. I'd better stay with the Indians, where at least I could sleep warm and eat, if it wasn't anything but parched corn. I picked up my load of wood and got back to camp quick as I could, and didn't none of them ever know I'd been away.

I never tried it again, but sometimes I'd sit there on the edge of the cliff and pick out the way I'd take if I did go. There was a ridge covered with black pines rose up right in front of the rockhouse. I thought if I could once get up there I could get down into the valley easy. I hadn't ever been over there, but I knew what the country would be like. I saw my-self slipping along through that divide, around the foot of the mountain and over some more mountains till I'd come out on a clearing. I'd slip up to some cabin, towards dark. They'd think I was an Indian at first, maybe, and then they'd see my eyes was light and they'd take me in and keep me till I could get back to my own folks again.

We stayed in that rockhouse a long time. The leaves all fell off the trees, and one or two light snows fell, but the real cold weather was late coming. The Indians hunted just enough to keep us in meat. They said the pelts were thin that year and not worth taking. Sometimes they would take me along to bring in the game, but mostly they left me to work by myself. When cold weather set in we built big fires in the cave and it was warm inside like a house. When the Indians weren't hunting they would lie around on buffalo skins and sleep. The smoke was terrible and the smell of Indians was all over everything. At first it bothered me, but after a while I got so I didn't notice it.

I wasn't in the cave much, even in bad weather. I had to gather all the firewood. The Indians didn't have an axe and I couldn't get anything but dead branches. There wasn't much down timber on the cliffside; so I'd mostly go up over the cliffs when I was hunting wood. There was a barren there, flat as the palm of your hand and covered with a thin kind of grass. It had plenty of trees on it but they were all twisty and stunted by the wind. The only sizable tree was a big elm. It was peeled for thirty or forty feet and had a rattlesnake painted on it—a monster snake coiling up around the trunk. You could see that snake from everywhere on the barren. I was feared to look at it. The Indians seemed to think a lot of it. Sometimes they would go up there a night and I would hear them singing and dancing and calling to the snake.

Somewhere on the barren there were lead mines. The Indians never let me go to them, but they would go off and stay two, three hours and come back with big balls of lead. They made me smelt it out for bullets. I had to have a mighty fire.

It would take me days and days to get up enough wood. I would heap it up in a big pile and then I would kindle the fire and keep it going for hours. When the lead melted, it ran down through little ditches into holes that I had dug to form the bullets. It would take the lead a long time to melt. Sometimes I would be up on the barren from sunup to sundown.

I would sit there and think about my husband and my children. I would wonder whether Tom went out in the woods hunting ginseng the way he used to do, and was he still looking for me or had give me up for dead. When I thought of Tom the house would be there, too, not burning down the way it was last time I saw it, but standing with the rooms just the way they always were. I could see both rooms plain, even to the hole that was burnt in the floor when a big log fell out one night. The children would be playing in and out of the house like they did. It was like they were all living; it was only me that was gone away.

I would think back, too, over things that happened long before ever I was grown and married to Tom Wiley. There was a man named Rayburn stayed at the settlement one winter. Lance Rayburn. A big, strong man and a mighty hunter. We ate bear of his shooting all that fall. He was handy with snares too, and took over a hundred beaver down in the bottom. He courted me some that winter, sitting in front of the fire after the old folks were in bed. I laughed and went on with him, but Tom Wiley had just started a-courting me and all the time my mind was on him more'n it was on the stranger.

Come time for Rayburn to pack up his pelts to take to the station, he saved one out for me. Beaver, and extra fine and soft. He give it to my sister, Sarah, and told her to hand it to me when I come to the house. She made one of the children bring it down to the creek where I was boiling clothes. I laid it there on the grass and I would stop and look at it as I went back and forth with my clothes, and sometimes I would wipe my hands dry and lay them on the soft fur for pleasure in the feel. But all the time I knew I wasn't going to keep it. When Rayburn come towards me through the willows I went to meet him with the pelt in my hands.

"Keep this," I said, "and give it to some girl where you're going."

"Don't you want it?" he asked.

"I ain't taking nothing from you."

He stood there looking at me and all of a sudden his eyes narrowed up like a cat's. "You're full young to be marrying," he said.

"I ain't too young to know my own mind," I told him and before I thought I laughed.

He come towards me, and before I knowed what he was up to he was on me and trying to bear me to the ground. He was a strong man but I was stout, too, and I stood up to him. We was rassling around in the bushes quite some while before he got me down, and then he had to keep both his hands on my chest. I laid there right still, looking up at him.

"What you reckon my pappy'll say when I tell him about this?" I asked.

He laughed, "I ain't a-feared of no Sellards that ever walked," he said, "but that Tom Wiley ain't no manner of man for you," he said.

"You can talk against Tom Wiley and you can hold me here till Doomsday," I told him, "but it ain't going to do you no good. I ain't going to have none of you no matter what happens."

His face kind of changed. Looked like it hurt him to hear me say it. He got up off me right away and he picked the beaver pelt up from where it lay in the grass and he throwed it hard as he could into the creek.

"It'll git to my girl that way fast as any other," he said.

I watched the pelt floating down the water and onto a rock and then off again. When I turned around he was out of sight and he was gone when I got back to the house. He stayed at the station a while and then he went off in the mountains hunting bear and wasn't ever heard of again. Some said he was killed by wild beasts. A rifle and a cap that they said was his was found up in the hills. The man that found the rifle kept it, but they give the cap to the Borderses. Wouldn't anybody wear it, and Sally hung it up in the dog alley. I used to look at it every time I passed and wonder whether it had ever been on Lance Rayburn's head and was he dead or still living. And sometimes I'd wonder how it'd been if I'd married him instead of Tom, but I knew all the time I wouldn't ever have married anybody but Tom because he was the one I fancied from the time I was a chap, living neighbor to the Wileys, back in the Roanoke country.

I thought about Lance Rayburn and I thought about a lot of other folks that had come to the settlement and stayed and then gone on and wouldn't anybody know whether they were living still or dead. And I thought about people dead long ago, my old granny back in Carolina, ninety-eight years old and turned simple. She'd sit in the chimney corner all day long, singing the likeliest tunes!

"Pa'tridge in the pea patch," she'd sing and call me to her and fondle me, liking gals, she said, always better than boys.

> "Pa'tridge in the pea patch
> Pickin' up the peas.
> 'Long comes the bell cow
> Kickin' up her heels . . ."

"Oh . . . h, the bell cow," she'd sing and catch me by my little shimmy tail. "O . . . O . . . hh, the bell cow . . ." and hist me up over the arm of her chair. "O . . . O . . . hh, the bell cow, kickin' up her heels. Call the little gal to milk her in the pail."

I used to call those songs to mind when I had to go down to the lick for salt. It was a place I didn't like to go. A deep hollow with three sulphur springs and a lick that covered nigh an acre of ground. The biggest lick ever I saw in my life. The way was white with the bones of beasts, and in between the piled up bones the long furrows that the buffalo made licking the ground for salt. I would walk down those furrows to the spring and fill my bucket with the salty water and go back up the hill to where my kettle was slung between two little birches. Sitting there waiting for the water to boil, I couldn't keep my eyes off the bones. I would take them up in my hand and turn them over and over, wondering what manner of beasts they had belonged to.

Once I made myself a little beast, laying all the bones out on some lacy moss, the front feet stiff like it was galloping off in the woods, the hind legs drawn up under him. A hare it might have been or a little fawn. Or maybe a beast that nobody ever heard of before.

There were beasts come to that lick one time or another not known to man. Bigger'n buffalo they must have been. One thighbone, I mind, longer'n I was and twice as big around as two goodsized men.

I thought of a man used to be around the station, Vard Wiley, second cousin to Tom. Folks said he was the biggest liar in the settlements. He would stay off in the woods hunting day after day and never bring in any game except maybe a brace of wild turkeys. And he told tall tales about a lick bigger'n any lick around those parts, where the beasts come up in tens of thousands. He would lay up in a tree all day and watch 'em, he said, and not take a shot for wonder. There used to be beasts there, he said, ten times the size of buffalo. He offered to take anybody there and show them the bones, and when they asked him why he didn't bring them back to the settlement he said couldn't no man carry them, nor no two horses.

Folks laughed at him, and the children round the settlement used to sing a song:

> "Vard Wiley's gone west, Vard Wiley's gone east,
> A-huntin' the woods for a monster beast.
>
> "He'll make him a tent out of the wild beast's hide
> And all the king's horses can stable inside.
>
> "He'll make him a wagon out of solid bone
> And it'll take ten oxen to draw it home."

I called that song to mind and I thought how if I ever saw Vard Wiley again I'd go up to him and say I knew him to be a truth-teller, and all the people would laugh at me maybe, the way they did Vard Wiley, but all the time I would be knowing it was the truth.

I thought, too, of other tales he told and of jokes he played. Of the time he borrowed my dress and sunbonnet and shawl and went and sat on the creek bank when the schoolmaster was in swimming. He sat there all evening with the sunbonnet hiding his face and old Mister Daugherty shaking his fist at him. "You hussy! You brazen hussy! Don't you know I'm naked?" and finally when he come up out of the water naked as the day he was born Vard took out after him and run him clean to the house. Old Mister Daugherty went around saying there was a woman ought to be run out of the settlements, and Vard would talk to him and make out it was me. But Old Man Daugherty knew wouldn't none of Hezekiah Sellards' daughters be carrying on like that. He was bound it was a woman from Ab's Valley.

I would think about 'em sitting there and arguing about how the hussy ought to be run out of the settlements, and I would laugh all by myself there in the woods. Throw back my head and laugh and then feel silly when the woods give back the echo.

I did a lot of work while I was with the Indians. It was hard on me at first but I got used to it. It was better after Mad Dog left us. The old chief was like a father to me, and the young ones knew I belonged to him and didn't bother me. I slept off by myself in a far corner of the cave and he would wake me up at daybreak and tell me what there was to do that day. He took pains to show me how to flesh pelts and cure them, and he showed me how to split a deer sinew for thread and how to make a whistle to call deer out of birch bark and sticks. And after I got so I could sew skins good he had me make him a pair of leggings and trim them with porcupine quills—porcupine quills colored with some roots he got out of the woods.

It bothered him the way I looked and he made me paint my face the way the Indians did. Fixed me up some of the red root mixed with bear's grease, and after I'd been putting it on my face for a while you couldn't told me from an Indian woman, except for my light eyes.

He'd stay in the cave with me sometimes all day, his buffalo hide wrapped around him so tight that his knees were up against him like a chair. He'd sit there and rock back and forth on his heels and talk while I worked. Down in the hollow the young braves would be practicing their war whoops. He would listen to them and laugh.

"Our young men give the war whoop loudly to cover up their fear of the enemy. It was not so when I was young. There was joy in the war whoop then."

He said he was a chief but he might have been something better. He might have been a medicine man. He had the gift of it from his grandmother. His own mother died when he was born, he said, and his old granny raised him. He told me about how she would take him into the woods with her looking for yarbs and roots, and how she knew where everything grew and which roots would be good to take and which had no strength in them. He said that after I was adopted into the tribe he would tell some of her secrets to me, but the Spirit would be angry if a white woman knew them.

I asked him wouldn't I still be a white woman after I was adopted into the tribe but he said no, the white blood would go out of me and the Spirit would send Indian blood to take its place, and then I would feel like an Indian and know all the Indian ways and maybe get to be a wise woman like his old granny.

He told me about his youngest daughter and how she come by her death, following what she thought was a fawn bleating. They found her days afterward, three enemy arrows in her. Her death had been paid for with three scalps of warriors, and he would say that he didn't grieve over her, but I knew he did. I got to feeling sorry for him sometimes to have lost his daughter that meant so much to him, and then I would think how I had lost all my children and my husband and I would cry, dropping tears on the skin I was sewing.

I got so after a while that the Indian way of doing things seemed natural to me. I thought nothing of seeing dark faces around me all the time, but in the night sometimes I would dream of white faces. White faces coming towards me through the trees. Or sometimes I would be in a house again and look up all of a sudden and all the faces in the room would be white.

One white face was always coming to me in my dreams: Tice Harman, the man whose house the Indians thought they were burning the day they burned ours. I always thought that if anybody came to save me it would be Tice Harman. I could see him plain in my dreams. A little man, wouldn't weigh more'n a hundred and twenty pounds, but he had a big head. A big head and a big beak of a nose and long yellow hair down to his shoulders. His eyes were blue and in my dreams they glittered like ice. I would dream about Tice Harman and when I waked I would think what I'd heard said of him—how he could go further and stand more than any man in the settlements, and how he loved to fight Indians better'n eat when he was hungry. I would think, too, of how folks said he would bring trouble on the settlements shooting that Indian down when there wasn't really any use in it; and I would think that since it was him that brought all my trouble on me, maybe it would be him that would get me away from the Indians. But time went on and nobody came, and after a while I got so I didn't think much about it.

One evening I was gathering wood on the cliffside and I heard a lot of whooping and hollering down near the mouth of the creek. The Indians come out from where they were sleeping back in the cave and stood looking over the falls. A long whoop came and the old chief put his hands to his mouth and answered it. There was more whooping back and forth, and then Mad Dog came up the trail by the falls with about twenty Indians following him. They were painted for war and marched single file, all except the last six or eight. They were in pairs and in the middle of them a white man, walking with his hands tied behind him. A white man? A boy. Couldn't have been more than eighteen years old.

I had to step out of the path to let them by. The dead branches rustled in my hands. The prisoner turned his head. He looked straight into my eyes. It was like he didn't know I was there. I spoke to him.

"I can't do nothing," I said. "I'm a white woman, but I can't do nothing. Christ!" I said, "there ain't nothing I can do."

He kept on looking at me but he didn't speak. They were hurrying him past. I dropped the branches and run after them. Mad Dog called to one of the young bucks and he caught me and held me. I fought him, but he held me till they had all gone up the path.

I went on to the rockhouse and kindled up the fire. After a while Mad Dog come down and told me to cook up some meat quick as I could. There would be singing and dancing, he said; they would want meat all night long.

I looked at him. "A present," I said. "A present for Kagahyeliske's daughter. Give me this boy. He is not good for anything but to gather wood."

His eyes were fierce. "Boy?" he said. "He has this day killed my brother." Then he laughed and smoothed my hair. "Jinny," he said, "pretty Jinny."

I made out I had to see to the fire and walked away. I put some bear meat on to boil and I told him I would call him when it was done, and he went on back up the path.

There was a moon coming. I sat there waiting for the meat to boil and watched it rise over the pines. Up on the barren the Indians were dragging up all the dead branches they could find into one pile. After a while I looked up over the rockhouse and saw the sky all light and knew they had kindled the fire.

The stamping and yelling went on, and every now and then a gun would go off. Then there was running around the tree. You could hear the feet pounding and the long calls. "Ai . . . yi . . . Ai . . . yi . . . Ai . . . yi . . ." One for each man that had died that day. And the sharp cry for the scalp taking. They would act it all out and the boy standing there watching. He was dazed, though; he wouldn't see it for what it was. He wouldn't know what they were doing, might not know what they were going to do. There on the path he looked at me and didn't know me for a white woman. I ought to have found out his name and where he come from. I ought to have done that much. But he wouldn't have answered. And what good would it do his folks . . . if I ever saw white folks again. Then Mad Dog's hand on my hair. "Pretty Jinny . . . pretty Jinny . . ."

The flames shot up and lit the whole valley. The moon looked cold where it hung over the pines. I kept the fire up under the kettle but I couldn't sit still. I walked back and forth in the rockhouse, back and forth, back and forth, waiting for the shrieks to start.

They were a long time coming. I thought maybe it was already going on. Indians can stand there burning and not make a sound, and there have been white men that could. But this was just a boy . . .

The first shriek was long and then they come short and quick, one right after the other. I got over in a corner of the rockhouse and held on tight to a big rock. After a while I let go of the rock and put both fingers in my ears and then I was feared to take them out, thinking it might not be over yet. The Indians were still yelling and stamping. The young ones kept running down and grabbing up chunks of meat from the boiling pot and carrying them up to the barren. I could see the old chief's shadow where he stood on the edge of the cliff calling to the new moon.

When he came down to the rockhouse Mad Dog was with him. They stood there dipping meat up out of the kettle. Mad Dog talked.

"It is too much. For five hundred brooches I could buy a girl of the Wild-Cats, young and swift, a fine worker in beads. A girl like a moonbeam, daughter of a mighty warrior."

His eyes were black in the circles of paint. His tongue showed bright between his painted lips. The red lines ran from his forehead down the sides of his cheeks to make gouts of blood on his chin.

A devil. A devil come straight from hell to burn and murder. Three white men killed that day and the boy brought back to torture. It was him that killed them, him that yelled loudest when the boy was burning. Him that set fire to my house and burned my children . . .

I saw him running through the woods, white men after him. I saw him fall, a dozen bullets in him. But he wouldn't be dead. He would lie there bleeding and look at me out of his painted eyes, and I would go up and stomp on him, stomp him into the dirt . . .

My hands shook so I dropped the sticks I was carrying. I was near enough now to hear all they were saying. Mad Dog was taking little silver brooches out of a buckskin. He poured them out in a pile on a rock and then counted them. The old chief stood there till he got through counting; then he swept them all up into a bag he took from around his neck.

"Brother," he said, "the woman is yours."

Mad Dog had left the fire and was coming towards me. I ran over and caught hold of the old chief's arm. I called him by his Indian name.

"Kagahye-liske, do not give me to this man. He has killed my children and burned my house."

He looked down at me and it was like he'd never seen me before. His face, not painted, was as cruel as the Cherokee's, the eyes bloodshot and the whole face swollen from the meat he had eaten.

"The war whoop drowns sorrow," he said. "This chief is my brother and a mighty warrior. He has this day killed three white men."

I hung on to his arm. "Keep me for one of the young men of your village," I said. "The Cherokee are old women. You have said so and you have promised. You have promised to take me with you wherever you go."

He shook my hands off. "A promise," he said, "to a white coward! Go to your work."

He turned around like he was going to leave the cave. I run after him and caught hold of his knees, but he broke away.

Mad Dog come and tied me up tight with thongs that he cut from buffalo hide, and then they both went on up to the barren where the other Indians was still screeching and stamping.

The screeching and stamping went on far into the night. The fire under the kettle went out and it was dark except for a little light from the moon. I laid there on the floor, listening to the Indians and thinking about how it would be when Mad Dog came down to take me for his wife. I laid there, expecting him to come any minute, but the singing and dancing went on and he didn't come, and after a while I went to sleep.

v

The white boy that they had burned came to me while I was asleep. He came carrying a lamp that was made from the bleached skull of a sheep. The brain hollow was filled with buffalo fat and there was a wick in it burning bright. He came walking between the trees like he didn't have need to look where he was going. His hair was light like I had seen it when he passed me there on the path, but it was long, too, like Tice Harman's. His eyes were the same eyes that had looked at me there on the path.

I said to him what I had said there. "I couldn't do nothing," I said. "There wasn't nothing I could do."

He didn't speak—only made signs for me to follow him. I got up and walked after him. The rawhide thongs were still on me but they didn't bind any more and I moved as easy and as light as he did. He went down by the falls and clomb up over the hill to where the elm tree stood that had the big rattlesnake painted on it. He walked past the elm tree and struck out through the black pines that were all over that ridge. Sometimes he would go so fast that I couldn't keep up with him, and then I would stand still and after a while I would see the light flickering through the trees and I would go on to where he was waiting for me. We went on through the pine

woods and started down the side of the ridge. I heard water
running somewhere far down below. I thought that would be
Mudlick Creek, but when I got to it it was a branch I'd never
seen before. We crossed it and went on up a path through a
clearing. There were little shrubs all round like the ones up
on the barren, and in the middle of them was a house. It was
my house and yet it wasn't. White all over and the walls so
thin you could see the light from the lamp shining through
the logs.

People were walking around in the yard and sitting on the
doorstep. They moved to let me go through the door, but they
didn't speak to me and I didn't speak to them.

The men that were sitting in front of the fire playing
draughts didn't even look up when I came in. I went over to
the hearth and tried to dry out my clothes. I stood there holding out my hands but no heat came. I looked at the logs and
they were white like the timbers of the house, and the same
light came from them. I saw that the men playing didn't have
a lamp and yet there was light all around them.

People kept walking in and out of the cabin, men and wom-
en and little children. I would go up to them and look in their
faces, but there wasn't anybody there I knew. I walked round
and round the room. Every now and then the people would
move out of the way and I would catch sight of the walls.
White, with patches of green on them. I put my hand up and
felt one of the logs. It was round and cold to the touch. No
log at all, but bleached bone. I knew then that all the house
was bone, the floor and the walls and the chimney, even the
table that the men were playing on, all made from the big
bones down at the lick.

One of the men at the table stretched his arm out and
pulled me over to him. He had on a beaver cap and his face
under it was pale like he'd been in the woods a long time. He

looked at me and I saw it was Lance Rayburn. He sang, pulling me up over the arm of his chair:

"Oh . . . the bell cow, kicking up her heels,
Call the little gal to milk her in the pail . . ."

Fiddling started up somewhere and all fell to dancing. They danced to one of my old granny's tunes:

"There was an old lord lived in a northern countree,
Bowee down, bowee down . . ."

There was bowing back and forth and balancing, and there were figures called, but wasn't any women dancing. I would see something going by and think it was a woman's skirt, but when I got up to it it would be fur or feathers dangling from a belt and all the faces around were dark, not like they were at first.

The great flames went leaping up the chimney, and all of a sudden I knew that they had built that fire to burn somebody by. I looked around for the one they were going to burn but he wasn't there. I said, "They will burn me next," and I saw what they would tie me to—the rattlesnake tree, going straight up from the table through the roof.

I went to the door and I saw through the black trunks a light flickering. I run and Mad Dog and the old chief were after me the way they were that day in the hollow. I thought, "They will kill me now when I go down," and I run faster and then they were both gone away and I was walking through pine woods, the light flickering on ahead of me.

I walked on and come to a creek that run along between wide banks of cane. The light shone on the water and made it light as mist. I stepped in, not knowing whether it was water or mist, and I could feel it coming up around my knees, water and yet not water. I moved along through it light as the wind till I come to where the creek forked. I could see the two forks and the white trunks of the sycamores along the bank, but I didn't know which way to go.

The light was all around me. I could see it shining on the reeds and on the little leaves of the cane and on the water where it broke on the rocks. Behind me there were voices talking.

"Jinny Wiley . . . Jinny Wiley, that was stolen and lived with the Indians . . ."

And then it was the old chief talking to the new moon:

"The white people . . . The white people are all over the land. The beaver makes no more dams and the buffalo does not come to the lick. And bees swarm here in the ancient village. Bees swarm on the graves of our fathers . . ."

The light that had been around me was gone. It was shining now through the tree trunks down a fork of the creek. I waded towards it through the light water, the voices following, and then they were gone and I was standing at the foot of a high mountain. I looked up and saw the light flickering at the top and I clomb towards it, pulling myself up by the scrubs and holly bushes.

I got up on the mountaintop but the young man wasn't there. I walked out onto the edge of a cliff and he was by my side. He said, "Look, Jinny!" and the flame of his lamp leaped up and lighted the whole valley and I looked across a river and saw a fort. I saw the roofs of the houses and the stockade and the timber burned back over the rifle range, and I saw men and women walking around inside the stockade.

I said, "I'm a-going over there," but the young man wasn't with me any more, and the dark that was all around was the inside of the rockhouse.

VI

When I woke up the next morning the Indians had a big fire going and were all sitting around eating. I laid there and made out I was still asleep. They had found trace of buffalo down at the lick and were making ready for a big hunt. I thought maybe they would take me along to bring in the game the way they did sometimes, and then I heard Mad Dog say they would leave me tied up in the cave till they got ready to start for their town.

I was laying with my face turned up and I was feared they could tell by my eyes that I wasn't asleep. I give a kind of groan and rolled over on my side. I laid there not moving while the talking went on all around me. Once footsteps come over to the corner where I was laying and I heard something slap down on the ground right by me but I didn't give any sign and the footsteps went away.

I laid there so still that I went to sleep again with the talking and the making ready for the hunt still going on. I was waked up by a kind of roaring sound. At first I thought it was the falls and then I knew the falls wouldn't sound that loud. I opened my eyes. The Indians were all gone and there was a big storm blowing up.

I laid there watching the pine tops lash back and forth in the wind, and the dream I'd had come back into my mind as plain as if it was something that had happened. I thought it was sent to me on purpose to tell me that now was the chance to get away. I knew that if the Indians come back with any game that night they'd feast high again and were more than likely to take me up on the barren and burn me like they done that boy.

I sat up. A piece of meat was lying on the floor right by me. That meant that the Indians would be all gone all day and maybe another day. If I could only get free of the thongs I might get a long way off before they knew I was gone.

There was a knife stuck in a crack of the rock where they laid the meat. If I could only get hold of that! I rolled over and over till I got to the rock and managed to get up on my knees, though the thongs cut into me bad. I could see the handle of the knife sticking up out of the crack and I laid my face down flat on the rock and tried to catch hold of it with my teeth. But it was too far down and all I did was get my mouth full of grit and sand. I gave up and laid down again. The wind wasn't as high as it had been, but the rain was coming down hard. It blew way back into the cave. I laid there with the big drops spattering in my face and a thought came to me. I rolled over to where the rain was pouring down off the roof and I laid there till I was soaked through. All the time I kept straining at the thongs and I could feel them giving a little, the way leather does when it's wet. I kept on, getting them looser and looser till finally I worked my way out of them and stood up free.

I listened and I couldn't hear anything but the roaring of the wind and the beating of the rain on the ledge. I tiptoed to the end of the cave and looked down the path. But I couldn't see any sign of living creature. I dug the knife out from between the rocks and I took the piece of cooked meat and a little kettle that the old chief had left laying around, and went off out of the other end of the cave and along the cliffside.

I kept to the path a little way and then I struck off through the trees down the hillside. The ground was wet and slid from under my feet in big chunks. I caught on to the trees all the way to keep myself from falling. When I got to the bottom I could look back and see where I'd come, as plain as if I'd blazed a trail. I knew I'd have to strike water. I run in among some pines and come to a wet weather branch. I waded right in. It was swift water and full of holes. I would step in one every now and then and go down, but I kept on as fast as I could. I felt all the time like the Indians were after me. I knew they had gone south towards the salt lick and I knew the whole cliffside and the barren was between me and them, but all the time I felt like they were right behind me. When I looked over my shoulder the top boughs of the rattlesnake tree showed from the barren. I was glad when I rounded a bend and it was out of sight.

When I come out to where the branch flowed into the creek I didn't know which way to go, and then I thought that in my dream I was following water and I struck right down the stream. It was harder going here than it was in the branch. The snows melting had filled all the dry weather branches, and muddy water kept running in till you couldn't tell anything about the depth. It was well I was going downstream, but even then the current was a hindrance to me, reaching in and sweeping me off my feet sometimes into a hole that I would have a time getting out of. More than once I was in danger of drowning.

I kept on like this all day. When it was drawing towards dark I crawled up on the bank under some cedars and I laid there and I ate a good-sized piece of the cooked meat I had brought with me. The rain had fallen off to a light drizzle and there was some color in the sky, sign of a clear day tomorrow. There was a flight of little birds over the water and then round and round the tops of the cedars. Some of them lit in the boughs of the tree I was laying under. I could hear them flying in and out and the quick cries and then the twittering as they settled down to roost. It was dark under the trees but the streak of light stayed on the water. I laid here and watched it fade and I wished I could stay there where the cedar boughs were like a little house. I wished I could stay there and not run any more. I thought I would maybe sleep a few minutes and then I could go on faster. But when I shut my eyes I would think I heard the Indians coming through the trees and after a little I got up and went on again.

I tried wading some more but I couldn't make it in the pitch dark. I got up on the bank of the creek and pushed my way through the bushes as best I could. Sometimes the undergrowth would be so thick I couldn't make it, and then I would have to get down in the water again. All the way I was worrying about losing time following the bending and twisting of the creek, and then I would think that was the only sure way to get out of the hill country and I had best stick to water, spite of all the bending.

Sometime during the night I lost my way from the creek and wandered in the pitch dark into a marsh that was all along the creek bottom. More like a bog it was. I couldn't seem to get out of it no matter what I did. I stood there bogged to the knees and couldn't even hear the creek running—nothing but the wind soughing in the trees. And I thought what a lone place it was and if I came on quicksand, as was more than likely, I could go down and even my bones never be found. And I thought of how Lance Rayburn's bones might have been laying all this time in some hollow of the mountain and nothing maybe but squirrels or deer ever going near the place, and it seemed to me I might better have stayed with the Indians. But I knew it wouldn't be any use going back now. They would put the fire to me sure.

I stood there and I heard some wild thing passing. Pit pat pit pat it went; feet falling on dry ground. I pulled out of the muck and made towards the sound, and a deer or something broke through the thicket and went off through the woods.

I followed and come out on high ground, a slope covered with pine needles. I threw myself down flat on my face. I must have gone off to sleep. When I come to myself light was growing through the trees, and all around me I could hear twigs snapping and little rustlings. I got up quick, thinking it was the Indians coming, and then I felt foolish, knowing it was only game stirring at break of day. I saw two deer go by, moving slow over the brown pine needles. The air was so still they didn't get a whiff of me until they were out of the thicket. The buck wheeled so quick he almost knocked the doe over, and then they were both clattering off over the hill.

I went down to the creek bank and washed my face and let the water run over my wrists where they were scratched by the branches. I ate the last of my meat sitting there on a rock. When I got ready to go I found out that one of my strings of jerked meat had slipped off during the night. I couldn't hardly believe it at first. I stood up and felt all over my clothes time and again but it warn't there.

"Well," I said, "it's gone and they ain't no use crying over it, but I wish to God it'd a been the little piece."

I got in the water and started wading again. The creek was shallow for about half a mile and then it run into a bigger creek. The two of them run on before me and I didn't know which way to go. I stood there looking. The sun was up and it shone on the water. I watched the riffles break on the black rocks where the sun caught them, and the place was not the same place I had seen in the dream and yet it was the same because of the light that was over everything.

I remembered the way I took in the dream. "Left I'll go," I said, "like it was in the dream, and if it don't turn out right it's no fault of mine."

I went on, wading half the time. All that day I was thinking about something to eat. Seems like everything good I ever had to eat in my life come back to torment me that day. The smell of herring, cooking, bothered me most. I would see myself, a chap, back in the Roanoke country, broiling herrings over the coals the way children did when their mammy wouldn't give them anything else to eat between meals. I would go over it all, time and again, the herrings hanging in rows in the smokehouse, like tobacco in a barn, and us climbing up on a slab of wood to get at them.

"Three," Dinny, that's my eldest brother, 'd say every time. "Three. You might as well get one apiece while you're at it."

I thought, too, about people wasting things, of a woman I knew used to give all her buttermilk to her pig, and I thought how it was shameful to have no mind for them that might be starving. And I thought how if I could have that pig's dinner one time, or even a moldy piece of bread, the kind I'd thrown away many a time as not good enough for the dogs. And yet I'd been as wasteful as any of them in my day—worse, even, with game. I used to go hunting just for the fun of it. Seemed like there warn't nothing I liked better than sighting down a rifle. Warn't none of the Sellards or Damron boys a better shot than I was, and I could throw a knife with the best of them. That time John and Dick and me and the two Damrons went to Sinking Fork on a big hunt I shot eighteen wild gobblers, and when we loaded up and there were more'n we could carry it was me that said to leave them laying, that there warn't no use in breaking yourself down and the woods full of gobblers. I thought about them gobblers more'n once that day and, Lord, how I wished I could git my hands on a rifle butt just one more time.

I threw my knife once or twice at some small game, mostly rabbits, but it was a rusty old thing and not fitted to the hand the way a knife has to be to turn proper. One rabbit that I hit square in the middle got up and skittered off like nothing had happened, and I saw then it was a waste of time to throw at them.

Late that evening I come on some forward wild greens in a sheltered place on the creek bank. I went down on my knees and gathered every shoot. I found some punk and went up to a rockhouse on the side of the hill and built a little fire way in under the ledge the way I'd seen the Indians do. I knew it was craziness to build a fire, but it might be days before I'd come on any wild greens again. "I'll eat," I said, "varmints or no varmints."

I put my greens on to boil in the little kettle with a piece of the jerked meat and sat there, thinking about how Indians would go up on a cliff to sight over the country and how the least little smoke curling up would be a sign to them. Once I was on the point of putting the fire out but I couldn't bring myself to do it. I feared to feed it much and yet I'd catch myself putting dead twigs to it. It was a long time before the bubbles started rising up in that little old kettle. I sat there rocking on my heels and talking to them.

"Boil," I said, "boil. God's sake, can't you boil no faster'n that? And me setting here starving."

I ate up every mite of the greens and drank the pot liquor and licked the kettle and then I put out down the hill as fast as I could. I could feel my stomach tight under my waistband and strength coming up in me from the vittles and I run faster than I'd ever run before. It was dark under the trees but there was still light down the water courses. I thought how in some cleared place or in a town it wouldn't be dark for two or three hours yet and I saw myself in such a place, moving around and talking to people but staying always in the light. And I said to myself, if I ever got into such a cleared place again it'd be hard to get me to set foot in the woods.

The creek I was following was a master tumbler. Straight down it went over big rocks and the water white everywhere with its dashing. Once I thought I would leave it and strike out through the woods again, and then I thought falling water'd take me out of the hills quicker'n anything else and I'd best stick to it long as I could.

I went on and then all of a sudden I come upon something that froze my guts cold: the print of a foot by the water. I knew it would be a moccasin but I stooped down and looked at it good. I told myself it might be a white man—might be a hunter wearing moccasins like most of 'em did; but I went on a little way and there were three, four footprints in some wet sand and all of them were moccasins. I thought then the game was up or would be directly, but I run on. I run on. I couldn't think of anything else to do.

It was still light when I come out on a big rock by some little falls. I stood there looking and I couldn't believe my eyes. A broad river ran there before me with clearings here and there on the bank and, right across from the rock I was standing on, a fort: a blockhouse with a stockade fence around it and the timber burned back over the rifle range.

I got off the rock and run down towards the water. A woman and some children were walking along outside the stockade. I called to the woman. She give one look at me and turned and run inside the fort, the children after her. I saw the gate swing to behind them and I knew they had shot the bolt.

I tore off my petticoat and waved it over my head and yelled loud as I could:

"Let me in! Let me in, I tell you!"

I could see heads at the upper story and one somebody standing up on a stump to look over the stockade. But nobody answered and there wasn't no sign of the gate opening.

I looked over my shoulder. The woods were dark behind me and there wasn't any signs of Indians, but I knew they'd be coming any minute. I felt like I knew the place in the woods they were at now. I saw them trotting, trotting through the trees, one after another, the way they went.

I thought, "I'll have to do something quick or they'll get me sure, after all my trouble." I started in to swim it but I couldn't make headway against that current. I saw I would be drowning in a minute, and I swum hard and got back to shallow water. It come to me then that the folks in the fort didn't know who I was. I stood up in the water and yelled, loud as I could:

"I'm Jinny Wiley . . . Jinny Wiley that the Indians stole."

The echo come back to me from the woods, but there wasn't

any sound from the fort. Then the gate opened a little way and an old man come out with a gun in his hand. He stood there looking at me and he turned around and said something to the folks in the fort and then he started down the path. I watched him coming down over the rifle range, an old man, gray-haired and feeble enough to a been my grandsire. I shouted at him.

"You can't do it. Send some young body over."

He stood on the bank and shouted back at me, his old voice quavering across the water:

"Where'd you come from?"

I jumped up and down and shrieked, top of my voice:

"God's sakes, man, you going to let me die right here before your eyes? I'm white! White, I tell you!"

"All of 'em's gone but me," he said, "and they ain't no canoe."

"Make a raft," I told him.

He nodded his head up and down. I could see his old gray beard a-shaking. "You better be ready to swim for it," he said. "I don't know as I can git across."

He called to the women in the fort and they come and brought an axe. There was a dead mulberry tree on the bank and they went to work felling it. The old man went off in the woods and come back with some grapevine. When the tree fell it split into three logs and he tied them together with a grapevine and then he and the women rolled them down to the water. They handed him two rifles and he laid them on the raft and started poling. The current caught him and he was going downstream. Yelling had started behind me somewhere in the woods. The Indians were coming.

I run down the bank till I got even with the raft and I swum out and clomb aboard. The old man poled hard. We got halfway out in the river and then the vines begun to come loose and the raft was spreading apart. I knelt down and held the logs together with my hands the best I could. The old man fell down on his knees and started praying.

"'Tain't no use," he said; "we can't make it."

I looked over my shoulder. The Indians were swarming down to the water. I knew they'd be swimming directly. The old man was still praying. I took the pole away from him.

"Go on and pray, you old fool," I said. "I'm a-going to git across this river."

I put all the strength I had into it and we made some headway. The yelling was closer now. The Indians were in the water. A shot rung out. I hoped to God one of 'em was hit. I poled harder and I saw some willow boughs ahead of me. I reached out and grabbed hold of 'em and we pulled ourselves to shore.

We went up over the rifle range fast as we could. I looked back once. The Indians had left the water and were standing on the bank. I heard Mad Dog calling:

"Whoopee! . . . whoopee! . . . pretty Jinny!"

We went through the gate. I heard the bolt shoot home and I knew I was inside the fort. I fell down on the ground and the women and children come crowding. The Indians were still yelling. I sat up and the high stockade fence was all around me.

"Lord God," I said, "I was lucky to git away from them Indians!"

NOTES ON THE
CONTRIBUTORS

JAMES APPLEWHITE is teaching again at Greensboro after an absence of several years for study at Duke. His poems have appeared in a variety of journals, including *Shenandoah, Red Clay Reader,* and *Southern Poetry Review,* and a number are forthcoming in the anthology *Young American Poets.* He was awarded an Emily Clark Balch prize by *The Virginia Quarterly Review.*

FRED CHAPPELL has published three novels, *It is Time, Lord, The Inkling,* and *Dagon,* plus a number of poems and stories. He spent the year 1967-68 in Florence on a Rockefeller Grant and has now returned to teaching at Greensboro.

KELLY CHERRY holds an M.F.A. from Greensboro. Her work, both poems and stories, has appeared in *The Greensboro Review, Carolina Quarterly, Red Clay Reader,* and *The Girl in the Black Raincoat.* She now lives in Greensboro where her husband teaches in the University's Art Department.

JEAN FARLEY, who was an undergraduate at Greensboro, now lives in Gambier, Ohio, with her husband Ellington White and helps with *The Kenyon Review* by reading poetry submissions. Miss

Farley has published poems in many national magazines including *The Reporter, Poetry,* and *The New Yorker,* and her poetry is widely anthologized.

CAROLINE GORDON taught at Greensboro during the late thirties. The winner of numerous awards, including a Guggenheim Fellowship and an O. Henry Award, she has pursued a long and distinguished career as a writer. She has published eight novels and a volume of stories, *Old Red and Other Stories.*

HIRAM HAYDN left Greensboro to become editor of *The American Scholar* in 1944. He has held many top editorial posts in New York, among them editor-in-chief of Random House, and is at present an independent publisher associated with Harcourt, Brace, & World, Inc. He is the author or editor of twelve books, including four novels; *The Counter-Renaissance,* a work in the history of ideas; and *The Portable Elizabethan Reader.*

BERTHA HARRIS, who as an undergraduate at Greensboro edited and contributed frequently to *Coraddi,* is now a M.F.A. candidate. For a number of years she worked as a free-lance editor in New York City. Her first novel will be published shortly by Harcourt, Brace and World.

RANDALL JARRELL taught at Greensboro over a period of eighteen years. He distinguished himself as a novelist, critic, and teacher as well as a poet. Among his seven volumes of poetry, *The Woman at the Washington Zoo* won the 1961 National Book Award. His last book of poems, *The Lost World,* appeared not long before his death in 1965.

X. J. KENNEDY, a former member of the English staff at Greensboro, has won many awards for his poetry, including the Lamont Award for his first volume of poems, *Nude Descending a Staircase.* He has taught writing at Wellesley and Tufts, has been the poetry editor of *The Paris Review,* and is a frequent contributor of book reviews to *Poetry* and *The New York Times.*

ROBIE MACAULEY left the University at Greensboro to become the editor of *The Kenyon Review* and at present is the fiction editor of *Playboy*. Many of his stories have been collected in the volume *The End of Pity*. Some of them have been reprinted in *O. Henry Prize Stories* and *Best American Short Stories*. He has also written a novel, *The Disguises of Love*, and much distinguished criticism.

HEATHER ROSS MILLER was an undergraduate at Greensboro, where she contributed to and edited *Coraddi*. Since her graduation she has published three novels, *The Edge of the Woods*, *Tenants of the House*, and *Gone A Hundred Miles*, and a book of poems, *The Wind Southerly*. She lives with her family at Singletary Lake in North Carolina.

THOMAS MOLYNEUX, who now teaches at the University of Delaware, is a graduate of Harvard and received his M.F.A. from Greensboro. He is a recent recipient of a Rockefeller Grant in writing to complete a novel. Recently his stories have been published in *Coraddi*, *The Greensboro Review*, and *The Sewanee Review*.

DIANE OLIVER graduated from Greensboro, where she contributed a number of stories to *Coraddi*, and went on to study at the Iowa Writers Workshop. Her first story in a national magazine appeared in the Spring, 1966, *Sewanee Review* shortly after her death in a motorcycle accident.

PATRICIA PETERS, a graduate of Skidmore College, received her M.F.A. degree from Greensboro. In 1967 she was a winner of a prize from The Academy of American Poets. Her poems have appeared in *The Greensboro Review* and *The Sewanee Review*.

LAWRENCE JUDSON REYNOLDS, who took his M.F.A. at Greensboro, is from Concord, Virginia. He was the first editor of *The Greensboro Review*. His stories have appeared in many publications, including Volume I of *Intro*, published by Bantam Books. He is now in London working on a novel.

WM. PITT ROOT received an M.F.A. from Greensboro. He has published poems in a wide variety of magazines, including *The Atlantic Monthly*, *The Sewanee Review*, and *The Virginia Quarterly Review*, and has won a prize from the Academy of American Poets. His first volume is forthcoming from Atheneum. He now teaches at Michigan State University.

JESSIE ROSENBERG, a native Mississippian, received her B.A. from Greensboro and is now working for her M.F.A. She has recently done teaching at Tulane University. Miss Rosenberg was first published in *The Atlantic* Young Poets section and then in *New Campus Writing*. Her first novel, *Sudina*, was published by Dutton in 1967 and her next one will appear shortly.

GIBBONS RUARK has published poems in a number of magazines, among them *Poetry, Massachusetts Review*, and *Southern Poetry Review*. One of his poems was awarded a prize by the National Council on the Arts and appeared in *American Literary Anthology*. After several years at Greensboro, he now teaches at the University of Delaware.

ALLEN TATE taught at Greensboro in the late thirties and again in 1966. His widely varied writings have been honored in many ways, among them the Bollingen Prize for Poetry in 1956 and the Fellowship of the Academy of American Poets in 1963. He is Professor of English at the University of Minnesota.

ELEANOR ROSS TAYLOR studied with Allen Tate as an undergraduate at Greensboro. She taught English in North Carolina high schools for several years and did graduate work at Vanderbilt before her marriage to Peter Taylor. Her poems have appeared in such magazines as *Virginia Quarterly Review, Poetry, Botteghe Oscure*, and *Accent* and have been collected in *A Wilderness of Ladies*.

PETER TAYLOR is now at the University of Virginia, after teaching at Greensboro over a period of twenty years. A recipient of many awards for writing, including Fulbright, Guggenheim, and Rockefeller fellowships, he has published a novel and four books of stories, the most recent of which is *Miss Leonora When Last Seen*.

ROBERT WATSON has taught at Greensboro for fifteen years. He has written criticism and plays and is the author of two books of poems, *A Paper Horse* and *Advantages of Dark*, and a novel, *Three Sides of the Mirror*. In 1959 he was awarded a poetry prize by *The American Scholar*. Mr. Watson has taught a third of the contributors to *The Greensboro Reader*.

www.ingramcontent.com/pod-product-compliance
Lightning Source LLC
Chambersburg PA
CBHW030626110726
47901CB00002B/337